An Introduction to Sports Tourism and Event Management

M. Saayman (ed)

This book is dedicated to my dad who loved sport.
Someone once said that the stars in the sky are the souls of those who died. Your star shines bright.

Institute for Tourism and Leisure Studies
Potchefstroom University for Christian Higher Education
Potchefstroom
South Africa
2520

FIRST EDITION: 2001

COPYRIGHT © 2001

ISBN: 1-86822-378-7

PRINTED AND MARKETED BY:

LEISURE CONSULTANTS AND PUBLICATIONS
PO BOX 20146
NOORDBRUG
POTCHEFSTROOM
2522

FAX: (018) 299 1426
TEL: (018) 299 1810
E-MAIL: ONTMS@PUKNET.PUK.AC.ZA

Index

CHAPTER 8 - Extreme Sports

by Lizl Steynberg: North West Department of Social Services, Arts, Culture and Sport, North West Province.

CHAPTER 9 - Planning a sports tour

by Lindie du Plessis: Porcupine Tours and Transfers, Potchefstroom.

CHAPTER 10 - Key success factors for a sports tourist destination

by Carina Uys: Institute for Tourism and Leisure Studies, Potchefstroom University for Christian Higher Education.

BIBLIOGRAPHY

List of tables

List of figures

A publication like this cannot be put together in isolation. I would therefore like to take this opportunity to thank those involved with this publication, especially the team at the Institute for Tourism and Leisure Studies, at Potchefstroom University for Christian Higher Education for their part in it. A special word of thanks goes to:

Lizl for your chapters on sensation-seeking and extreme sports.

Lindie for your chapters on the historical development of sports tourism and how to plan a sports tour.

Carina for your chapter on determining key success factors for a sports tourist destination.

Alvera Visser for making this document presentable.

Dr Amanda van der Merwe for the editing.

Anelle Wickens and Katja Swart at Ons Drukkers for editing and layout of this document as well as designing the cover.

Prof GJL Scholtz for your support and motivation as well as preparing the preface. I believe this publication will encourage sports tourism, even though this is a small beginning.

Lastly our Heavenly Father for inspiration, energy and enthusiasm to complete this publication but also for the opportunity to work with wonderful people.

Something about the authors

Prof Melville Saayman

Prof Melville Saayman is currently the director of the Institute for Tourism and Leisure Studies at the Potchefstroom University for Christian Higher Education. He was also a director of the South African Tourism Board (SATOUR) for three years (1997-2000). He is also a director and deputy chairman of the North West Parks and Tourism Board, executive member of the Institute of Environment and Recreation Management as well as board member of the National Zoological Council. He further holds the position of chairman of the marketing sub-committee of the North West Parks and Tourism Board. He is an executive member of the South African National Recreation Council (SANREC), as well as president of the North West Provincial Recreation Council (PROREC-NW). At an international level he is a member of the advisory board of the International Sports Tourism Council and a member of the Marco Polo Committee on Statistics of Travel and Tourism (COSTT), member of the Association of International Experts in Tourism (AIEST) and he is the first South African to be nominated as resource editor of the leading tourism journal, Annals of Tourism Research. He is currently active in the field of tourism marketing and development. Prof Saayman became the first South African tourism and leisure academic to be included in the Marqui's Who's Who in the World.

Miss Lizl Steynberg

Lizl is currently busy with her PhD on sensation seeking in sports tourism. Which is the first of its kind in South Africa making Lizl a leader in this field. Except for been busy with further research she is also responsible for organising leisure management in-service training courses. She holds the position of administrative official and secretary of Provincial Recreation Council (PROREC-NW) and Recreation Northwest (RECSA-NW). She is employed in the Department of Arts, Culture and Sport in the North West Province and was seconded to the Institute for Tourism and Leisure Studies in 1996.

Mrs. Lindie du Plessis

Lindie du Plessis is currently busy with her master degree in Tourism Management at the Potchefstroom University for Christian Higher Education, where she does research on the competitiveness of South Africa as a tourist destination. Lindie is involved at the Institute for Tourism and Leisure Studies helping with research projects and the development of business plans and tours. She is co-author of the practical guideline series of publications. The first booklet was published in 1999 titled - Practical guidelines for starting your own tourism business.

Lindie is an executive member of NOWATOTA (North West Association of Tour operators & Travel Agents) and is well known in the North West Province. She is the proud co-owner of Porcupine Tours & Transfers cc which is known for quality tours and specialised in safari's, adventure, and golf tours.

Miss Carina Uys

Carina is a lecturer in tourism management at the Potchefstroom University for Christian Higher Education. Her love and participation in sport (athletics) contributed to research which determined the key success factors for Potchefstroom as an international sports tourist destination, from which she wrote a chapter for this book. She received the South African Tourism Board (SATOUR) trophy for the best third year tourism student in 2000 at the Potchefstroom University for Christian Higher Education and is currently busy with her master degree in tourism management.

PREFACE

In South Africa, sports tourism is a relatively new phenomenon. However, its economical, political, social and marketing potential are thoroughly realised and utilised by countries across the world. With tourism as the world's largest and fastest growing industry, and sports tourism as one of its most virile branches, our country and its institutions should be eager to become part of this new and dynamic national, international and even inter-continental trend. Furthermore it should also be reflected in the tourism training offered by its institutions. And this is exactly what this book on sport tourism in this novel field is trying to achieve.

The book starts by defining sports tourism as a vibrant branch of the tourism industry in general. More specifically, it focuses on the sport person in its multiple tourism roles, such as participants; spectators, facilitators and entrepreneurs in private tourism-oriented enterprises. To obtain a broader perspective, sports tourism in South Africa at present is analysed from a historical and international perspective. This book differs from other available books on sports tourism, in that it extensively deals with motivational factors, and analyses relevant sensations and factors underlying participation in sports tourism. This is a novel and most useful contribution of this book. To make it an even more useful tool for the student and practitioner, it deals extensively with the skill of catering for sports events; the social and economic impact of sports tourism; and the planning of hallmark events.

Seen from an academic, practical and applied perspective, this book is strongly recommended for general application and practical usage, but also for its intrinsic value as one of the first in this new and vibrant field.

Prof. Gert J.L. Scholtz
Professor in Sport Tourism, University of Pretoria.

CODE OF MUTUAL UNDERSTANDING FOR SPORTS TOURISM

A CODE of understanding must be developed, introduced and nurtured by the Sports Tourism Industry (the "sports hosts") as well as the "sports guests" to achieve, uphold and maintain world PEACE.

The following are a few "global mix" recommendations for such a Code of Mutual Understanding:

- Regardless of race, culture, language and geographic territory, any community of peoples is entitled to respect for their lifestyle models, peculiarities, standards, and philosophies, whether sports guests approve of these or not.

- Active or passive membership within the Sports Tourism Industry, regardless of geographic location, exacts a responsibility to objectively recognise, understand and appreciate the lifestyle peculiarities, standards and philosophies of any given community of peoples, without pre-judging or prejudice in accordance to some other collective or individual behavioural norms.

- Members of the Sports Tourism Industry should honourably and scrupulously offer, discuss and debate ideas, opinions and actions of any community of peoples in terms of the latter's lifestyle COMPOSITES, communications and dialogue being the greatest enhancer.

- The Sports Tourism Industry leaders should as far as possible emphasise to all interested travellers (sports guests) that no two communities of people are identical in all lifestyle respects, even though, at any time, composites may appear to be concomitant.

- The Sports Tourism Industry should educate all sports travellers to share a responsibility in coordinating their behavioural attitudes in terms of existent community of peoples composites and not exact their sense of lifestyle upon other communities of people.

- The Sports Tourism Industry should emphasise in all its activity forums that appreciation, closeness and, in many instances, acceptance of certain lifestyle COMPOSITES require changes in overall personal attitudes, not overlooking the fact that such movements require skills.

- In all its ways and means, the Sports Tourism Industry should educate worldwide communities of peoples (sports hosts) on their specific roles and responsibilities in guest-host relationships.

- The Sports Tourism Industry, through all its workings and networking, should impart to all industry leaders, professionals, workers and volunteers the inherent potentials of PEACE through the worldwide channels of Sports Tourism.

- The Sports Tourism Industry should develop support services to spur PEACE dynamics, enhancing all positive relationships among communities of peoples.

- Leaders in the field of Sports Tourism should discover avenues by and through which sport guests and hosts could communicate with one another, expressing feelings and meanings in other words, to grow and mature together.

- The Sports Tourism Industry should insist that sports visitors (guests) and/or sports host communities not allow negative experiences to harden their hearts but that they rather use sports tourism experiences for better awareness and sensitivity to others, as growth is impossible in smothering environments.

- Leaders in the Sports Tourism Industry should continuously examine the nature of community COMPOSITE relationships for no relationship remains static. Changes always occur; at times quickly and on other occasions gradually and progressively.

- Sports visitors/guests should be educated by the Sports Tourism Industry to expect what is reasonable and not perfection.

- Compassion, must be nurtured in the hearts of all involved, be they the Sports Tourism Industry, the sports hosts or the sports guests, to encourage better understanding and greater acceptance by both the sports guest and the sports host (**Kurtzman et al., 1993:5-6**).

Chapter 1

Sports Tourism: A Growing opportunity

Not only is there an art in knowing a thing, but also a certain art in teaching it.
Cicero Do Legibus

1.1 INTRODUCTION

Baron Pierre de Coubertin, father of the modern Olympic Games, inspired the development of sports tourism (**Firenze, 1998:1**). According to **Kurtzman et al. (1998:2)** De Coubertin ones stated that "competition produces harmony between competitors and the organisations or nations they represent." It was his belief that sport brings people and nations together. It was De Coubertin's concept that gave sports tourism its vitality and foundation, according to **Firenze (1998:1)**. Other schools of thought believe that sports tourism existed long before the modern Olympic Games. As a result the profession of sports tourism became a growing reality - and gave impetus for the pursuit of business entrepreneurship, economic impact and profitability within the tourism industry. Sports tourism developed over many years to what it is today. Tourists travelling to see pyramids, visit seaside resorts, and attend festivals and athletic events, needed food and accommodation. They spent money for these services, which qualified them as tourists and more specifically as sports tourists. The economic expenditure was difficult to measure as it still is today (**McIntosh et al., 1995:40**).

The tourism potential of sports tourism and consequently of sports events have been addressed in several studies. In all cases these events have been established to appeal to tourists as well as to the relevant sports community or cultural group (**Murphy & Carmichael, 1989:32**). According to **Burgan & Miles (1992:700)** the foreign tourism growth in Australia over the past decade has been an average of 10 percent annually. Special sporting events have played an important part in this growth. Australia hosts over 400 sporting events each year, many of which are international tournaments and world championships. Some of the major events were the Commonwealth Games in 1982 with 6 000 foreign visitors, the America's Cup Defence in 1986-1987 with 700 000 visitors, the World Expo in 1988 with 427 000 visitors (**Burgan & Miles, 1992:701**) and the Olympic Games in 2000.

In addition to the participants, sporting events often involve tourism numbers via spectators, medical personnel, participants, family and friends, media personnel,

3

and officials. Tourism authorities in Australia realised the potential for using sporting events as part of their promotion of Australia as a tourist destination and 1993 had sport as its theme in the tourism promotion programme. Like Australia, South Africa offers an excellent climate, value for money and a sports culture, which are obvious benefits as a host to major sporting events. Rising world incomes and reduced airfares reduce the disadvantages caused by travel time and cost in getting to these destinations from the main population centres of the Northern Hemisphere (**Burgan & Miles, 1992:701; Saayman, 2000**). It is the aim of this chapter to address the concept of sports tourism and what it entails. Firstly the relationship between sport and tourism, is addressed.

1.2   THE RELATIONSHIP BETWEEN SPORT AND TOURISM

Tourism is an industry and a physical, emotional, intellectual and spiritual experience (**Marsh & Henshall, 1987**). Tourist activity consists of a number of organisations that feed the collective dreams of the tourists and carry out a liberating function in a society dominated by logic but in need of the legendary and the mythical (**Dufour, 1977**). It is a liberating myth and a great adventure for a lot of workers. The main representative of this thought is **Jafari (1989)**, who compares tourist travel to a "springboard dive" that allows the tourist to be suspended for a while. In this space the daily world remains behind and the traveller becomes absorbed in another dimension (**Miranda & Andueza, 1997**).

According to **Saayman (2000)** tourism can be defined as the total experience that originates from the interaction between tourists, job providers, government systems and communities in the process of attracting, interacting with, transporting and accommodating tourists. In analysing tourism and what it is all about various researchers have analysed the phenomenon of tourism. Some of their findings are explained below.

Janse Verbeke (1988) and **Saayman (1997)** are the only authors who have divided the core aspects of tourism in certain categories, namely primary, secondary and additional aspects. The models of **Trigg (1995)** and **Jansen Verbeke (1988)** are the only two models that exclude transport. All the authors include the aspects of accommodation and catering, although in many different forms, such as hotels and restaurants, food and drink and hospitality. Attractions (man-made and natural) and culture were included in the models of **Gunn (1988), Jansen Verbeke (1988), McIntosh et al. (1995), Sessa (1994) and Lundberg (1990)**. The fourth largest mutual element in the models was entertainment, addressed by **Trigg (1995), Jansen Verbeke (1988), Chadwick (1994), Saayman (1997), Sessa (1994) and Lundberg (1990)**.

As shown in Figure 1.1, main elements include transport, accommodation, catering, attractions and entertainment. Other aspects identified by these authors may be classified as secondary aspects. Although they are important to the tourism industry, they are not vital elements such as the primary aspects which are seen as the core of the tourism industry (**Saayman, 1997 and McIntosh et al., 1995**). These aspects which were identified earlier need more detailed explanation due to the complexity of the tourism industry. For the purpose of this book only the primary aspects will be discussed.

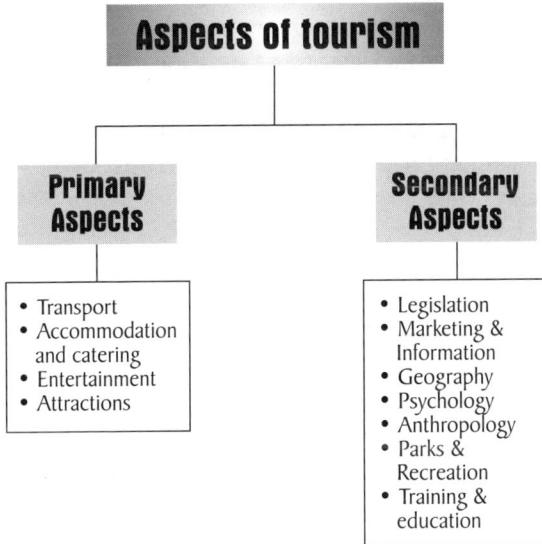

Aspects of tourism

Primary Aspects

- Transport
- Accommodation and catering
- Entertainment
- Attractions

Secondary Aspects

- Legislation
- Marketing & Information
- Geography
- Psychology
- Anthropology
- Parks & Recreation
- Training & education

Figure 1.1: Aspects of tourism

- **Accommodation and catering**

  Accommodation includes hotels, guesthouses, bed-and-breakfast establishments, holiday resorts, camping facilities, game reserves and game farms. Catering includes restaurants, coffee shops, informal bars, tearooms, shebeens and kiosks (**Saayman & Swart, 1997**). These sectors are vital to the tourism industry, for tourists need overnight facilities at hotels, guesthouses and caravan parks. In South Africa there is a growing need for more accommodation because of more tourists. As a result bed-and-breakfast establishments and guesthouses are emerging at a rapid rate.

- **Transport**

  According to **Bukkart & Medlik (1981)**, "tourism is about being somewhere else...". This quotation illustrates not only the extreme importance of transport suppliers in the tourism industry, but in fact indicates that without transport there will be no tourism industry. The transport sector includes all types of transport, namely ships, bikes, motorcars, aeroplanes, taxis, busses and trains (**McIntosh et al., 1995; Lundberg, 1990**). Needs for transport include accessibility of tourism attractions, the availability of transport to attractions, route maps and road signs.

- **Entertainment**
  Recreation activities and facilities include entertainment, gambling, festivals, visiting friends and relatives, sport, public parks, picnic spots, markets and shopping centres (**McIntosh et al., 1995; Trigg, 1995**). Tourism attractions and facilities must have the necessary equipment and be accessible to everyone and information regarding the facilities must be available to the general public as well as to tourists. The quality and accessibility of entertainment centres are of the utmost importance to attract tourists. Bookings and reservations as well as services in general must be of a high standard to ensure that tourists will return (**Saayman & Swart, 1997**).

- **Attractions and culture**
  Attractions can be natural or man-made (**White Paper on Tourism, 1996**). Natural attractions include beaches, caves, rivers, lakes, mountains and fauna and flora. According to **Swarbrooke (1995:5)**, two main categories of man-made attractions may be distinguished, namely attractions not originally designed primarily to attract visitors and, secondly, attractions purpose-built to attract tourists. Attractions not originally designed primarily to attract visitors include cathedrals, churches, archaeological sites, ancient monuments, historical gardens and steam trains. Purpose-built attractions include museums, game reserves, zoos, cultural heritage, garden centres, amusement parks, picnic sites, galleries, waterfront developments and marinas. Figure 1.2 gives an analysis of attractions.

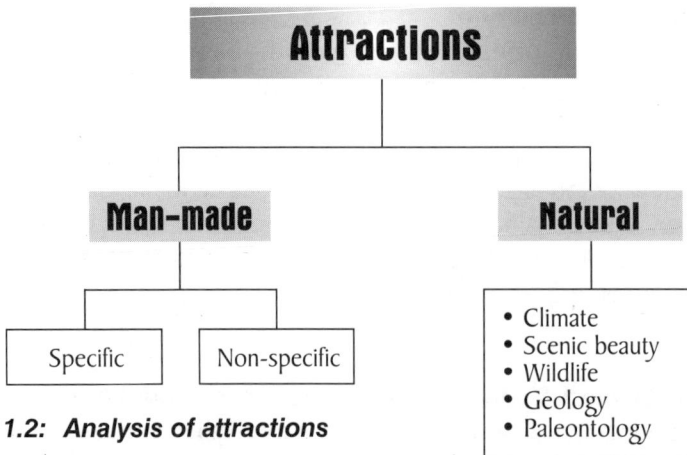

Figure 1.2: Analysis of attractions

Tourism and sport have joined forces to build an international competitive sports tourism industry worldwide. It is an industry that works with communities and sport governing bodies to strategically pursue sports events to be hosted in these communities generating a substantial economic income, media exposure and quality of life impacts (**Olsthoorn, 1998**). Sports tourism focuses not only on international events, but it includes local, regional and national events.

Gibson (1998:155) noted that travel related to sport and physical activity is one of the fastest growing segments of the tourism industry. Redmond (as quoted by **Gibson, 1998:155**) suggested that "a symbiotic relationship" exists between sport and tourism. Tourism is directly or indirectly part of most of the world's industries, including sport, sporting goods, promotions, infra- and suprastructure development and equipment.

Sport provides people with the opportunity to realise their desire to be self-complete through the testing and development of the body. This purpose has a special attraction for spectators because they share a common identity with the participants. **Kurtzman et al. (1998:3)** remark that "… the revolution in communications makes greater numbers aware of sport competitions. Governments use sporting events to political advantage. Sport can strengthen identification to the nation - with positive consequences."

Sport has become a social phenomenon of great complexity. It has considerable implications for the success of both the domestic and international tourism industry. The spectator factor creates an urgency for an achievement ethic, a widespread system of sport programmes, and general access to the mass media. This applies to all the categories of sports tourism. In addition, sport represent a highly organised social structure that may be divided into the spectators, the officials, the athletes (competitors), the sponsors, and many more (**Kurtzman et al., 1998:3**).

Tourists, be they domestic or international, are motivated to visit these sports events and attractions and to satisfy their various desires, needs and interests. But they are also motivated to visit these destinations because of certain factors such as planning, organisation and uniqueness in a well-constructed facility or site (**Kurtzman et al., 1998:3**). The above implies a strong relationship between sport and tourism that goes back to the beginning of tourism.

During the last 40 years there has been a dynamic articulation of both sport and tourism. Both went through a constant period of adaptation and transformation which affected the social intervention spheres of each. This period was characterised by two types of processes: the emergence of a "leisure society" (**Dumazedier, 1988**) and the advent "of a consumer society" in Europe (**Baudrilled, 1970**). By acquiring an economic value from its different facets and by increasing its symbolism, the field of sports grew. In the same way, tourism, in the search for the development of new products and new markets, pursued a constant extension and adaptation towards strong sectors or economic niches such as sports declinations. In this way, the creation of synergetic relations between sport and tourism has generated new horizons through the use of appropriations of the image and the symbol or by accountable integration (**Pigeassou, 1997**). Gammon and **Robinson (1997)** states clearly that a clear theme runs along the existing sport and tourism literature. This relationship gained momentum because of the following five directions, namely:

- Popularity of national and international events.
- An understanding of the health benefits of sports participation.
- A realisation of the value of these events.
- A greater variety of events all over the world.
- The impact of globalisation on sport and tourism.

The clarification of the relationship between sport and tourism is based on a public reference framework, and depends on at least two conceptual structures. Firstly, symbolism plays an important role in all psycho-sociological interpretation frameworks which centre on the signification of choices and conditions of sport participation or tourism. These frameworks refer to a comprehension of the anthropological links and roots which work with the imaginations. The second kind of conceptual structure is an economic framework with of a pragmatic and operational approach. This framework identifies the areas of interaction, characterises the synergies and locates the stakes. Most of the research on sports tourism is done from the perspective of the latter framework.

Tourism and sport are social activities which have developed since the industrial revolution in the English society. The development of tourism preceded sport by several decades in the 19th century. Yet the relationship between these two spheres of activity developed, throughout the 19th century and into the first part of the 20th century. The reason for this relationship was that both were part of the largest category of activity leisure, and more specifically of the category of leisure activities away from home, which include outdoor recreation.

The development of physical leisure was progressively realised through sport and sport activities. However, birth of a leisure industry and the consequent emergence of mass tourism were only part of the general principle of paid holidays. The extension of these holiday periods and the decrease of weekly working timetable accentuated the social role of leisure activities. Television acquired a major part in this process and, sport and tourism gradually involved more and more people (**Pigeassou, 1997**). The role of the media in sports tourism is thus paramount.

Sport and tourism in Africa, and particularly South Africa, went through a similar process, but at a much later stage. The sport industry only got momentum over the last approximately forty years. South Africa has only been a global player in sport as well as tourism since 1994.

The word sport was derived from the word disport meaning to divert oneself (**Edwards, 1973**). Sport can be defined in many ways and from different viewpoints or distinctive perspectives. Definitions are mere tools which serve to specify some level of precision and characteristics. The following definitions have been selected to demonstrate that sport as part of our social world:

- Sport is viewed as game occurrence (**Hart and Birell, 1981**).

- Sport is a diversion, amusement or recreation; a pleasant pastime which can be pursued in the open air as hunting, fishing, skiing or trekking (**Zeigler, 1984**). Recreation is the positive usage of one's leisure time (**Saayman, 1997**).

- Informal sport is free in that participation is totally voluntary (**Chu, 1982**).

- Competitive sport is an institutionalised competitive activity that involves vigorous physical exertion or the use of relatively complex physical skills by individuals where participation is motivated by a combination of intrinsic and extrinsic factors (**Coakley, 1982**).

- Competitive sport consists of physical activities which involves the coordination of large muscle groups which have a set of universally recognised rules and which produce a winner and a loser (**Coakley, 1982**).

- Recreational sport is characterised by playfulness involved and enjoyment of play that serves the primary reason for participation (**Chu, 1982**).

Stevenson and Nixon (1972) isolated five basic functions of sport, namely:

1. The socio-emotional function which operated at the level of the individual and is

concerned with the socio-psychological stability of the individual.

2. The socialisation, which also operates at the level of the individual, and is concerned with the inculcation of cultural mores and beliefs, and with the development of personality characteristics.

3. The integrative function, which operates at the level of the collective, and is concerned with the harmonious integration of disparate individuals into, and their identification with, the collective.

4. The political function, which is predominantly operative at the level of the Nation State, is concerned with the function of sport as a political instrument.

5. The social mobility function, which operates at the level of the individual's position relative to socially defined categories.

Saayman and van Niekerk (1996:64) and Tow (1997) further identified the following benefits of hosting sports events, which relates to the relationship between tourism and sport:

- The development of an accommodation infrastructure.
- The improvement of the transport infrastructure.
- Publicity of the host community through television broadcasts of the sports event.
- As a result of new facilities brought by the hosting of an sports event, more international sports events will follow, resulting in more sports tourism.
- Creation of jobs; one direct and two indirect jobs are created for every 30 new tourists in South Africa.
- Improvement of other facilities such as banks, water, and electricity.
- Improved wealth in urban and rural regions.
- Creates a multiplier effect, which supply four to seven persons with an income.
- Generates investments.
- Contributes to the upliftment of communities.
- To profile and promote your country's great sports.
- Earns valuable foreign exchange.
- Mutual understanding and goodwill are promoted.
- Provides valuable funds for conservation and the balanced utilisation of resources.
- To give athletes the "home ground" advantage.
- To recruit and train volunteers.

According to **Firenze (1998:3)** the primary qualifier for sports tourism is the fact that tourists are participating in or attending a predetermined sports activity. The latter defined sports tourism as the use of sport as a vehicle for tourism endeavours. Having made this distinction, a broad definition for sports within sports tourism was given in terms of the "physical" aspect of running, jumping, walking, racing, throwing, shooting, hitting, and the like.

An important annotation to this definition was that a sports tourist might be a participant or a spectator. **Saayman (2000)** emphasises that the concept sports tourism is based on travel motivation. Nevertheless, it is the "physical" aspect of sport that is the "polariser" for tourism (**Firenze, 1998: 2**). The term tourist industry which is often used to describe the economic sectors supplying the tourist, who is the consumer of the industry's products (**McIntosh et al., 1995: 15**). An industry is often defined on the basis of a product, and in tourism the product is what attracts the tourist to a certain place (**Law, 1996: 6**). Therefore in sports tourism the product is the specific sport or sports event and the experience derived from that, including the sports event organisers and all the goods and services needed to host the event form part of the sports tourism industry.

1.3 SPORTS TOURISM PHENOMENA

Kurtzman (1993) developed the model below giving one a clearer understanding of the sports tourism phenomenon. The model depicts movement on a Wavy Roadway over time; whereby each sports tourist can adapt and adjust according to his/her needs, interests and desires (**Kurtzman, 1993**).

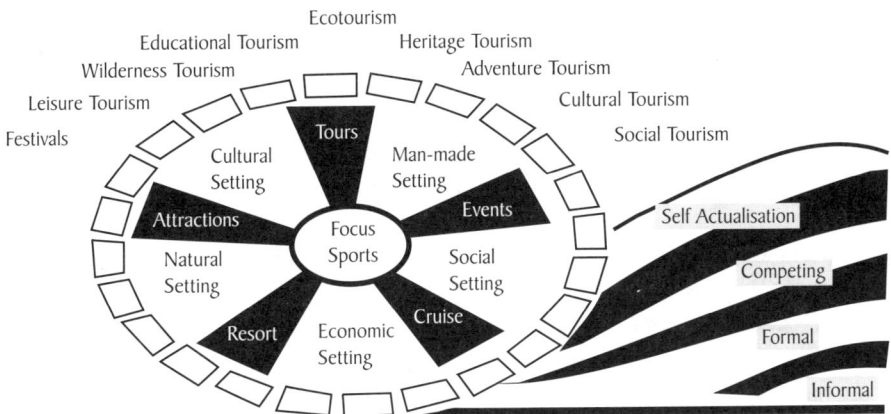

Figure 1.3: The sports tourism phenomena

1. The Hub represents the main focus of sports tourism around which the respective physical activity (be it recreational, competitive or both) evolve.

2. The Spokes illustrate the five different sports tourism categories according to specific touristic endeavours.

3. The Spoke interspaces represent five potential settings in which the sports tourism activity, for participant or spectator or both, could take place.

4. The Outer Rim indicates different building blocks that potentially could and do contribute to the overall development of sports tourism.

5. The Roadway suggests motivation elements, which impel tourists, be they participant, spectator or both, in varying degrees and different directions to be involved in specific sports offerings and opportunities.

Five specific activity categories have also been determined for sports tourism with a "touristic endeavour" foundation (**Firenze, 1998:4-6**):

a) Sports events
b) Sports attractions
c) Sports tours
d) Sports resorts
e) Sport cruises

These categories are discussed below.

SPORTS TOURISM EVENTS

Sports tourism events refer to those sports activities that attract tourists of which a large percentage are spectators. Furthermore, these sports tourism events have the potential to attract non-resident media, technical personnel, athletes, coaches and other sport officials (**Kurtzman and Zauhar, 1997**).

In some instances sports tourism events may have a cultural association - for example the Hong Kong Dragon Boat Festival which developed from a semi-religious ceremony into an international sports tourism event (**Sofield and Sivan, 1994**).

Tourism hallmark events or mega events have also been associated with this category. They include the Olympic Games, world cup and major regional, national and international contests/competitions.

Other distinctions that qualify a sport event to be touristic in nature are:
- Tourists travelling distances to see present and past star athletes or winner teams.
- Tourists attending or participating in sport activities, formally planned or informally organised.

The sports tourism activity category of sport events include:
- Olympic Games
- Regional/national/international multiple sport games
- Championships/bonspiels
- Invitational
- Meets/marathons
- Scheduled league games (professional and amateur)
- Twinning games/friendship games
- Sport specific world cups/trophies
- Races/regattas
- Derbies
- Stampedes
- Sport festivals
- Bowl Games (**Kurtzman, 1993**).

SPORTS TOURISM ATTRACTIONS

This category includes those attractions providing "energising power" with sports-related physical activities as their principle focus. Such attractions are usually on-location in places within regions, country sides or urban settings offering the tourist things to see and do, where personal and social expectations are realised to varying degrees (**Gunn, 1988**). Attractions can be natural (parks, mountains, wildlife), or man-made (museums, buildings).

General characteristics represented in this core area of sports tourism product include visitations to:
- State-of-the-art sports facilities and/or unique sports facilities which generally house sports happenings, such as stadiums, arenas, bowls, domes, etc.
- Museums dedicated to sport heritage, such as those at Ancient Olympia in Greece.
- Sport heritage sites dedicated to and honouring particular sport heroes, leaders and organisers.
- Colossal and unique sport facilities such as water slides, summer ski jumps, bungee jumping stations.
- Sport theme parks such as Disney World of Sports.
- Sport shows and demonstrations such as tall ships visitation, aquatic

performances.
- Adventure events such as the river rafting and the Duzi Canoe Marathon.

The sports tourism attractions category includes:
- Sport museums/hall of fame
- Sports conferences
- Sport shows/displays/demonstration
- Sport theme parks
- Bungee jumping
- White water rafting
- Golf courses/ ski facilities
- Balloon fests
- Water slides/wave tech pools
- Stadiums/arenas
- Sports clinics/courses/schools
- Fantasy camps
- Stampedes/rodeos.

SPORTS TOURISM TOURS

In effect, sports tourism tours characteristically consist of:

- Specific visitations to one or more sport attractions over a specified number of days (sport museums, halls of fame, stadia, theme parks, etc.).
- Combined visits to sports attractions and major sport events (heritage sites, walls of fame, wave tech pools and sport events).
- Attendance at a specific number of major sport events (soccer, rugby, cricket and hockey, in one or more locations).
- Participation in conferences, workshops, clinics, forums and attendance at major sport events (scientific congress prior to the Olympic Games).
- Tours related to the natural characteristics of a region pursued by tourists for aesthical and/or physical reasons (trekking, cycling and canoeing).

In essence, this category may be indicative of "novelty seekers" and "explorers" in pursuit of authentic and quality sports tourism experiences.

The sports tourism activity category of sport tours include:
- Professional sport games tour
- Sports study tours
- Sport adventure tours
- Facility/site/event tours
- Game safaris

- Training tours
- Cycling/hiking tours
- Trekking/climbing/caving tours
- Ski-doo excursions
- Outdoor expeditions
- Adventure tours
- Scuba/diving tours.

SPORTS TOURISM RESORTS

This category represents well planned and integrated resort complexes or villas with sports as their primary focus and marketing strategy. In many situations, these vacation centres have high standard facilities and services available to the sports tourist (Smith, 1989). Generally speaking this resort category offers:

- Teachers, trainers, coaches with a great deal of expertise and personal visibility.
- High-tech instructional apparatatus for practice and game play.
- Opportunities to compete and practice fundamentals, fine-tuning and comprehensive strategy.
- Areas, sites and facilities for general sports activities.

The sports tourism activity category of sport resorts includes:
- Golf resorts
- Ski resorts
- Snorkel/scuba resorts
- Fitness & spa resorts
- Ranches
- Tennis resorts
- Outfitters
- Multiple sports resorts
- Camp sites
- Sports hotels
- Golf and ski condos
- Fishing resorts
- Golf and country clubs.

SPORTS TOURISM CRUISES

Although the technology of ship construction evolved slowly, cruise ships are becoming more and more resemblant of hotels and resorts (**TTRA, 1986**). The cruise category designates boat trips that have sports or sporting activities as their principal marketing strategy. In South Africa this is a fast growing market with more and more cruise ships in our coastal waters. Some ships may offer unique sport events as well as sports celebrities on board. The use of watercraft for sporting activities (yachting, sailing, barging and the like) is also an important dimension of this category.

General characteristics enhanced by this cruise area are as follows:
- Special transportation for tourists from one land location to another providing opportunities for golf, tennis, snorkelling etc. in unique and varied water environments.

- High profile sports personalities on board sharing anecdotes, discussions and coaching opportunities for tourists.

- Provision of on-board facilities for phisical activiteis, sport competitions, and/or modified games.

- Hosting of a sports conference with experts offering seminars and special sessions.

There are also cruise-and-drive programmes, where tourists board private vehicles to facilitate transportation to desired sports destinations or centres. In addition, fly-and-cruise programmes provide both air and sea transportation to distinct sports environments. Another example of a sports cruise involves the classy and serene ambience of a cruise ship combined with the intimacy and luxury of a private yacht.

The sports tourism activity category of sports cruises include;
- Sports celebrity cruises
- Golf cruises/tennis cruises
- Sailing cruises
- Whale boating cruises
- Scuba/snorkel cruises
- Sports fishing/deep sea fishing
- Sports conference cruises
- Sports attractions cruise visitation
- Canoeing/kayaking/rowing
- Sailing
- Jet boating
- Yacht charters/catamarin cruises
- Bare boat cruises/barging
- Health and fitness cruises (**Kurtzman, 1993**).

Table 1.1 gives a summary of the information mentioned above.

Table 1.1: Sports tourism categories

ATTRACTIONS	RESORTS	CRUISES	TOURS	EVENTS
Sport museums Halls of fame	Fishing/hunting resorts	Sports celebrity cruises	Golf/tennis scuba tours	Regional/national international sport events
Sports symposial conferences/ meetings	Outfitters	Golf cruises	Heritage site tours	Championship bonspiels/meetings contest
Sport heritage sites	Ski/golf/scuba/ tennis resorts	Tennis cruises	Sports study tours	Invitational marathons/bowls
International sports congresses	Health/fitness spas	Snorkel cruises	Mountain climbing tours	Professional league games/ championships
Sports demonstrations	Sports seminar/ conference resorts	Multiple sports cruises	Facilities/sites/ tours	Twining games Peace games Friendship games
Gymnastic displays	Sport fantasy camps	Sports attractions visitations	Game safaris	World cup
Sport ice sculptures/sports art	Sports clinics/ camps	Sports fishing	Multiple sports tours	Regattas/car rallies
Theme parks	Training camps	Deep sea fishing	Basketball participation tours	Horse racing
Bungee jumping	Volleyball camps	Motor boat racing	Soccer participation tours	Sports festivals
White water rafting	Basketball schools	Boating/ sailing	Training tours	Olympic games/ Asian games/ Pan Am games
Golf courses	Soccer schools	Yacht charters	Cycle/walking tours	Commonwealth games European games
Ski facilities	Summer sports camp	Bareboat chartering	Ski doo excursions	World championships

Water slides	Multiple sports resorts	Card cruises	Outdoor expeditions	Unique sports events Games
Wave tech pools	Recreational/ sports camping		Trekking tours	Dragon boat racing/camel racing/ caber tossing
Stadiums/arenas			Adventure expeditions	Ski doo jumping Donkeyball Extreme games Recreation sports

(Source: Kurtzman, 1993)

1.4 MOTIVATIONAL ASPECTS OF A SPORTS TOURIST

Throughout history man has been impelled to travel because of sport - it has been the motive, the drive or the concern for travel. A motive can be explained as a person's basic disposition to react or strive towards a particular goal or goals. A "drive" can be defined as an inner factor predisposing on to react either positively or negatively towards some particular object or act. A concern deals with a person's commanding role to become involved (**Bhatiz, 1991**). In other words, a sports tourist is motivated by the specific sporting activity.

Sports tourism can either be participatory or non-participatory in nature. The Olympic Games, for instance, attracts a good number of spectators in addition to skilled participants. Both groupings are considered to be sports tourists and the Olympic Games are the "sports tourism environment" (**Firenze, 1998:4**). At the Sports Hall of Fame or a sports museum there are principally spectators, which are sports tourists too. **Gammon and Robinson (1997)** developed the following model to explain the characteristics of sports tourism, including definitions of a sports tourist.

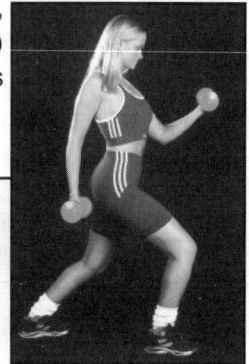

Sport & Tourism

Sports tourism		Tourism sport	
Hard definition	**Soft definition**	**Hard definition**	**Soft definition**
Passive or active participants at a competitive sporting event	Primary active recreational participation in sport	Visitors who engage in some minor form of sport or leisure; their participation is purely incidental	Tourists who at a secondary reinforcement passively or actively participate in sport
EXAMPLE National/International events Olympic Games Rugby matches (Tri-Nations) Wimbledon International cricket Comrades Marathon	EXAMPLE "Fun runs" Hiking/walking Skiing Cycling tours (Argus) Canoeing (Duzi-Marathon) Caving	EXAMPLE Mini-golf Bowls Swimming Tennis Rowing Pool/snooker	EXAMPLE Adventure PGI Health & fitness clubs Sport cruises

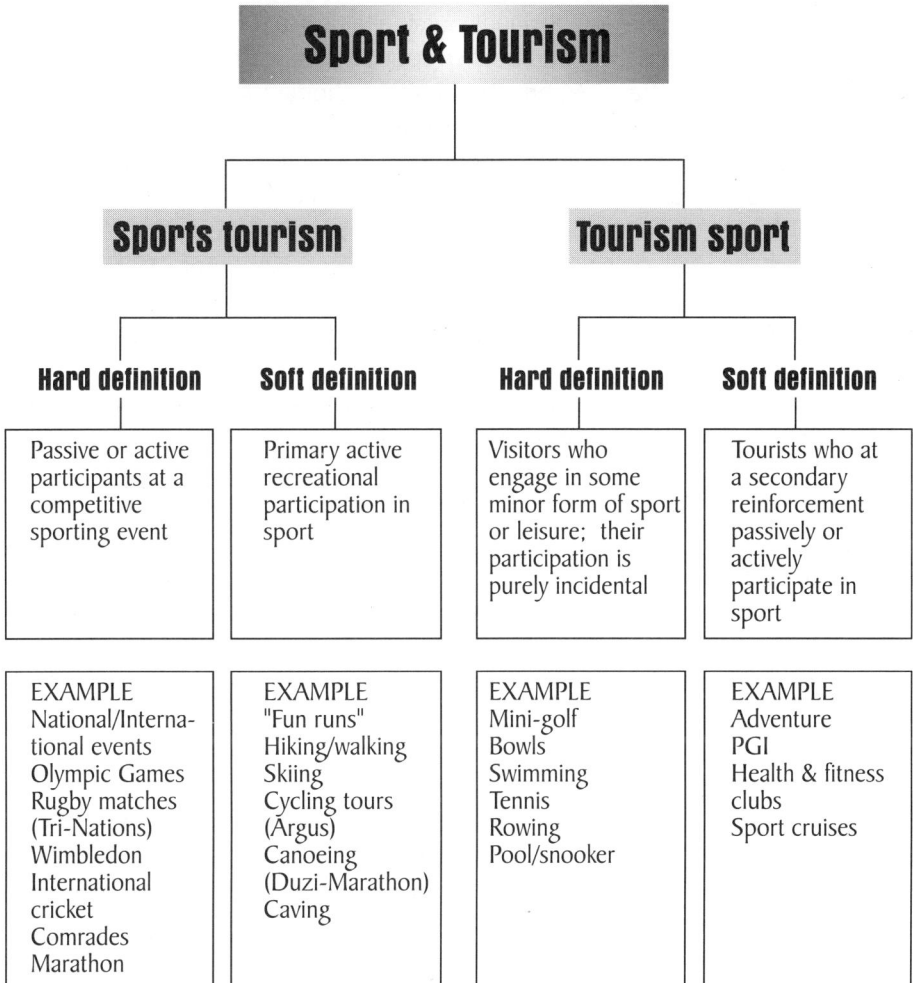

Figure 1.4: Sport and Tourism characteristics
(Source: Adapted from Gammon and Robinson, 1997)

In Figure 1.4, **Gammon and Robinson (1997)** divided sports tourism and tourism sport in two definite categories, trying to give more meaning to these concepts. The following section will give more detail on these concepts.

SPORTS TOURISM
Hard definition:
A hard definition of the sports tourist is based on the active or passive participation at a competitive sporting event. One can define a hard sports tourist as someone who specifically travels (staying in places outside their usual environment) for either active or passive involvement in competitive sport. Therefore the sport is their prime motivational reason for travel. One should stress the fact that sports tourists are also normal tourists, but they travel because of or primarily for sport. It does not imply that they do not participate in other forms of tourism. Examples of sporting events are the Olympic Games, Wimbledon and the major marathons, such as the London, Comrades, New York and Boston Marathons. The competitive nature of these events is the distinguishing factor (**Gammon and Robinson, 1997**).

According to **Saayman and Van Niekerk (1996:61)** tourist arrivals related to the Olympics Games include:
- Pre-Olympic visitors - These include all members travelling to the host country or region to help with the organisation of the event, and the IOC evaluation team.

- Olympic-specific visitors - Officials, athletes, media personnel and spectators.

- Induced visitors - The increase of international tourism as a result of the increased media coverage for the event, and therefore increased awareness of the host country.
Thus an event such as the Olympic Games attracts three different types of tourists.

Soft definition:
A softer definition of the sports tourist would be someone who specifically travels for and who is primarily involved in active recreational participation of a sporting/leisure interest. Skiing and hiking holidays would for instance involve travelling to the Alps. The active recreational aspects are the distinguishing factors in this definition.

TOURISM SPORT
Hard definition:
The hard definition includes holidaymakers for whom the sporting elements act as a secondary enrichment to their holiday (passive or active). In other words the primary motivation for travel is something. Competitive or non-competitive sport may be applied, examples of which can be found in holidays such as Butlins and Centre Parks. This category fits the hard definition of tourism sports because the holiday is the tourists' primary motivation to travel, although they will also expect to participate in some sport. Therefore sport will act as a secondary reinforcement to their vacation.

Soft definition:
A soft definition of tourism sport involves visitors who engage in some form of sport or leisure on a purely incidental basis as a minor part of their trip. For example, whilst visiting Skegness for the day they may play or watch bowls or play putting on a local park; or visitors to Cambridge may punt on the river. This is deemed "soft" sports tourism because their participation is purely incidental (**Gammon and Robinson, 1997**).

Plog Research Incorporated, found in their research distinctive travel personality traits, with two extremes of sport tourists, namely the allocentric and the psychocentric. The former is seen as the trend setter, the challenger, the courageous person who wilfully desires to be the first traveller to a new destination, setting or environment. In effect this tourist could be referred to as a leader. An example of the allocentric sports tourist would be the individual to first experience paragliding or paddle down a historical river. This group can also be found participating in dangerous and extreme sports. The psychocentric, on the other hand, is a follower who prefers to travel to familiar and safe sports tourism areas, after some family member or acquaintances have already experienced the sport and after the novelty of the sport has worn off (**Plogg, 1987**).

Table 1.2: Allocentric and psychocentric travellers

ALLOCENTRIC	PSYCHOCENTRIC
More frequent travel	Less travel
Venturesome	Less venturesome
Self-confident	Less self-confident
Less inhibited	More inhibited
Less anxious	More anxious
Travel by various means	Travel most likely by car
Select more exotic sports destinations	Select familiar and safe destinations
Spend more money on destinations	Spends less money on travel while on vacation

(Source: Plogg, 1987)

An understanding of the consumer is very important for successful business in the tourism industry. When the different facets of the tourism, travel and hospitality world meet the needs of the consumers, there is some chance of business success, provided that other financial and managerial inputs are appropriate. More than just an understanding of human needs is required for predicting the effects of motivation on behaviour. An understanding is needed of the process whereby these needs are transformed into motivated behaviour and the way in which the sport tourist's expectations give this motivated behaviour its direction (**Witt and Wright, 1993:44**).

Thus, if tourist expectations are met or exceeded by tourism operations, repeat business and positive word-of-mouth advertising can be expected, as well as the ability to maintain or even increase the current level of charging for the existing tourism service. Understanding tourist needs falls within the area of the psychology of the tourists' behaviour. It is concerned with what motivates tourists, how they make decisions, what tourists think of the products they buy, how much they enjoy and learn during their holiday experiences, how they interact with the local people and environment, and how satisfied they are with their holidays (**McIntosh et al., 1995:167**).

Many trips are motivated by a number of factors. In sports tourism the primary purpose of a trip to a city is to attend a sports event, but the traveller might also have secondary motivations, such as sightseeing or visiting friends and relatives, as described by **Gammon and Robinson (1997)**. But when a tourist primarily travels to visit friends or relatives, and decides to attend a sports event while there, the sports event becomes a secondary motive to travel.

There are many unique sports activities associated with sports tourism. For example, if a particular marathon attracted tourists, then the marathon would be considered a sports tourism activity. In this situation, both the participants and the spectators might be sports tourists. It has been suggested that people travel to authenticate their lives. Ordinary, everyday life is judged to be of no value and people therefore travel in order to experience the 'high life' (**Law, 1996: 13**). People do not want to stay in the same place all year round and are drawn to lustrous events and landscapes if they can afford it or know about it.

Attending sport is the primary element in travelling in sports tourism. **Law (1996:7)** also identifies other facilities which are important for the experience of the tourist, but are unlikely to be the cause of the visit. These include hotels, shops, attractions and other services and are described as the secondary elements.

Visitors travel to purchase one product only, or to consume a number of products during their stay. Many of these products are unique to a certain place and they can only be consumed by travelling to the city where they are found. But the uniqueness these attractions alone does not guarantee an influx of tourists. While people have special interests for which they will travel long distances, most people will only travel for something that they perceive as really impressive (**Law, 1996:7**).

Great sport events are usually held in large cities, which have many products. Although these products are not the primary element for travelling or do not appear unique to the outsider, it does not mean that they are valueless for sports tourism. Visiting one of these secondary attractions can enhance the enjoyment of the trip. Tourists or consumers focus on or value things differently. **Robinson (1997)** identified the following five consumer values:

- **Economically orientated consumer**
  This sports tourists places great emphasis on economy, luxury and well-organised activities. Additionally, his or her interest lies in gaining knowledge of the activity. A prime example of such a person would be a sports tourist vacationing at one of the top ski resorts where lessons, skiing, amenities and accommodation refinements are available (**Robinson, 1997**).

- **Intellectually orientated consumer**
  This vacationer appreciates aesthetics, comparisons, and contests, particularly in highly skilled athletic performances. He or she analyses, contrasts and studies particular movements and strategies. An example could be a sports tourist spectator viewing an Olympic gymnastic event (**Robinson, 1997**).

- **Socially orientated consumer**
  Social values are the basic motives for such a traveller-consumer. The love of people, the affiliation rapport, the social interactions and cooperative spirit are the main characteristics. The sports contests and/or competitions are not necessarily the primary focus interest. An example of such a consumer would be a sports tourist golfer who, as a participant, would travel to various golf courses, enjoying the social contacts, the scheduled leisure activities and amenities (**Robinson, 1997**).

- **Politically orientated consumer**
  For the sports tourist, the importance of participation or visitation is highly influenced by status, power, sport icons and symbols. At times, the value is dependent on personal contact, association or residual influences. "Come ski where the Olympic Heroes competed" is an example of such consumer orientation. Another would be travelling to the official opening of a hall of fame where politicians as well as sport celebrities would be in attendance (**Robinson, 1997**).

- **Complementary orientated consumer**

  The drive and motive here for the complementary orientated consumer is a combination of two or more "core" consumer values in varying degrees. Nevertheless, there is a basic affinity for sports travel. For instance, a person may attend a professional baseball game for different reasons - social atmosphere, autograph sessions, skill appreciation, strategy analysis, and or because it is the "in thing to do". Also, a sports tourist combining different visitations/participation's within a particular geographic region or urban area would be another example (**Robinson, 1997**).

Tourists visiting an area because of a sport event spend money getting there and back, some of which is sport in the destination area, as well as at the event itself. It is tempting to consider all tourist expenditure at the event as a benefit to the area, - after deducting the costs incurred by the area. These include the cost of all imported goods and services; cost of bringing in staff or talent from outside; and organisational and marketing expenditure outside the area.

There may be uncertainty about calculating the expenditure of a tourist who happened to be in town for a business meeting and incidentally spent money at the sport event. The tourist would have possibly spent money somewhere else in town if the event did not occur. Therefore, all this spending by the business tourists in town should be considered as a benefit of the meeting, and not the sport event.

Attributing the expenditure to both the conference and the sport event would be double counting, so some sort of allocation is required. The best way to determine the allocation is by asking all visitors a set of questions about their reasons for visiting the destination and what proportion of their spending in the area, including the event, was due to the attraction of the event itself. From the answers, the proportion of tourist expenditure attributed to a given event or attraction can be estimated (**Getz, 1994:441**).

There is certain arbitrariness in these attribution procedures that might best be handled by doing a "sensitivity" analysis. Consultants use different attribution weightings. For example, 79% to 100% of the expenditure of residents and 10% to 27% of day-tripper expenditure may be excluded before concluding that the results were not affected in a major way.

Time-switching is another complication (**Naude, 1998**). Some tourists attending events might have simply rescheduled a planned visit to the area, while others might have stayed away because of perceived congestion or expense associated with an event. Some residents might even decide to leave town while a major event is held, thereby generating an economic loss for the area. It is difficult to take this considerations into account, but at a minimum visitors should be asked if their visit to the area would have been made at another time and had merely been rescheduled to co-incide with the event (**Getz, 1994:442**). The expenditures of time-switchers should not be taken into account in the calculations of incremental income.

1.5   CONCLUSION

It was the aim of this chapter to give clarity on the concepts tourism, sport and sports tourism. Kurtzman did a lot of work on this theme and could be seen as the father of sports tourism. His work reflects that devotion. He is devoted to growth in the field of research in sports tourism. This chapter also explained the criteria for classifying a tourist as a sports tourist. The author's view is that a sports tourist is a person who travels primarily for a sporting activity or event but who does not necessarily refrain from participating in other forms of tourism during his/her trip. In other words, one can be a sports tourist and also visit eco-attractions, conferences and museums, etc. It is, however, important from a research point of view that more work needs to be done on themes like sports tourism in South Africa.

Sports tourism has definite economic, social and ecological impacts. In economic terms it generates revenue and jobs. Its social impacts involve communication and exposure to other communities and cultures. Ecologically it impacts on the creation of infra- and suprastructures. For the purpose of this book, the emphasis will be on its economic and social impact.

Chapter 2

History of sports tourism

Your legacy should be that you made it better than it was when you got it
Lee Iacocca

2.1 INTRODUCION

Travel is ancient behaviour. It laid the foundation for sports tourism as we know it is today (**Saayman, 2000**). The realities of travel in earlier times were harsh, with the restrictions of civilizations and constraints in modes of travel, accommodations and services. Furthermore, in primitive societies people rarely had the leisure time required for pleasure travel. Travel was therefore not an activity of relaxation, but dangerous and undertaken for very specific reasons. As the quality of life increased, people began to move more readily from one place to another. Shorter workweeks and the phenomenon of holidays contributed to mass travel, relaxation and self-development. Gradually, travel and tourism were transformed; more travel for more reasons and motives took place and the activity is still growing at a rapid rate. In addition, technological, political and social events made tourism a worldwide leisure experience (**Bhatia, 1983:6**). It is thus the aim of this chapter to give an overview of the evolution of sports tourism. This evolution culminated in billions of dollars in global business. From an academic point of view it is also important to see what lessons can be learnt from the past and to make some predictions about the future.

2.2 HISTORICAL OVERVIEW

In the annals of history, sport seems to have played a minor or secondary role in touristic popularity and trust. Since the term "tourism" did not appear in the English language until the early 19th century, the word "tour" was more closely associated with the idea of an individual being temporarily away from his/her home environment (**Laverty, 1989:13**). Globally people are participating more in sport and travelling to certain destinations for the pleasure and enjoyment of physical activities, both on an amateur and/or professional level. These travellers are more conscious of the inherent values emanating from sports and are prepared to financially support their inclinations. This led to global sporting practices which generate a considerable amount of money. It was pointed out in chapter one that there are different role players in sport tourism, therefore there are different motives for travel.

Sports travel is rapidly increasing for all levels and ages of society, especially in South Africa, where it gained momentum after the 1994 democratic election.

Furthermore, many sports destinations are being organised and marketed according to knowledgeable approaches and human legacies.

The history of sports tourism, has never been analysed for the purpose of gaining insight that can help current planners and marketers to prepare for the future. Little background has been provided to indicate lessons and relationships that still exist today. There is a notable legacy that has never been explored.

Stone Age man had more leisure time than any of his descendants (**Reader's Digest, 1974:24**). He did not wander aimlessly; rather, he moved in an annual cycle developing a deep knowledge of his environment and territory. They found more time for leisure activities, games and story-telling after their hunting for the day was finished. Groups moved and travelled in relation to other groups and food resources. Leadership amongst such groupings would be "informal - based on a combination of age, strength, intelligence and success in hunting" (**Zauhar: 95:1**). Movement from one place to another was based on basic needs in terms of finding food and shelter. According to Maslow's motivation hierarchy, their emphasis would be on primary needs. The following section will give an overview of how sports tourism developed in various nations and/or phases over a period of thousands of years.

2.2.1 EGYPTIANS

Sports tourism certainly flourished during this Egyptian era. In effect, certain authors and historians have suggested that the "sporting tradition" can be attested to the Kingdom of the Pharaohs (**Habashi, 1992:24**). A variety of sporting activities took place involving spectatorism. Royalty also seemed very interested in the promotion of and participation in such activities.

The Egyptians enjoyed watching performances in which strength and dexterity were manifested. Ball games, hunting, fishing and fowling as well as wrestling contests, boxing matches and bullfights were at the order of the day (**Durant,1954:168**). Proof of tug-of-war also exists. It was also important to have spectators to watch, while other people had to name and promote performers or had to be directors of events or managers of participation (**Olivova, 1984:59**). In fact, the king would name and promote performers to be directors of events, managers of court activities and producers of royal festivals. It was considered as a great honour to be selected in one of these positions.

Ancient murals have been discovered depicting a good number of wrestlers, ranging from 59 couples to 209 pairs (**Zauhar, 95:48**). Various stages and styles of wrestling are also sketched. Relics dating from 1190 to 1160 BC show spectators eagerly watching contests of wrestling and fencing with sticks (**Carroll, 1988:121-122**). On one particular frieze, grandstands are shown with ten pairs of wrestlers in the ring (**Olivova, 1984:49-50**). Some of the "most interesting scenes illustrate Egyptians fighting with foreigners".

There is also evidence that swimming was very popular. Boats were a common means of transportation and the Nile played a major role as a water highway. In effect, boat yards were to be found at various points. The existence of professional rowers armed with long poles trying to capsize vessels is implied and can thus not be excluded (**Olivova,1984:49-50**). The Pharaohs delighted themselves in many forms of sporting activites; which included horse riding, hunting and fishing (**Olivova, 1984:49-50**). They particularly enjoyed fishing in artificial ponds in the royal gardens, and they derived great pleasure performing for an audience. Festival events in Egyptian times were connected to the different phases of the vegetation cycle and the start of summer floods. The general public took an active part in all festival processions and celebrations. The kings most often were the chief performers who demonstrated their physical powers (**Zauhar, 1995:52-55**). A picture on a tomb wall of "King Akenaton seated on his throne awaiting tribute from Nubia" depicts a celebration of activities including sports competitions. Usually, these contests took place in front of the Pharaoh, his court, nobles, soldiers and ambassadors from foreign countries.

Although there is assertion that "women enjoyed equal rights with men throughout Egyptian history", wall paintings and sketches mostly depict male athletes (**Guttmann, 1981:9**). The female role was usually considered supportive, and artefacts testify that Egyptian women swam, participated in aquatic games and races, and played ball. From about 1500 BC onward, signs of tourism which include travel for simple curiosity or pleasure, were quite discernible (**Casson, 1974:32**).

Throughout the history of Greece, people lived in separate communities called city-states, which were mostly found along the coast. Although separate, these city states were built in a uniform standardised fashion (**Zauher, 1995: 96**). They never amalgamated nor united to constitute larger urban or rural entities and were constantly engaged in bickering, struggles and wars. Yet, these contentious conflicts never stopped the Olympic or festive competitions (**Casson, 1974:77**). These activities might have contributed to these competitions. Even in the modern era countries or regions use sport as a vehicle to demonstrate their strength.

Various factors contributed to the indulgence of Greeks in sporting events and physical activity. Amongst the most prominent were geography, climate, social appreciation and political drive. It was all about the strive to link men to their gods. Their obsession with victory, especially in athletic ventures, was a distinguishable and discernible feature. Greeks valued recognition and they idolised danger and pain. Much of their daily life was spent in physical rivalry. Their motto, in sum, was "live to fight and fight to live". They admired speed in running, skill in wrestling, bodily strength, physical beauty, eloquence and form (**Durant, 1954:231-233**). The Greeks showered their victors with various gifts: oils, iron, silver, gold and money. That varied with contests. The first prize usually represented five times the value of the second prize. Athens was the most rewarding venue for athletic powers and fortitude.

Participatory citizens to the forty festivals listed came from all parts of Greece and even beyond the borders of the country in veneration of certain gods such as Prometheus, Hermes and maid Palaistra (**Woody, 1949:339**). Athletic events varied from contest to contest. For instance, the Ancient Olympics comprised the running of races, long jumps, discus and javelin, wrestling, boxing, bare-knuckle boxing, chariot racing and horse racing (**Casson, 1974:78**). Some festivals even featured stud races, gymnastics, double races, and races in heavy armor. Games and festivals were held over three to seven days. Some were scheduled every other year - alternating between summer and winter - such as the Nomian and the Isthmian Games. At times, contests and competitions were arranged by age categories. Some Greek inscriptions record up to nine rounds of competition.

Homer, in Odysseus, makes mention of crowds - thousands of people following running, wrestling and discus events. He describes, in dramatic fashion, incidents where emotions have swayed the spectators; particularly where there were greedy entertainers anxious to win and eager to reap the highest rewards. There is also mention of onlookers gasping in amusement or responding boisterously and raising raucous noise (**Miller, 1992**).

Spectators formed a large part of the people who were involved in sport at that stage. The people found some pleasure in watching how men and women participated.

In the hippodrome, horses paraded before crowds of spectators, delighting the fans. During the Panathesian festivals, special varied programmes were offered to foreign visitors, particularly during the 2nd century BC. Some entertainment included gambling, tavern hopping and dancing girls. The aim was to give onlookers something to do during their stay. This could have been the start of entertainment for tourists and locals who attended events. The Marathonian Games drew vast numbers of spectators from abroad. The big event programme included gymnastics, chariot racing, horse races and wrestling, establishing a precedent leading to a long-term tradition (**Guttmann, 1981:347**).

Athletes began to hire trainers and coaches. The increase in numbers of idle passive onlookers also gradually became evident. More time and interest were devoted to observing contests. Celebrations became forms of rest, recreation, and manifestation of patriotism. Women were, to a large degree, excluded from certain games, not only as participants, but also as mere spectators (**Guttmann, 1981:18**).

To attract tourists, certain services were required for travelling. Travelling was strenuous and dangerous and roads offered little in terms of amenities. People were obliged to travel in groups, with plenty of slaves. One reason for this was safety; another was baggage conveyance. These major events emphasised needs other than just the event itself. Aspects such as transport and transport routes, accommodation, entertainment and others come to the fore. These aspects were the foundation of the tourism industry, as we know it today. Groups of city-states came together for many festivals. The most important of these festivals are discussed below.

Olympic Games
No one knows exactly when or how the Olympic Games started, but certain explanations are offered in the mythology of the ancient Greeks. According to Greek mythology it started with Hercules, the strongest of all men challenged his four brothers to a race before the Gods in the fields of Olympia. The recorded history of the Games dates back to actually begins in 776 BC - a point at which the Greeks marked their calendars in four-year periods called Olympiads (**Anon, 1999(a)**). The

work of recording the Games was done by the scientist Hippias van Elis and was continued by the well known Greek philosopher Aristoteles (**Van der Merwe, 1990: 34**).

The development of the Olympic Games may be describe in the following terms: "In ancient Greece, the Olympic Games became one of the world's most enduring and hallowed institutions. They were celebrated continuously for almost 1,200 years. The athletes who won were lauded as heroes for life, and often elevated to the status of royalty in their hometowns. Statues were erected in their honour around the extraordinary Temple of Zeus, near the Sacred Grove of Altis and the stadium at Olympia.

In 393 AD, the Roman Emperor Theodosius declared the Olympic Games corrupt and put an end to them. Earthquakes and floods buried Olympia and the temple of Zeus until the German excavations of the 1870's. When the statues emerged from the vaults of antiquity - and the overwhelming cultural beauty of Greek sport was put on display - Europe went into a frenzy for all things classical.

A young Frenchman, Baron Pierre de Coubertin, found the sacred ground of Olympia particularly fascinating. In his inspiration, he conceived the idea of Modern Olympic Games - and successfully proposed it to a gathering of the world's leading sports authorities on 23 June 1894 in the Grand Hall of the Sorbonne in Paris. Coubertin's dream of creating the world's greatest sporting event - a truly international spectacle that would travel among the capitals of the world every four years - was always a means to a far greater end. Coubertin and his colleagues - like their heirs in the Modern Olympic Movement - believed that global sport could become a global platform for peace. During the last century, the Olympic Movement has succeeded in many ways beyond Coubertin's dream. It has survived the traumas of two World Wars, endured the horrors of modern terrorism, suffered political boycotts and overcome economic hardships that threatened its very existence. Today, the Olympic Movement is stronger and healthier" (**Anon, 1999(a)**).

The Olympic Games is one of the great inheritances from the Greeks. Over the years it grew to a global event. The following table indicates some of the statistics of participation in the Olympic Games.

Table 2.1: Participation in the Olympic Games

YEAR	CITY	PARTICIPANTS
1896	Athens	311
1900	Paris	1330
1904	Saint-Louis	625
1908	London	2035
1912	Stockholm	2547
1920	Antwerp	2607
1924	Paris	3092
1928	Amsterdam	3014
1932	Lost Angeles	1408
1936	Berlin	3959
1948	London	4099
1952	Helsinki	5867
1956	Melbourne	3184
1960	Rome	5348
1964	Tokyo	4457
1968	Mexico City	5531
1972	Munchen	7123
1976	Montreal	6085
1980	Moscow	5217
1984	Los Angeles	6797
1988	Seoul	8465
1992	Barcelona	9959
1996	Atlanta	11 000
2000	Sydney	

(Statistics: Van der Merwe, 1990; Cape Town 2004 Olympic Bid, 1997 In Scholtz: 1999, and Anon(b), 1999)

Pythian Games

The god of the Delphi Kingdom, namely Apollo himself was the founder of the Python Games when he defeated the snake Python. After 582 BC, when the games were re-introduced, it was held every four years in the months of August/September in the third year of the Olympiad. In 275 BC an impressive station was built in the mountains of Delphi. The programme of these Games was known for its music competitions before the sport programme. The winner of each section received a Lourier crown of the Louriertree, which was a symbol of the holiness of Apollo. The

Pythian Games died together with the ancient Olympic Games, by order of Theodosius I in 394 AC (**Van der Merwe, 1990: 43-44**).

Isthmian Games

Sisufos started the Isthmian Games as a funeral game in remembrance of the hero Melikertes-Palaimon. Its importance lay in the fact that it was situated along one of the important trade roads between Corinth and Athens. The Games were characterised by the hippios - a running activity in the sport section. The programme also included music, art and recital competitions. The interesting thing about these Games was the reference by Walton (**see Van der Merwe, 1990: 43**) of women competitors later on.

Nimian Games

There are two interesting myths about the origin of the Nimian Games, told by Yalouris in **Van der Merwe (1990: 44)**. The first one is about the little baby boy of king Lukoergos who was bitten by a snake and died. The second is the story of Hercules, who ordered to kill the "immortal" lion. Hercules killed the lion with his bare hands and gave it as sacrifice to Zeus.

The games were held every two years and were mainly based on sport activities. It did not have the same importance of the previous three games but it managed to bring different cultures together (**Van der Merwe, 1990: 43**).

These games polarised tourists. At any one time, there was a large concentration of travellers. They stayed in a location in order to attend the religious festivals. They wanted to be part of the great events. Some came days prior to the scheduled activities; others lingered on after the closing ceremonies. Incidental attractions were organised with the specific aim to entertain these people. Many visitors had enough time to arrive early and enjoy the atmosphere of excitement before returning home. There is also mention of tens of thousands of visitors, apart from the number of active participants. Hence, vendors of essential and non-essential services, like food, drink, souvenirs, guided tours, transportation and the like, became omnipresent (**Casson, 1974:66-78**). For visitor lodging, two-story inns were with twenty rooms, each measuring 15 feet square. Special Oracles were available for government officials, statesmen, generals and notables. In time an abundance of inns offering rest and life necessities were established along different roadways, for the comfort of travellers. Some had sufficient amenities; others simply offered sleeping quarters. Nonetheless, this hospitality trend diminished the risks and perils of travel to some degree. Such improvements assisted in the promotion and promulgation of sports tourism and tourism in the broader sense.

2.2.3 ROMANS

The Roman Empire was one of the strongest empires of the time. Therefore it was the destination of visitors all over the world, who wanted to settle there. It was difficult to keep peace among all the different cultures, and something had to be deviced to keep them occupied. Large festivals and sport events were consequently held. These events were supported by the Romans and their slaves who were captured mainly in Antigua, Alexandria, Constantinople and Jerusalem (**Scholtz, 1999: 35**).

The Romans were known as sensation seekers, and their sport activities were more bloodthirsty and cruel than those of the Egyptians and the Greeks. They had quite a few public holidays that were spent watching fights between humans and "beasts". Scenes of criminals who were prosecuted and battles between gladiators and animals were often presented. Crowds went wild, money was spent and organisers smiled. Sports tourism was a growing economic phenomenon. They spent much money on the preparation of leisure activities, for example the Roman Baths, which can still be found in Europe and in Britain.

Large numbers of tourist were attracted to act out their cruel fantasies, although it could mean their death. During these feasts spectators as well as gladiators lost their lives when crowds got out of hand. Over 20 000 gladiators were trained in Rome and this became a huge tourism attraction. Zauhar, in **Scholtz (1999)**, states that ancient Roman life demonstrated the love of brutal and cruel festivals. Spectators, especially the educated Romans, took the death of men and beast for granted. Combats between beast and beast, beast and men, and between men and men were common entertainment.

Pleasure associated with watching bloodthirsty sports was also prevalant in the prosecution of Christians. Large numbers of crowds gathered to watch Christians burn or being thrown into lion cages as a sports activity at a major event.

Activities such as boat races, horse races, wrestle boxing, ball games and hunting also took place (**Scholtz, 1999:36**). "The underlying principle or cult was to consolidate all parts of Roman Empire by sports and entertainment. In occasion, thousands of birds were set free amongst onlooker crowds and lottery tickets were thrown into the mass of spectators offering vessels, garments, gold and pearls as gifts - all to encourage attendee retention, interest and satisfaction. At times, large processions were held prior to certain Games in honour of particular gods, men or victorious warriors which was a delight to onlookers" (**Zauhar, 1996(a): 14**). The

Romans left the modern world one of the architectural wonders of the world, namely the Coliseum. It was initially known as the Flaviance Amphitheater, because Emperor Vespasianus built it in 72 AC. The opening of the Amphitheater lasted for 100 days during which, 9000 wild animals and 2000 gladiators lost their lives. The coliseum was the first indoor stadium in the world, and could be used in rainy as well as sunny weather (**Van der Merwe, 1990: 54**).

Roman games

When Generals who returned from war as conquerors they wanted to win the favour of their people by arranging a sports feast for the people. The people of Rome could attend the games free of charge. One of these famous games was known as the Ludi Magni and started in September each year. These games started at the Temple of Jupiter on the Capitolium and moved to the Circus Maximus. The Circus Maximus could host more than 150 000 people.

The major event of the Games was the chariot race. Two or four horses pulled the chariots. The driver was tied to the chariot with the rein. The drivers usually wore the colours of the team they represented. The colours were white, red blue and green. The competition was between the different teams, dressed in different colours. The winner was rewarded with a palm leaf. The horses were specially bred for this game and were trained in Africa and Spain.

Another item was fencing. This eventually became more popular than the chariot races. It probably had its origin with the Etruscans, who had organised fights between people to the death and which were part of a funeral game for an important leader. The tradition of Gladiators was born out of this funeral game.

Julius Caesar held fights of 320 pairs of fighters, and the sport grew each year. In the time of Augustus, 63 BC until 14 AC, Gladiators was a national sport. After a gladiator fight the spectators would decide if he could live or die by a simple thumbs-up or thumbs-down sign for the editor of the arena. A gladiator who was killed would be burnt with a red-hot iron to make sure that he was really dead.

Other Roman games included ball games which were played before supper or dinner. These games were named trigon, harpastum and follis. On days when there were no show games the Romas kept themselves busy with hiking, gambling, exercising, or just relaxing in the Roman baths. At these baths there were warm and cold baths, as well as massage rooms, gyms, palaistrai, conference rooms, lounges, libraries, dining rooms, show rooms and shops.

Athletic games such as the Pan-Helenistic Games were not very popular with the

Romans.

2.2.4 SUMARIANS

During the Sumarian period, wrestling became the first highly developed sport. A cylindric seal from the middle of the third millennium BC depicts two pairs of naked wrestlers, while a relief carving from the same period shows a boxing match (**Olivova, 1984:38**). Furthermore, " in the context of military campaigns, swimming, using inflated animal skins, has been attested" (**Grun, 1991:3**). There is no information on how many spectators were present at Sumarian physical activities. People were mostly interested in the performer-participant rather than in those who glorified physical skills or cheered them on (**Guttmann, 1981:1**). However, women of the Minion civilization (2000 to 1200 BC), living on the Island of Crete, held a position superior to men. A number of artifacts portray women occupying the best seats while men are pictured crowded together (**Howell, 1976:9**).

2.2.5 BABYLONIANS

The Babylonians, on the other hand, were traders as well as devoted travellers (**Reader's Digest, 1974:58**). Their ships sailed the Euphrates to the Persian Gulf, principally to Arabia and India. Their caravan routes extended eastward and westward. Public and private celebrations provided adequate opportunities for hunting and fishing. Skills in using the bow were perfected and men learned to ride horses, although the chariot still remained quite fashionable (**Olivova, 1984:90**).

2.2.6 CRETE- MENONIANS

During the Crete-Menonian period, onlookers played an important role in all social classes. Performances were public and open to men and women. They undoubtedly enjoyed great popularity. Wrestling was fashionable but boxing was most revered. Minonian art depicts grandstands, terraces and windows for spectator purposes. In effect, "a fragment of Knosses well portrays over three hundred and fifty people, with considerable realism, gesticulating and talking animatedly as though commenting on the performance. Apparently, public festivals were a striking feature of this culture" (**Zauhar, 96:69-95**).

Civilisations, regardless of their origin, historical evolution, or presumed disappearance, tended to have some types of festivities and celebrations within their structural governance. These included athletic competitions with local and visiting participants and spectators. Some records also show specific facilities for these purposes. Sport entertainment and amusement was undoubtedly a part of everyday life - regardless of daily chores and regular social and political obligations.

2.3   CONCLUSION

The Greek, Roman and Egyptian civilisations laid the foundation for sports tourism. Greeks devoted much time to the preparation of Games. The Games were most probably their biggest contribution to what we know of sport tourism today. They dispatched messengers or runners well in advance to announce the exact dates of their festivities. These messengers would invite various city-states to participate, actively or passively, even to the point of assuring peace and security in their projected travels.

Games were also of great economic significance, including housing, special services, souvenirs and gifts bought by delegates and visitors. This led to the development of facilities: swimming pools, steam baths, massage halls, semicircular auditoria, gymnasia and promenade colonnades. The Romans put a lot of emphasis on leisure in the preperation of athletes for the contest.

Particular esteem was accorded to the victors of game events. All basked in glory, popularity, and hero-worshipping. Professional athletes as well as spectators from different areas and countries moved from city to city and festival to festival - a sports touristic phenomenon.

Sports tourism in the ancient days was managed along, the same principles as today. The essence of this is that business will grow if people are given what they need or want. Sports tourism has developed into a business with many facets. Sports tourism is one of the components that contribute to tourism globally. It forces organisers to cater for international needs in order to manage events successfully.

Major findings or implications of the historical evaluation of sports tourism have to be seen in the context of the development of tourism in general. All the different motivations for travel contributed to the tourism industry as it is known today. The important aspect is that each aspect is developing in a mega-tourism business, creating jobs and breaking down barriers. These barriers include political, economical, cultural and social barriers.

Chapter 3

Sensation-seeking & participation in risky sports tourism activities

It is only by risking our persons from one hour to another that we live at al
William James

3.1 INTRODUCTION

Among the biologically rooted theories of personality, Marvin Zuckerman's sensation-seeking model has proved to be very effective to explain and predict certain types of risky behaviours, including specific types of sports tourism. Current views on optimal level of stimulation and arousal can be traced back to **Wundt (1893)** who first formulated it to explain the curvilinear relationship between affective reactions and intensities of stimulation. **Leuba (1955)** suggested that organisms prefer some intermediate range of stimulation, which may be considered optimal for that organism. The clearest definition of the optimal state of arousal came from **Berlyne (1960:194)**, namely:

For an individual organism at a particular time there will be an optimal influx of arousal potential. Arousal potential that deviates in either an upward or downward direction from this optimum will be drive-inducing or aversive.

Although activation can be seen as a perceptive global theoretical construct, it lacks empirical exactness. In the place thereof and based on the general concept of optimal arousal, **Zuckerman (1979:10)** composed the sensation-seeking tendency as alternative which moved beyond the optimal level of arousal, defining sensation-seeking as:

a trait defined by the need for varied, novel, and complex sensations and experiences and the willingness to take physical and social risks for the sake of such experience.

Since then, a few minor changes have been made, thus defining sensation-seeking as:

a trait defined by the seeking of varied, novel, complex, and intense sensations and experiences, and the willingness to take physical, social, legal, and financial risks for the sake of such experiences (**Zuckerman, 1994:27**).

A sensation-seeker can thus be described as a person who needs varied, complex, novel and intense forms of stimulation and experiences, and who is capable of taking physical and social risks inherent in such experiences. Sensation-seeking is regarded as a stable individual trait according to which individuals can be distinguished as low, medium or high sensation-seekers. The latter are characteristically under-aroused and subsequently they seek stimulation to raise their arousal to a level that is optimal for their functioning. They have a stronger tendency towards experiences which include variation, complexity and risks, as well as toward tourism and leisure (**Schwartz, Burkhart and Green, 1978**). Low sensation-seekers, on the contrary, tend to be over-aroused and they attempt to avoid excessive stimulation in order to reduce or maintain a level more optimal for effective functioning (**Farley, 1976**). Since 1960, **Zuckerman (1994)** has designed six Sensation-seeking Scales (SSS). These scales have proved to be most profitable and valid psychological instruments to assess the personality trait of sensation-seeking.

Travel, among a large variety of tourism activities, provides the individual with a diverse variety of alternative experiences (**Zuckerman, 1994**). At the extremes, a vacation may consist of anything from unusual and exotic activities to relatively repetitive, commonplace experiences. One possible explanation for the wide variation in vacation preferences among individuals is the need for novelty or stimulation. Persons seeking stimulation can express a preference for vacations characterised as invigorating and/or innovative; whereas those avoiding stimulation will prefer vacations described as structural and/or enriching. Studies carried out in the field of tourism have demonstrated that high sensation-seekers are prone to be drawn to vacations and activities that involve high physical and social risk taking. Low sensation-seekers like the comfortable familiarity of their usual environment. Thus, when they travel they like to plan their trips carefully or have it planned for them so that there will be no unexpected events. When they vacation they often go to the same place every year. High sensation-seekers, on the other hand, like to travel to exotic places and do not worry much about making all their reservations in advance. They may change their itinerary on impulse as they travel (**Zuckerman, 1994**). It is the aim of this chapter to give some theory on why people travel for different sports activities. This chapter will also indicate how tourism can benefit from the research findings on sensation-seeking, in order to promote a greater variety of tourism events. This furthermore has the advantage that it makes market segmentation easier.

3.2   A SPECTRUM OF SENSATION-SEEKING BEHAVIOUR

Research have shown that high sensation-seekers are inclined to participate in risky activities such as skydiving (**Breivik, 1991; Freixanet, 1991; Steynberg, 1997**), water-skiing (**Freixanet, 1991**), gliding (**Zaleski, 1984; Freixanet, 1991**), rock-climbing, kayak paddling and acrobatic flying (**Calhoon, 1988; Connolly, 1981; Zuckerman, 1983b**), scuba-diving (**Biersner and LaRocco, 1983; Freixanet, 1991; Steynberg, 1997**), auto-racing (**Freixanet, 1991; Straub, 1982; Zaleski, 1984**), Alpine skiing (**Bouter, Knipschild, Feij and Volovics, 1988; Calhoon, 1988; Landeweerd, Urlings & DeJong, 1990**), mountain-climbing (**Cronin, 1991; Fowler, von Knorring and Oreland, 1980; Freixanet, 1991**), caving (**Rossi and Cereatti, 1993**), hang-gliding (**Breivik, 1991; Freixanet, 1991; Wagner and Houlihan, 1994**), elite rock climbing (**Robinson, 1985**), rugby (**Potgieter and Bisschoff, 1991; Steynberg, 1997**), ballooning (**Freixanet, 1991**), racing of motorcycles (**Freixanet, 1991**), racing of boats (**Freixanet, 1991**), adventuring (**Freixanet, 1991**), white-water canoeing (**Breivik, 1991**), as well as anti-social youth behaviour and delinquency (**Newcomb and McGee, 1991; Simo and Perez, 1991; Zuckerman, 1979**), criminal behaviour (**Haapasalo, 1990; Horvath and Zuckerman, 1993**), gambling (**Hayes, 1988; Zuckerman and Kuhlman, 1978**) and sexual behaviour (**Clement and Jonah, 1984; Zuckerman, 1994**). It was found that factors such as gender, age, ethnicity, nationality, language, culture and religion have a strong meditating role in sensation-seeking (**Zuckerman, 1979; 1983b; 1994**).

Sport and leisure seem to provide a relatively social form of sensation-seeking in that they stimulate arousal, require skills, and sometimes provide a competitive-aggressive outlet that only rarely results in serious injury to oneself or others. Watching sports is practically risk-free but less arousing than actual participation. Nevertheless, for millions of people the excitement of watching their teams compete is the greatest thrill they could have.

The next section gives a profile of the high sensation-seeker and certain behavioural tendencies of the high sensation-seeker. An individual high sensation-seeker will not necessarily exhibit all these characteristics.

High sensation-seekers have the following characteristics:

- They exhibit risky behaviour (**Burkhart, Schwartz and Green, 1978; Zuckerman, 1994**) and enjoy participation in risky sport and tourism activities (**Breivik, 1991a; Rowland, Franken and Harrison, 1986; Watson, 1985**). They enjoy to travel to exotic places (**Zuckerman, 1979; Zuckerman, 1994**) and to gamble at high stakes (**Waters and Kirk, 1968, Zuckerman, 1974; 1994**).

- They stop participating in the activity when the stimulation value is insufficient (**Zuckerman, 1979**) and high sensation-seekers easily get bored (**Zuckerman, 1979; 1994**).

- They have a bigger tolerance for high intensity stimulation (**Zuckerman, 1979; Zuckerman, 1994**) and can make quicker observations than low sensation-seekers (**Neary and Zuckerman, 1976**).

- They are creative (**Emmons, 1981; Okamoto and Takari, 1992**), uncomfortable and flexible (**Farley, 1976**). There is a relationship between sensation-seeking and general intelligence (**Anderson, 1973; Zuckerman, 1979; 1994**). Sensation-seekers have primary process thoughts and vague images, dreams, day-dreams (**Giambra, 1977; Zuckerman, 1994**), unrealistic fantasies (**Bailey et al, 1982; Franken and Rowland, 1990**) or even hallucinations (**Zuckerman, 1979**).

- They prefer blue and green colours (**Berkowitz, 1967; Zuckerman, 1979**).

- They prefer classical music or jazz (**Zuckerman and Hopkins, 1979; Zuckerman, Persky, Hopkins, Murtaugh, Basu and Schilling, 1966**) and enjoy heavy metal music (**Zuckerman, 1979; 1994**).

- They prefer vacations which offer personal interaction and are interested in crisis vacations (**Irey, 1979; Kish and Donnenwerth, 1969; 1972**), but avoid cosmic vacations (**Kish and Donnenwerth, 1972**). High sensation-seekers are usually found in unusual (**Kish and Donnenwerth, 1972; Piet, 1987; Zuckerman, 1979**) and dangerous vacations (**Montag and Birenbaum, 1986; Musolino and Hershenson, 1977; Zaleski, 1984**).

- They are liberal in their social behaviour (**Looft, 1971; Pearson and Sheffield, 1975**).

- They can be sexually permissive (**Hendrick & Hendrick, 1987; Kish and Donnenwerth, 1972; Zuckerman, 1979**). They also display on interest in visual and audio-visual stimulation, as well as tangible sexual stimulation (**Brown, Ruder, Ruder and Young, 1974**). They can participate in a wide variety of sexual activities and with a variety of people (**Emmons, 1981; Zuckerman, Bone, Neary, Mangelsdorf and Brustman, 1972; Zuckerman, Tushup and Finner, 1976**). High sensation-seekers are relatively more attracted to persons perceived as dissimilar to themselves (**Thorton, Ryckman and Gold, 1981; Williams, Ryckman, Gold and Lenney, 1982**).

- They have a charismatic type of religion, but outgrow religious puritanism (**Zuckerman, 1979; Zuckerman and Need, 1980**).

- They sometimes use a wide variety of drugs (**Kaestner, Rosen and Appel, 1977; Zuckerman, 1983a; 1994**).

- They are smokers (**Zuckerman, Ball and Black, 1990; Zuckerman, 1974; Zuckerman and Need, 1980**).

- They may sometimes drink heavily (**Johnson, 1988; Mookcherjee, 1986; Schwartz, Burkhart and Green, 1978**).

- They prefer spicy, sour and crunchy foods (**Logue and Smith, 1986; Kish and Donnenwerth, 1972; Wolowitz, 1964**).

- They are impulsive extroverts (**Gerbing, Ahabi and Patton, 1987; Zuckerman, 1994**).

- They show a psychopathological tendency toward mania (**Blackburn, 1969; Cronin and Zuckerman, 1992; Zuckerman, Bone, Neary, Mangelsdorf and Brustman, 1972**) and sociopathy (**Zuckerman, 1979**) and may be narcissistic (**Zuckerman, 1979; Emmons, 1981**).

- They may participate in criminal violence (**Daitzman, Zuckerman, Sammelwitz and Ganjam, 1978; Haapasalo, 1990**).

- They reveal an internal locus of control (**Blenner and Haier, 1986; Zuckerman, 1994**).

- They can cope with intense levels of pain (**Petrie, Collins and Soloman, 1958; Zuckerman, 1979**).

- They reveal positive behaviour, but can get angry (**Zuckerman, 1979; 1984**).

- They tend towards antisocial behaviour like traffic violations and reckless driving (**Arnett, 1991; Heino, van den Molen and Wilde, 1992; Furnham and Saipe, 1993**).

- They are independent and hedonistic (**Zuckerman, 1979; 1994**).

- They are hermaphroditic (**Zuckerman et al., 1972**).

- They are self-dependent, but not devoted, caressing or affiliated (**Zuckerman and Link, 1968**).

- They may show certain field-independence tendencies (**Baker, 1988; Cohen et al., 1983; Zuckerman and Link, 1968**).

- They are dominant, autonomous, aggressive, radical and have a need for chance (**Gorman, 1970; Zuckerman, 1979; Zuckerman, Bone, Neary, Mangelsdorf and Brustman, 1972**). Subsequently the high sensation-seeker is inclined to conflict-intensity reactions in conflict situations, rather than conflict weakened situations (**Pilkington et al., 1988; Sternberg and Soriano, 1984**).

OTHER POSSIBLE SOCIAL FACTORS

- Parents can delegate the sensation-seeking model by giving an example, as well as through their genes (**Fulker et al., 1980; Zuckerman, 1979**).

- Birth order studies (**Bone et al., 1973; Zuckerman, 1979; 1994**) show that first-born and only children are more often high sensation-seekers than other children. These children receive more attention and stimulation.

- Family and environment can have a influence on the sensation-seeking model, because of a lack of opportunities and funds (**Zuckerman, 1979; 1994**).

- Criminal delinquency can be the only outlet for the sensation-seeking tendency in low socio-economical groups (**Farley, 1967**).

  The probability exists that social and genetic influences are in interaction with each other. In that case the biological theory is a bio-social theory which can facilitate or inhibit sensation-seeking behaviour.

3.3 GENERAL PARTICIPATION IN SPORT AND LEISURE

Sport and leisure activities and the types of activities and skills associated with specific sports and activities, as well as the experiences that are gained from practising them, may be classified in various ways. Some activities, for instance, contain a larger measure of competition or aggression than others. Characteristics such as intensity, exertion, power, exhaustion, speed, skill, strategy, risk of injury and danger, are associated in varying degrees with each of the more than 130 types of sport that are currently pursued (**Scholtz et al., 1997**). The same applies to other activities that are pursued for leisure and those that contain elements of risk, either physical or social. Sport and leisure activities such as boxing, parachuting, hang-gliding, free falling, rock-climbing, cave-climbing, bungee jumping, acrobatics, rugby, kayaking, river-rafting, motor-racing, motorbike racing, etc. involve the risk of injury, death and various forms of social and psychological harm. Rock-climbing involves the risk of losing one's grip, injury and even death. In competitive sports participants risk losing not only the competition, but also status, prestige, popularity, prize money, credit-worthiness or a cherished title. It is accompanied by disappointment, which includes the disappointment of failing to live up to the set standards.

Sport and leisure seem to provide a relatively pro-social form of sensation-seeking in that they stimulate arousal, require skills, and sometimes provide a competitive-aggressive outlet that only rarely results in serious injury to oneself or others. Watching sports and leisure is practically risk-free but less arousing than actual participation. But for millions of people the excitement of watching their teams compete is the greatest thrill they could have.

From the above it is clear that risk-taking in sport does not affect participants only, and that many risks of different kinds involving various degrees of danger can be linked to sport and leisure activities.

3.4 RISKY SPORTS AND LEISURE ACTIVITIES

It has been remarked that: "there is no stress like landing on an aircraft carrier, especially at night - not even being shot at by the enemy" (**Alkov, 1988**), and that nothing compares to "the intense emotional stress, before, during, and after a parachute jump" (**Schedlowski and Tewes, 1991**).

High sensation-seekers tend to choose risky sport and leisure activities like skydiving, scuba-diving and fire-fighting. These people apparently have a lack of fear or achieve fear levels which are manageable to them. It is also possible that their fear levels are not perceived by them as fear, but rather as excitement or a challenge. Low sensation-seekers, in contrast with high sensation-seekers, withdraw to a lower self-estimated risk level (**Zuckerman, 1979**). People who engage in sensation-seeking activities are inclined to experience less anxiety in physically dangerous situations. High sensation-seekers appraise risk as less dangerous and therefore experience less anxiety on high-risk levels than low sensation-seekers. Participation in risky leisure activities can thus be seen as a indicator of sensation-seeking. **Kusyszyn et al. (1973)** contrasted sensation-seeking in males which participated in high physical risky activities with sensation seeking in government officials and male students. They found that participants in high-risk activities achieve higher scores in sensation-seeking, excitement-seeking and adventure-seeking, general risk-taking, achievement-motivation, internal locus of control and a need for social approval than government officials and students.

Perceived risks are associated with sport and leisure activities, which involve two major dimensions, namely functional and psychological risks (**Cheron and Ritchie, 1982**). Functional risks refer to the potential inability to perform an activity and the danger of physical injuries. Activities which are classified as high in physical risks involve activities like snow-mobiling and snow-skiing, because of the danger of physical injuries involved. Psychological risks include dangers of personal failure or the failure to meet social standards, and frustration which arises from unsatisfactory experiences and the associated waste of valuable leisure time (**Cheron and Ritchie, 1982**).

High sensation-seekers are usually drawn to sport and leisure activities which are characterised by excitement, adventure or high physical or social risks. **Bouter et al. (1988)** found that Dutch skiers achieve higher sensation-seeking scores than non-skiers. It appeared that sensation-seeking differs according to different types of sport and leisure activities. Wagner and **Houlihan (1994)** used the Sensation-seeking Scale to differentiate between sensation-seeking levels of hang-gliders and golfers. It was found than hang-gliders had higher sensation-seeking scores than golfers. With reference to age, these results are in line with earlier results which show that younger sensation-seekers have higher sensation-seeking levels than older sensation-seekers. To explain this phenomenon, **Zuckerman (1979:126)** postulated that the decline in sensation-seeking with age can be due to the phenomenon that "experience in life leads to increasing conservatism and decreased risk taking", but that a alternative explanations for the age decline may be suggested from biological correlates of sensation-seeking".

Rowland et al. (1986) found that with time, high sensation-seekers tend to get involved in more sport and leisure activities than low sensation-seekers, but low sensation-seekers participate in leisure and sport activities for longer periods of time than high sensation-seekers. Their findings show that the need for new experiences and the attraction to high-risk sport and leisure activities characterise high sensation-seeker's participation in sport and leisure activities (**Rowland et al., 1986**). High sensation-seekers' need for new experiences lead to the findings that they will be interested in and participate in a wider variety of sport and leisure activities than low sensation-seekers (**Rowland et al., 1986**). In earlier research by **Schalling et al. (1988)** it was found that high sensation-seekers have a greater susceptibility for boredom than low sensation-seekers and their scope of participation shorten. **Rowland et al. (1986)** came to the conclusion that if high sensation-seekers are motivated by the need for new activities, as well as their susceptibility for boredom, they will exhaust the novelty of popular and easily accessible activities and will be forced to participate in less popular, less accessible and less risky sport and leisure activities. From a tourism perspective, and specifically sports tourism, events or activities mentioned above can attract sports tourists from across the globe to participate in one way or the other.

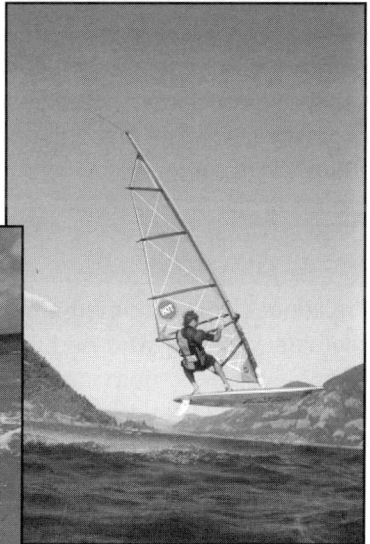

3.5   HIGH RISK SPORTS AND LEISURE ACTIVITIES

A review of the literature on sensation-seeking and sport identified riskiness as a major factor in sport, showing a positive relationship with sensation-seeking (**Zuckerman, 1983b**). High-risk sport participation, like skydiving, hang-gliding, auto-racing, scuba-diving, mountain-climbing, and skiing, were reported to be associated with high sensation-seeking in various studies (**Zuckerman, 1994**). Medium-risk sport participation, such as contact sports, were also associated with sensation-seeking. Lower-risk sport participation, requiring intensive training and practice, such as running and gymnastics, were not associated with sensation-seeking. Running were actually more common among low sensation-seekers (**McCutcheon, 1980**).

Rowland et al. (1986) found that the athletes who were currently active in risky sport activities, such as climbing, skiing and skydiving, were generally above average on sensation-seekers. But high sensation-seekers were also attracted to some low-risk sports and leisure activities, like playing pool, snooker, target-shooting, and modern dancing (**Zuckerman, 1994**). **Kerr and Svebak (1989)** used the risk classifications of **Zuckerman (1983b)** and **Rowland et al. (1986)** to compare those engaging in risky and non-risky sports and leisure. The results confirm the tendency of high sensation-seekers to engage in more risky sport and leisure activities (like canoeing, downhill-skiing, and motor-racing), whereas the low sensation-seekers choose less risky sports and leisure (like archery, golf and bowling). However, risk is not the only aspect differentiating high- and low-risk sport and leisure. Most high-risk sports and leisure activities provide arousing sensations like speed, suspension of gravity (as in free fall) and novel views (like an underwater scene) (**Zuckerman, 1994**). In the following sections a summary of comparisons between selected sports groups is given:

3.5.1 Mountain climbing

Freixanet (1991) compared four groups of this sport: (1) experienced mountain-climbers (Alpinist) who had participated in several expeditions to the Himalayas; (2) mountaineers, both climbers and mountain skiers; (3) a group engaging in a variety of other risky sports including skydiving, scuba-diving, water-skiing, gliding, hang-gliding, ballooning, racing of cars, motorcycles, or boats, and adventuring; (4) a control group not engaging in any risky sport and leisure activity. All three groups engaging in risky sport and leisure activities are higher sensation-seekers than the control group. Mountaineers and the sport and leisure group are also higher sensation-seekers than the control group. None of the differences between the Alpinists and the other risky sport and leisure groups were significant. The study shows that the primary difference in sensation-seeking tends to be between all risky sport and leisure activities and any other kinds of sport and leisure, rather than among the different types of risky sport and leisure activities. Experience in mountaineering also did not make a difference, as judged from comparisons between the Alpinist and the other mountaineering group. The results further suggests that thrills and adventure are not the only goal of risky mountaineering, but rather that the climber is looking for some more general kinds of experiences through the mind and the senses.

3.5.2   Skiing

Downhill-skiing involves both speed and heights and has been associated with high sensation-seeking in the USA (**Calhoon, 1988; Connolly, 1981**) and in the Netherlands (**Bouter et al., 1988; Landeweerd et al., 1990**). In the Connolly study, skiers are higher sensation-seekers than the control group of non-skiers. It is therefore evident that higher sensation-seeking leads to greater risk-taking and consequently a higher incidence of injuries in which experience does not play a role. Calhoon's skiers were all ski instructors and ski patrolmen, and they are higher sensation-seekers than the college student non-skiers. Skiers in the Netherlands are also higher sensation-seekers than the control group. In the study by **Landeweerd et al. (1990)**, where skiers were compared with a high-risk vocational group of construction workers, the skiers also were higher sensation-seekers. People who earn their living from skiing (at least during the season) seem to be more generally sensation-seekers. For less experienced, recreational skiers, sensation-seeking is limited.

3.5.3   Other high-risk sports

The broadest comparisons of participants in various sport and leisure activities has been done in Norway by **Breivik (1991a)**. It showed that climbers, canoeists and parachutists are higher sensation-seekers than physical education students and military recruits. The various groups did not show much differentiation, although the distinction between experience and intention was important here. The climbers were actively seeking sensation in both areas, whereas the students and recruits were not as active in sensation-seeking, but their intentions were at the same level as those of the climbers. The skydivers, however, showed higher sensation-seeking tendencies than any of the groups, as well as higher current sensation-seeking activity.

Zuckerman (1994:163) notes that skydivers are characterised by both higher sensation-seeking ambitions and a search for thrilling experiences, more so than most other participants of other risky activities. An earlier view of psychologists was that skydivers had an inherent death-wish. However, it is noted that risk itself is not the attraction. Instead, participants are attracted by the challenge to reduce the risk as far as possible, by "developing skills..., careful planning..., and intense concentration" **(Zuckerman, 1994:175)**.

In a study involving a high-risk population of base jumpers, **Biron (1990)** found that they are higher sensation-seekers than other high-risk populations like hang-gliders and automobile-racers **(Straub, 1982)**. **Straub (1982)** compared groups of hang-gliders, auto-racers and bowlers. The results show that auto-racers are higher sensation-seekers than hang-gliders, and that both these groups are higher sensation-seekers than bowlers. Hang-gliders and automobile-racers indicated that they obtain more injuries during participation than bowls-players. The former group (hang-gliders and auto-racers) also regard their sport as a high-risk activity; none of the bowlers considered their sport as risky. Both risk-taking groups were higher sensation-seekers than the bowlers.

The literature above shows that participants in high-risk sport and leisure activities tend to be higher overall sensation-seekers than participants in medium and low-risk sport and leisure activities involving fewer unique kinds of experiences. High-risk sport and leisure participants' evaluation of risk bear out the suggestion that maximising risk in not the goal of their activities.

3.6   MEDIUM-RISK SPORTS AND LEISURE ACTIVITIES

Although contact sport and activities seldom result into fatal injuries, temporary bone injuries occur regularly. Because of these injuries in certain sport and leisure activities, they are characterised as medium-risk sport and leisure activities. **Stirling (1977)** compared three test groups. The first group consisted of contact sports and activities (rugby, boxing, wrestling and American football), the second of non-contact sports and activities (racket activities, golf, swimming and athletics) and the third group of non-participants (low participation on all activities). The three test groups did not differ much from each other. People in the non-contact sports and activities group were higher sensation-seekers than those in the non-participant group. The contact sports and activities group were higher sensation-seekers than both the other groups. This is consistent with results from **Cellini (1982)**.

3.7 LOW-RISK SPORTS AND LEISURE ACTIVITIES

Svebak and Kerr (1989) classified sport and leisure as endurance (requiring strenuous and persistent activity) and explosive (requiring intense concentration and activity for relatively short periods of time). Cricket, soccer, hockey, baseball and surfing are given examples of explosive sports and leisure activities. Long-distance running, rowing, and jogging on the other hand, are regarded as endurance sports and leisure activities. In one study long-distance runners were compared with tennis and field-hockey players. The long-distance runners were more planning-oriented and arousal-avoiding than the tennis and hockey players. This is consistent with other data showing that long distance runners tend to be lower sensation-seekers (**McCutcheon, 1980**) and more introverted (**Eysenck et al., 1982**). **Potgieter and Bisschoff (1990)** found marathon runners (low-risk, endurance sport and leisure) to be lower sensation-seekers than rugby players (medium-risk, explosive sport and leisure). Both rugby players and marathon runners rated rugby as a higher-risk sport and leisure activity than marathon running.

However, there is one running activity in which high sensation-seekers do participate: the streaking fad of the early 1970s. This activity is not a sport or leisure activity and participants are generally university students who run naked on university grounds, sports fields or in roads. Due to mass participation, no arrests can be made for exhibitionism or disparagement of the public. The individual motivations of streakers are not yet determined. **Bone (1979)** found significant correlations between sensation-seeking and the streaking tendency. Streaking provides a novel and exciting experience for most participants, with few risks involved.

Babbitt et al. (1990) found that aerobics participants were quite dedicated to this activity, attending every week and not participating in many other sports or activities. Their main motives were health, appearance and weight control. As with regular running or jogging, the low sensation-seekers are the most persistent and regular practitioners of this physical activity. High sensation-seekers sometimes try these kinds of activities, but they rarely persist or practice.

High sensation-seekers are drawn to sports and leisure activities which involve physical risk-taking, such as skydiving and scuba-diving (**Hymbaugh and Garrett, 1974**). Low sensation-seekers are moderately phobic, even in low-risk situations, such as looking down from heights (**Zuckerman, 1979**). The nature of different sports and leisure activities which attract high sensation-seekers is important to predict possible influences of sports and leisure participation on the leisure preferences of high sensation-seekers.

3.8   CONCLUSION AND OTHER PERSPECTIVES

Zuckerman (1979) predicted that cognitive differences between high and low sensation-seekers can be the cause of the sensation-seeker's participation in sport or leisure activities that are avoided by low sensation-seekers. This cognitive difference assumes that high sensation-seekers evaluate risk and danger differently than low sensation-seekers (**Zuckerman, 1979**). The high sensation-seeker's need for adventure and excitement can be based on a biological tendency which is partially inherited. The choice of the type of sport or leisure activity can influence leisure preferences.

According to **Zuckerman (1979)**, high sensation-seekers are inclined to participate in more sports and leisure activities than low sensation-seekers; while low sensation-seekers are inclined to participate in sports and leisure activities for longer periods of time than high sensation-seekers. Gender also plays a mediating role. It was found that sensation-seeking and gender are in interaction in the choice of sport and leisure activities. Furthermore, low, but generally positive correlations are expected between sensation-seeking and participation in risky activities. **Zuckerman (1979)** assumes that the need for novel experiences and the attraction of high risks characterise the high sensation-seeker's participation.

The anxiety levels of low sensation-seekers are prone to rise more quickly and their sensation-seeking levels also decline more quickly than those of high sensation-seekers. **Jacques Cousteau (1972)** describes play behaviour as follows:

It's fun to do things you're not made to do, like going to the moon or living under the ocean. I was playing when I invented the aqualung. I'm still playing. I think play is the most important thing in the world (New York Times).

Sensation-seeking is important for sports tourism because it explains some aspects of travel motivation. This information can be used to shape marketing strategies in general, but also strategies to market a specific segment of the tourism market and to better understand sports tourists. Sensation-seeking can be divided in three categories, namely high, medium and low, each of which will attract spectators and participants accordingly. This chapter gives some clarity on why people participate in different activities. Sensation-seeking is identified as a motive, with strong potential to explain not only high-risk sports and adventurous types of tourism behaviour, but also low-risk tourism behaviour.

Chapter 4

Socio-cultural impact of sports tourism

If I have learned one thing in life, it is that it is only through human contact that our differences be overcome and dialogue opened. Perhaps that is what our world today lacks the most

Juan Antonio Samaranch
IOC President

4.1 INTRODUCTION

Sport has an integrating effect when introduced into a social system. In essence, sport is a vehicle for improving social relationships in surroundings, for attaining relationships with one another, for strengthening abilities to understand one another and for the well-being of peoples (**Kurtzman et al., 1998:2**). No South African will probably forget the moment when South Africa won the Rugby World Cup in 1995. Never before were South Africans brought closer together than at that occasion. All cultures were united as a wining nation.

Today it is easier than ever before to travel to sport events. This is due to rising standards of living, changes in the population age composition, the increasing levels of educational attainment, better communication, increased social consciousness of the welfare and activities of other people throughout the world, and the psychological shrinking of the world by means of globalisation.

People travel to exotic locations to experience unfamiliar environments, not only geographically but also personally, socially, and culturally. Thus, the traveller faces certain problems, and if the trip is to be fully enjoyable and rewarding, solutions must be found for these problems. Travellers must manage their time and money in situations that differ from those at home, as well as their social interactions and social relations, to obtain sustenance, shelter, and other needs and possibly to find companionship.

When travelling to sports events, people make different degrees of contact with the new culture in which they may find themselves while travelling. The extent of the "cultural distance" they may wish to maintain, influences decisions on how unfamiliar the traveller wants his or her environment away from home to be. Sports tourism is concerned with the movement and interaction of people in different geographical locations. Visitors to a community or an area create social relationships that differ greatly from their own traditions (**McIntosh et al., 1995**).

From a sociological perspective there are usually certain social relations between people in the tourism context:

- The confrontation of different cultures, ethnic groups, lifestyles, languages and levels of prosperity.

- The behaviour of people freed from many of the social and economic constraints of everyday life.

- The behaviour of the host population, which has to reconcile economic gain and benefits with the costs of living with strangers.

Culture refers to a way of life of a particular group of people and their patterns of behaviour, values and perceptions of themselves and the world. Cultural differences are differences between groups of people who do things differently and percieve the world differently. This can cause differences in behaviour and the interpretation of behaviour, and therefore misunderstanding (**Reisinger&Turner, 1998:82**). **Saayman (1999)** points out that culture entails the knowledge, experience, meanings, values, attitudes, religion, concept of the self, concept of a relationship, hierarchy of status, role expectations, spatial relationships and time concepts commanded by a group of people which are transferred from generation to generation, through individual and group aspirations.

Culture can thus be seen as the "glue" that keeps people together. The degree to which conflict will occur between host and guest depends upon the similarity in their standards of living, the number of tourists at any time, and the extent to which tourists adapt to local norms (**Mill & Morrison, 1985**). Tourism act as a medium for social change rather than the cause itself.

The host-guest interaction offers the opportunity for each to learn more about the other, and as such it can contribute to a greater understanding between people. Each destination must weigh the potential cultural gains (e.g. revived arts, theatre, exposure to new ideas) against the potential losses (e.g. overcrowding and exploitation of the culture and possible social change) (**Mill & Morrison, 1985**).

4.2   SOCIO-CULTURAL IMPACTS

Tourism has been a major source of intercultural contact (**Slabbert and Saayman, 2000**). Research on many tourist countries suggests that the socio-cultural structures of many tourist countries have changed considerably under the influence of tourism. These changes have varied from country to country. The reactions of the hosts in the face of these changes have been quite diverse, ranging from an active resistance to a complete adoption of Western culture. Tourism, and specifically sports tourism, has certain consequences, as will be described in the following paragraphs.

Increase in undesirable activities

Many people in the tourism destination areas believe that tourism attracts or facilitates undesirable activities such as gambling, drug abuse, crime and prostitution. These result in changes in the local system of values. The industry has introduced one phenomenon to many countries: and increase in the number of "beachboys", young men who do not look for jobs because they know that they can be supported by the female visitors to the area. Local residents are also often offended by the brief attire of sports tourists, women wearing shorts to town, or bathing suits in the street. However, this reaction varies from city to city. Another fear is that crime will increase as the sports tourism industry grows and affluent tourists are envied by poor residents (**Crandall, 1994**).

Social dualism

Another social cost of tourism is what has been called the "premature departure to modernisation", producing rapid and disruptive changes in the host society. Foreign values, ideologies and lifestyles come to be accepted by local residents, influencing their lives and behaviour. Some may copy tourist behaviour and attitudes and ignore cultural and religious traditions (**Crandall, 1994; Shaw & Williams, 1994**).

Under these circumstances social tension develops as hosts become divided between those adopting new values and those retaining a traditional way of life (**Shaw & Williams, 1994**). Social dualism may be observed in a person who is partly Westernised, while partly holding on to traditional values. Families may be driven apart and disruptions can occur in societies.

Demonstration effect

The demonstration effect is the adoption by local residents, especially the young, of sports tourist behaviour and attitudes, consumption patterns, and even their language. Such a process can have some benefits if local people are encouraged to get a better education in order to improve their living standards. However, most evidence points to social detriments, as locals adopt the rich lifestyle of of affluent tourists and live beyond their means. This can lead to spending on diverse items, such as blue jeans, track suites, fast-food items and sunglasses. The consumption of imported goods is further increased (**Crandall, 1994; Shaw & Williams, 1994**).

Culture as a commercial commodity

Another impact of tourism is that art, ceremonies, rituals, music and traditions can become marketable commodities and lose their relevance and symbolic meaning to the local people. The result may be lowering the dignity of the people and their culture, a deterioration of the standard of local arts and crafts and a watering down of local music, crafts and ceremonies for mass tourist consumption. Pseudotraditional art forms (i.e. cheap, portable souvenirs) develop. Ceremonies and rituals now become meaningless and are used primarily to attract tourists who feel no respect for the local beliefs or traditions (**Crandall, 1994**). Local communities and cultures are thus exploited and situations arise where one finds people from certain tribes, for example the Ndebele, will sit in the sun, posing for tourists to take photographs of them, or where locals in the Amazon will pose naked to be photographed by foreigners.

On the more positive side, however, the tourist industry is also credited with the revival of craft activities and cultural heritage of a destination area. A sense of pride in one's country is promoted as tourists seek things not found elsewhere (**Crandall, 1994; Shaw & Williams, 1994**).

Figure 4.1 illustrates the main cultural aspects which attract tourists:

MAIN ELEMENTS OF CULTURE THAT ATTRACT TOURISTS:	
• Handcrafts	• Traditions
• History	• Architecture
• Local food	• Art Music
• "Ways of life"	• Religion
• Language	• Dress
• Folklore	• Sport and games

Figure 4.1: Main elements of culture that attract tourists
(Shaw & Williams, 1994)

Increase in animosity to tourists

There is a strong increase in the feelings of resentment and animosity towards the sports tourist on the part of the local resident. Resentment, hostility and violence against sports tourists can also grow as hordes of people descend on regions with limited space, thus straining infrastructure, such as roads, and water and sewage systems (**Crandall, 1994**).

4.3 THE POSITIVE AND NEGATIVE EFFECTS OF THE SOCIO-CULTURAL IMPACTS OF TOURISM

Tourism has both a positive and a negative socio-cultural impact. If host communities recognise that indigenous culture will attract tourists and serve as a unique factor in distinguishing one destination from another, attempts may be made to keep the culture alive.

In some cases, traditional ways and goods may be restored because willing buyers (tourists) can be found. In other cases, festivals and competitions are produced for tourists by the community, which is thus encouraged to keep its culture alive. Entertainment of the tourist may therefore be the impetus for the performing of cultural activities or the production of goods, but the effect of such behaviour on the local community is that of preserving part of their old culture (**Mill &Morrison, 1985**).

The existence of cultural differences between countries may be one of the principal stimulants to the tourism industry. Sports tourists are by definition strangers in a destination. Their dress codes and patterns of behaviour are different from the residents. The local culture and customs may be exploited to satisfy the visitor, sometimes at the expense of local pride and dignity. In undeveloped and isolated areas, the arrival of too many visitors may even move/force local people to lease their settlements and move to new areas where they remain undisturbed. The negative and positive impacts of tourism are discussed in more detail below.

The Negative impacts
In less advanced countries, where cultural differences between tourists and hosts are greater than in more advanced countries, the negative effect of direct tourist-host contact is increased. Tourists are percieved as aggressive. The tourism-host contact generates exploitation, assault and victimisation. These processes occur due to big cultural differences that are important elements in shaping tourists and hosts mutual perceptions of each other (**Reisinger & Turner, 1998:83**).

The negative impacts of sociocultural contact include the following:

• Stereotyping of the host and guest.

• Xenophobia. Due to previous experiences the host tends to hate the tourist even before he arrives at a particular destination.

- Social pollution. Because of the number of people who go to a destination during a major event the residents leave the city.

- Commodification and exploitation of culture and traditional ways of life. The culture tends to be common and not special.

- Threat to traditional family life in host communities. Tourists introduce new ideas and new ways of doing. They could also contribute to high levels of violence. This confuses the host and he has to find a compromise between the traditions and the new way of doing.

- Prostitution. Sex tourism develops and expands where there are many people together, especially where major events are taking place.

- The sex industry is also associated with child sex, pornography, gangsterism and drugs.

- Conflicts in the host community (**Shaw & Williams, 1994**).

The authenticity of culture packaged for the tourist may be questionable. Many people feel that when a cultural event is prepared for tourist consumption, its original, often spiritual, meaning is lost (**Mill & Morrison, 1985**). **Crandall (1994)** points out that socio-cultural tourism can lead to the growth of servile attitude, violence and conflict due to different lifestyles.

The positive impacts
The socio-cultural impact of tourism may also be positive. Tourism appears to act as a medium for social change (because of the contact between host and guest) rather than as the cause itself. The host-guest interaction offers the opportunity for each to learn more of the other, and as such it can contribute to a greater understanding between people(**Mill & Morrison, 1985**).

Shaw and Williams (1994) identify the following positive socio-cultural impacts of tourism:

- Broadens education. The sports tourist and the host learn more of each other's culture and customs.

- Promotes international peace. Due to the contact the host and the sport tourist can understand each other better. Tourists can understand why certain people behave in a certain way.

- Breaks down racial and cultural barriers.

- Promotes pride for one's country.

- Reinforces preservation of heritage and traditions.

- Enhances an appreciation of cultural traditions.

Changes brought about by host-guest encounters are transmitted through social and cultural impacts.

4.4 EFFECTS OF TOURISTS ON A HOST SOCIETY

Regardless of economic considerations, sports tourists tend to be viewed in a negative way in most societies. "Whatever the tourist does, he does wrong", by being the "rich tourist", the "uncultured tourists", the "exploiting tourist", the "polluting tourist" and so on **(Krippendorf, 1987)**. A generally held view is that the impact of tourism on a host community will vary according to the differences between the tourists and their hosts. Such differences may be meassured in terms of race, culture and social outlook, while the number of tourists is also significant. Relations between the tourists and their host community tend to be characterised by four main features:

- **The transitory nature of encounters between hosts and guests**
  These are viewed differently by visitor and host. To the former they are facinating and perhaps unique. To the host they may be just one of many superficial encounters experienced during the holiday season. Visitors are only in a community for a short period, so any interaction between hosts and guests has little chance to progress beyond casual and superficial levels.

- **Temporal and spatial constraints on relationships**
  These influence the duration and geography of visitor-host relationships. Tourists want to see as much as possible of culture in a short period of time, but they are also very often restricted in tourist enclaves. Visits are usually seasonal and non-repeated events, so the hospitallity business often becomes exploitative to take advantage of this situation.

- **A lack of spontaneity in most encounters**
  Sport tourism turns traditional human relations into economic activity; package

tours, planned attractions and cultural events become nothing more than cash-generating activities. Money is more important for the host than the people who stay over at his guest-house. Because of the development of mass tourism visitor-resident meetings lack the spontaneity associated with individual schedules. If that could be changed, value can be added to the visit for the tourist.

- **Unequal and unbalanced relationships**
  This is especially the case in developing countries: because of the wide disparities in wealth, hosts often feel inferior. Resentment of such differences may often motivate host communities to compensate by exploiting the wealth of tourists (**Shaw & Williams, 1994**). The visitor is on holiday and enjoying novel experiences, while for the resident such events and meetings have become routine and represent work, not fun (**Murphy, 1986:117**).

Host and guests not only have diverse socio-cultural backgrounds but also very different perceptions. The tourist is living in terms of unordinary time and place, while to the host it is ordinary life and home. These unordinary worlds are structured and conditioned by respective cultures. The degree of contrasting values and conflict will obviously depend on levels of differences, together with each world's inherent flexibility and ability to adapt.

The structure of the community is of particular importance, especially the way it opens to other cultures and its traditions of hospitallity. The main operating force within the community is the host culture, which structures community life and defines the degree of outside influence. Some host communities are multicultural, which produces a far more complex response to tourists (**Shaw & Williams, 1994**).

Both the tourist culture and their residual culture in turn, structure the unordinary world of the tourist. Sports tourists come from diverse social, ethnic and cultural backgrounds; yet their purpose to observe rituals and their behaviours and pursuits bind them into one collectivity. In contrast, residual culture stresses the differences between tourists, since it denotes the "cultural baggage" that tourists bring from their home cultures. Such residual culture shapes the behaviour of sports tourists and can play an important role in the host community.

The whole nature of host-guest relationships is therefore conditioned by the complex interactions between these different elements of culture, together with the level and nature of tourism development (**Shaw & Williams, 1994:86-86**). The diagram below (Figure 4.2) indicates what factors influence the contact and relationships between hosts and tourists.

Tourist-host Encounters

Social Impacts				Cultural Impacts		
Social Change	Language	Health	Religion	Moral Behaviour	Moral Behaviour	Moral Behaviour

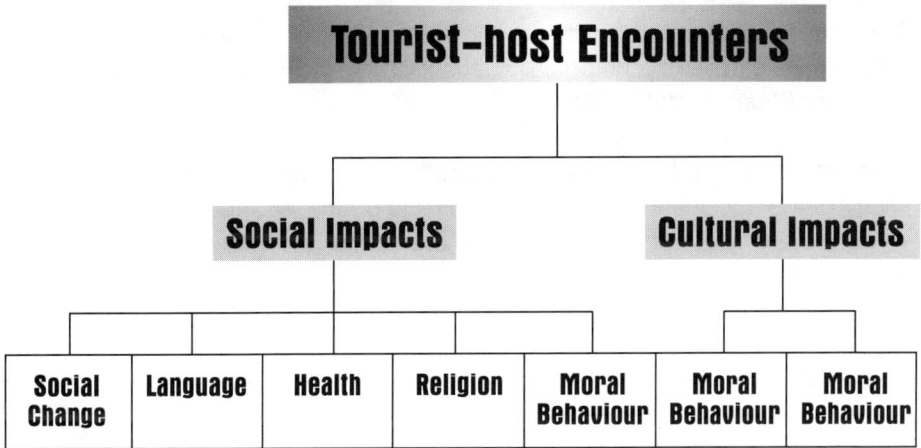

Figure 4.2: Influences on the contact and relationships between host and tourist (Shaw & Williams, 1994)

Dimensions of tourist-host encounters

The social and cultural impacts of tourist-host encounters may be explained in the following terms:

Social impacts: The destination community's more immediate changes in quality of life and adjustment to the industry.

Cultural impacts: Longer-term changes in a society's norms and standards, which will gradually emerge in a community's social relationships and artifacts (**Murphy, 1986:117**).

Tourist-host contact effects

Where there is contact between people, there is change, whether it is good or not. Tourists influence residents and vice versa. Some visitors are intensely interested in interacting with residents, while for others the local people are little more than a part of the scenery. Additionally, the size and technological sophistication of the host community plays a crucial role in mediating the impact of tourism and the nature of the resident-host contact. The following types of contact are identified:

- **Direct contact influences for isolated and poor communities**

  Direct contact between tourists and the local people of Third World and poor communities often generates discord, exploitation and social problems. The simple process of tourists observing the local people can have profound effects.

Certain cultural, economic, and day-to-day activities of ethnic groups seem to appeal to tourists and are promoted as tourist attractions.

For some small, technologically unsophisticated host communities, direct contact with tourists can be psychologically beneficial if they come in small, manageable numbers (**Pearce, 1994:106**).

- **Indirect-contact influences for isolated and poor communities**
  Many of the social and psychological effects on the local people are of a less direct nature and not all such effects are negative. There are some strong arguments for the view that sports tourism can provide social benefits to Third World/technologically unsophisticated communities.

  Many cultures attach enormous symbolic and spiritual importance to their ceremonies and art objects. An adequate interpretation of these symbolic meanings may require considerable anthropological knowledge on the part of the consuming tourist. Without an understanding of the significance of cultural activities, tourists will merely see these events as "pretty" customs. This not only trivialises the local event, but it also wastes an opportunity for tourists to appreciate the ethnocentrism of their own culture.

- **Direct-contact influences for technologically advanced communities**
  Studies showed that the popular opinion about the impact of tourism in the region should not be confused with residents' views. They found a combination of seemingly contradictory positive and negative attitudes to tourists and their effects, suggesting that there is a hierarchy of community needs in which attitudes are balanced against the survival of the community.

  In some parts of the world sports tourism plays a major role in meeting the needs of communities. When the basic needs are met, attention turns to other needs or to the negative side-effects of tourism, which once were suppressed.

Local stereotypes of international visitors can emerge very quickly and negatively influence the quality of the host resident encounter. These stereotypes are readily applied to the visitors, who are easily identified and whose behaviour is distinctive or culturally different, thus promoting prejudice and attributions to nationality rather than to individual personality. There is general consensus that international contact promotes goodwill and that the direct interpersonal encounters soften or modify harsh images of the parties in contact (**Pearce, 1994:109**).

Tourists appear to have maximum social and psychological impact on their hosts when the host communities are small, unsophisticated and isolated. This impact may be a powerful one, either in direct interpersonal encounters or in subtle, indirect influences on the visited community. When the receiving society is technologically more advanced and the affluence gap between tourists and the hosts are smaller, tourism has less impact. Sports tourists may develop friendships with the hosts, and the visitors can sustain local social institutions as well as promote pride in the visited community. The negative effects are not restricted to interpersonal friction, but also include indirect stress to the hosts through environmental degradation and infrastructure costs (**Pearce, 1994:110**).

REASONS FOR THE IMPACTS OF TOURISTS ON A HOST SOCIETY
In trying to understand the effects, stage or step models, such as the ones below, have been popular.

- **Smith's model of cross-cultural contact**
  Smith (as quoted by **Pearce, 1994**) saw the development of tourism in terms of distinct waves of tourist types. He directly relates social impacts on local communities to the expansion of tourism and distinguishes seven categories in order of expanding community impact. As shown in Table 4.1, the more tourists visit the community, the higher the impact will be.

  When the number of tourists is limited the impact on the community is small in fact, the tourists are hardly noticed. With the arrival of masses there will be an increase in the impact.

  Normally this can be found during peak seasons when people travel to the coasts and overcroud the space. When the community feel overwhelmed by the tourists, not even the economic benefits can change their attitude toward tourists.

Different types of tourists have the following effect on their host communities:

Table 4.1: Effects of tourists on host communities

TYPE OF TOURIST	NUMBER OF TOURISTS	COMMUNITY IMPACT
Explorer	Very limited	
Elite	Rarely seen	
Off-Beat	Uncommon but seen	
Unusual	Occasional	STEADILY
Incipient Mass	Steady flow	INCREASING
Mass	Continuous influx	
Charter	Massive arrival	

- **Doxey's Irridex**

  At about the same time Smith's work was gaining momentum, Doxey proposed an irritation-index or "irridex" to assess host-guest interactions and relationships. Doxey noted that the existence of local tolerance thresholds and hosts' resistance to further tourism development was based on a fear of losing community identity. The model represents the changing attitudes of the host population to tourism in terms of a linear sequence of increaing irritations as the number of tourists grows **(Shaw & Williams, 1994)**.

  In this perspective, host societies in tourist destinations pass through stages of euphoria, apathy, irritation, antagonism and loss in the face of tourism development. The progression through this sequence is determined both by the compatibility of each group, which is related to culture, economic status, race and nationality, as well as by the sheer numbers of tourists.

  In the early stages of development, visitors are likely to be greeted with enthusiasm by local residents. The new industry brings employment and revenue. Furthermore, the early visitors are appreciative of local customs and lifestyles. This state of euphoria is particularly noticeable in areas where there are few alternative forms of employment, and when the level of tourist activity is not overwhelming.

  As the volume of visitors increases, contact between resident and visitor becomes less personal and more commercialised, and visitors demand more facilities, built specifically for them. The industry is now taken for granted and local people develop a more apathetic attitude to the activity.

  If development continues, it may exceed community-tolerance thresholds because of increased congestion, rising prices, and its threat to traditional ways of life. Then apathy can turn to annoyance, as residents feel their community is being changed around them and the costs of accommodating the industry are beginning to exceed perceived benefits (**Murphy, 1986:124-125**).

As the development continues, annoyance turns to antagonism. At this stage open hostility to tourism facilities and visitors can occur, as local residents perceive it to be the cause of all their economic and social problems. The final two stages occur when local residents have perceived changes to their lifestyle and identity, which they will not tolerate. This can include dimensional changes such as crowding and traffic jams, or structural changes, such as interfering with the changing of the nature of the society by outside investment priorities and politics. Structural changes are more difficult to control and remedy, requiring political decisions at the highest level before any effective management can be applied.

Doxey's model suggests a unidirectional sequence, where residents' attitudes and reactions will change over time in a predictable sequence (Figure 4.3).

Euphoria	• Initial phase of development
	• Visitors and investors welcome
	• Little planning and control mechanism

Apathy	• Visitors taken for granted
	• Contacts between residents and outsiders more formal (commercial)
	• Planning concerned mostly with marketing

Annoyance	• Saturation points approached
	• Residents have misgivings about tourist industry
	• Policy makers attempt solutions via increasing infrastructure rather than limiting growth

Antagonism	• Irritations openly expressed
	• Visitors seen as cause of problem
	• Planning now remedial but promotion increased to offset deteriorating reputation of destination

Figure 4.3: Doxey's index of irritation

• **Butler's model of intercultural perception**
Another stage-development model relating to tourism was proposed by Butler (as quoted by **Pearce, 1994**). He contends that a community's emerging attitude toward tourism is likely to be more complex, and will be affected by the varying degrees of contact and involvement its residents have with the industry. He identified two groups of factors that can influence visitor-resident relationships.

Firstly, the characteristics of visitors will have a bearing that extends beyond the physical impact of their increasing numbers. Butler indicates that the tourists' length of stay and their racial and economic characteristics need to be considered as well as their number.

Secondly, a destination's own characteristics will help determine its ability to absorb the growing number of visitors. Characteristics like its level of economic development, the spatial distribution of its tourism activities in relation to its other economic activities, the strength of its local culture, and political attitude will determine how well a destination can mold and manage its tourist product and visitors. In addition to visitor and destination characteristics, Butler considers resident reactions to more complex than those envisioned by Doxey. Butler contends that the attitudes and behavior of residents, in turn, may be expressed via active or passive behaviour (Figure 4.4).

The resulting combination of responses allows four reactions to occur. It is quite impossible that all four options can take place in an area simultaneously. With this model, combinations of attitudes and reactions to tourism become possible and understandable. Businessmen who are involved with tourism are likely to be favourable and aggressive in their support, through Chamber of Commerce activities and personal promotion.

Lobbyists, such as conservation or neighbourhood protection groups, could be unfavourable towards and aggressively opposed to certain tourism developments, using letters to the editor and protests to the council as their expressions of dissent. In general the public is likely to be passive and silent because they derive some personal benefit from the industry, because it has no direct bearing on their lives, or because they see no way of reversing the process (**Murphy, 1986:125-126**).

In this model the impacts of tourism are not the direct focus of attention. Instead the model is concerned with more general issues of the evolution of tourist areas (marketing, organisation, ownership of tourist services and attractions), although the attitudes of residents and the community support for tourism are discussed as a part of the larger process.

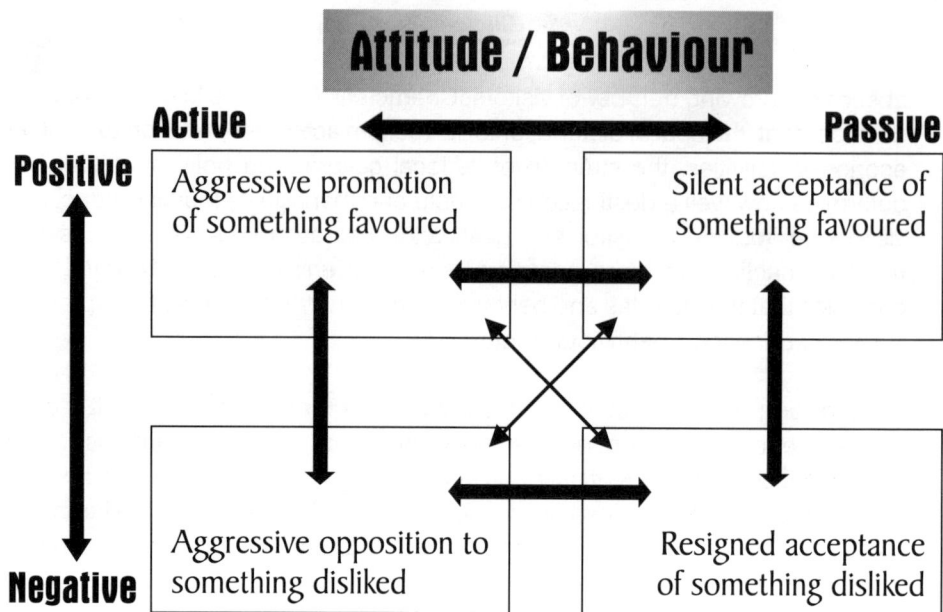

Attitude / Behaviour

	Active ◄────────────► Passive
Positive	Aggressive promotion of something favoured
	Silent acceptance of something favoured
Negative	Aggressive opposition to something disliked
	Resigned acceptance of something disliked

(Arrows indicate possibility of change)
Figure 4.4: Attitudinal/Behavioural attributes of intercultural perception (Murphy, 1986:125)

All three models have poor demarcation between the stages or steps. It is also unclear whether shifting from one stage to another precludes the continued existence of the previous stage. For example, will tourism communities who have moved from the development phase to the consolidation phase retain and exhibit many of the features of the development phase, or are these necessarily superseded? Additionally, stage models prompt the question of whether or not the order of the stages is invariant. The Doxey and Smith models appear to assume this point, but Butler notes that some tourism destinations may move directly into a higher level without the preceeding steps (**Pearce, 1994:114-117**).

Factors that influence the tourism-saturation point of a country
These factors will let the host decide that he/she had had enough of the tourists. This could occur when cultural performances are put on only for the tourists, while local people never participate in them and never get to enjoy them when the tourists are absent. The performance thus becomes more important than the performers. For example, in many countries there are shopping centres primarily for the tourists, with the local people a secondary consideration. In turn this changed the local residents' shopping and transportation patterns, as they tend to go elsewhere to

shop in order to avoid the crowds of tourists.

Certain characteristics of the visitors have different effects on the host population, while the characteristics at the destination area itself also influence the relationship between the tourists and the hosts. The characteristics of each respective group are discussed in more detail below.

Characteristics of the visitors

- **Volume:** A small number of visitors in a country with a large population will have little effect, while a large number of tourists visiting a small island or resort town, especially over a short season, will have a major impact.

- **Length of stay:** The longer the visitors stay, the greater will be their contact with the host population and their socio-economic penetration.

- **Racial characteristics:** The greater the differences between the tourists and locals in terms of colour, language and culture, the greater will be their impact.

- **Economic characteristics:** The greater the difference in levels of affluence, the stronger will be the resentment and desire for equality on the part of local residents.

- **Activities of tourists:** Their activities determine the amount of contact, for instance visiting local hang-outs versus spending a week on the beach. When they are visiting local hang-outs, there will be more contact with locals.

Characteristics of a destination area

- **Economic development:** A general rule is that the more developed the local economy, the less the dependence on the tourism industry and the less its impact.

- **Spatial characteristics of the destination:** This includes the size of the destination area, the size of the population, location of resorts, capacity of facilities, number of hotels, properties of the beach area and other physical variables. Ratios are then calculated between visitor arrivals and the population and land area, and between tourist-nights and land area, beach area and restaurant capacity. Obviously, the higher the ratios, the more likely it is that friction will occur.

- **Degree of local involvement:** The amount of contact is also a function of whether tourist enterprises are run and owned by local or foreign companies (the former situation is better for the economy).

- **Strength of local culture:** The stronger the local culture (i.e., unique, clear traits) and language, the better the ability to withstand the impact of a foreign culture.

- **Other:** This can include the political attitudes and degree of nationalism in the host country, as well as its historical background. It can also include the stage of development of the tourism industry, the length of its existence, and the rapidity of its development.

The point of physical saturation may be determined, but social attitudes are equally important and must also be taken into account, since what one person finds irritating often might not bother someone else (**Crandall, 1994:417**).

Regardless of the degree of local participation, the individual sports tourist must at least study the country to be visited and reach some level of decision on how these problems of environmental differences are to be resolved. Advance preparation is an intelligent approach. Travel experiences, and therefore sports tourism, have a profound effect on the traveller as well as on society, as travel experience often is among the most outstanding memories in the traveller's life.

With the costs that tourism can impose in mind, governments should attempt to optimise the benefits which sports tourism provides. The social benefits and the cost of sports tourism should be viewed similarly. While the host community seeks to optimise the benefits, it must weigh these against the social costs. In an area that still possesses a traditional social structure the social costs are higher in both probability and magnitude when tourism is being considered for development.

4.5 THE SOCIAL BENEFITS

The social benefits of sports tourism may be described as a sports event's or sports festival's value as a leisure or cultural phenomenon (**Getz, 1994: 442**). The hosting of a sports event by developing countries may act as a stimulus for infrastructural and human development and as an attraction for sports tourists to an area with a weak tourism image. According to **Fayos-Sola (1997:243)** this was the main reason behind the Cape Town bid for the 2004 Summer Olympic Games.

Ebersohn (1995:19) pointed out that sport events and tours have social benefit effects. In particular he mentioned the Australian tour in the summer of 1994, which

74

provided R2 million for cricket development and considerable amounts for business people from disadvantaged communities.

Travel, and particularly domestic travel, is encouraged by government policies in progressive nations, as a means of acquainting citizens with other parts of their country and building appreciation for the homeland.

The presence of visitors in a country affects the living patterns of the local people. The way they behave themselves and their personal relationships with the citizens of the host community often have a great effect on the way of life and the attitudes of the local people. On the other hand, the visitors are influenced by the contrast in culture, which generally leads to an increased appreciation for qualities of life in the society visited by the sports tourist.

When the sports tourists and the members of the host community mingle and become better acquainted, a favourable situation develops in which the awareness of each other's character and qualities is greatly increased, building respect and appreciation in both groups.

Wiseman, as quoted by **Melnick (1993:47)**, suggested a relationship between sociability and mental health, when she observed that "people, regardless of where they live, need a certain amount of close interpersonal interaction to develop socially and will determinedly seek out such relationships for their continued psychic survival." **Wakefield & Sloan (1995:153)** suggested that many spectators seek social interaction and entertainment through sports events.

Over the past few centuries the satisfaction of our sociability needs have changed. The traditional institutions such as the family, the work place, and the neighbourhood can no longer satisfy our needs for social interaction, and we are forced to less personal, less intimate, more public places (bars, discos, etc.) to fulfill these needs (**Melnick, 1993:48**). These venues offer casual interaction with strangers of a quasi-primary kind, it offers the willing participant the opportunity to be cheerful yet anonymous for the duration of the encounter. These places are attractive because the risk is minimal and parties understand that they are not going to move into each other's private spaces.

According to **Melnick (1993:50)** the watching of a sports event provides a most appropriate opportunity for initiating conversation, because it has the right ecological setting. It provides an absence of temporal restraints, and openness on the part of most fans to interact with each other. Although the person next to you is a total stranger, the two of you are likely to indulge in the same behaviour such as clap, boo, yell, or scream, because you share the same position. Unlike strangers in other circumstances, such as in a supermarket, spectators at a sports event share a silent enthusiasm for what is about to happen; a commitment to the event. This shared interest, excitement and the possible trading of useful information makes casual sociability that much easier.

Melnick (1993:51) also noted that spectators do not feel hurried or pressured to socially interact at a sports event, because there is plenty of time to approach the stranger next to you if that is your desire. Frequent time-outs and intermissions at sports events provide spectators with enough opportunities to comfortably interact with one another, because there are clear-cut starting and ending points to the engagement-these are determined by the temporal duration of the sports event. Unlike silence that can inhibit the initiation of a conversation between strangers, the ever-present noise at a sports event makes it easier for words to simply flow. It is a place where the party-like atmosphere of the occasion makes interaction between strangers not just possible but highly probable.

Thus, according to (**Melnick, 1993:55**), sports events offer spectators possible opportunities to experience "bottom-up", individuated identities and a sense of empowerment, by giving them the chance to escape from oppressiveness of the work place. It contradicts the spectator's everyday experience; it reverses the social order.

The social and communal possibilities of sports events should be promoted. If such events could help satisfy the sociability needs of the spectators, greater numbers of spectators will be likely to attend them, which will encourage sports tourism and increase its benefits in the community.

Law (1996:28) remarks that potential residents (including professionals and executives) will be persuaded of a city's lifestyle opportunities, in reaction to the expansion of certain activities, such as sports - even if this expansion is only partly directed at the tourism market.

With the redefining of districts and the new image provided by big sports events, it will be easier to persuade middle-class residents to return to the inner city. The money that tourists spend may make these activities economically more viable, which will be of benefit to the local community. The physical regeneration of areas, the development of facilities and the arrival of sports tourists may increase local pride. Local residents with pride for their community will take much greater care of the environment (**Law, 1996:28**).

An example of a mega event contributing to the development of a destination is the Olympics in the Chamsil Area of Seoul. Studies demonstrated that urban areas generally benefit from the Olympic Games and that in anticipation to the 2000 Olympic Games in Sydney, work has been carried out to ensure these benefits (**Fayos-Sola, 1997:243**). Sport and sporting events has community health benefits, because it raises the community's interest in sport and leads to greater participation (**Burgan & Miles, 1992:708**). The region may also gain longer-term tourism promotion benefits from a major sports event.

According to **Burgan & Miles (1992:709)**, large events that attract international attention to the host region, often seem to have positive psychological benefits in the local community. For example, the citizens of Brisbane were proud of their city's effort in hosting the 1982 Commonwealth Games, and as a result of media attention and the presence of international athletes, they enjoyed a feeling of importance. This is referred to as "psychic income", and is manifested in civic pride, self-confidence, or a festival atmosphere. Putting financial value on such effects is known as "contingent evaluation" and involves questioning the population on how much they are willing to pay for it (**Burgan & Miles, 1992:709**). "With regard to cultural flows, major sporting events (Olympic Games, tennis tournaments, the Soccer World Cup, etc.) are ideal vehicles for multinational firms in their world market penetration strategies, thus contributing to the commodification and homogenisation of cultures" (**Harvey & Houle, 1994: 346**).

4.6   NEGATIVE SOCIAL EFFECTS

On the negative side, the huge amount of tourist that are attracted by a sports event over a short period of time, bring social costs to the host community in the form of crime and vandalism, sports hooliganism, pollution, traffic congestion, new cultures, ideas, values and norms, and the disruption of the lifestyles of residents.

In the case of recurring sports events in a city, contingency plans based on previous experience can be made by authorities to overcome these problems, but it may be difficult to plan for the short-term congestion problems of a once-off sports event such as the Olympic Games. It is possible to put some of these impacts into financial value, and in order to provide a comprehensive analysis, these non-multiplier impacts should be taken into account when analysing impacts (**Burgan & Miles, 1992:708**).

Crime

Tourists can be an easy target for criminals as they are unaware of dangerous areas or local situations in which they might be very vulnerable to violent crimes. They are therefore easy targets. As they are readily identified and are usually not very well equipped to ward off an attack, they become an easy prey for robbers and other offenders. Tourists sometimes seek accommodation within walking distance from the attraction. By walking to or from the hotel and to an attraction, tourists may pass through a high-crime area, and efforts must be made to inform tourists about such high-crime areas (**Bennett, 1995:338**).

McIntosh et al. (1995: 223) states that "crimes against tourists result in bad publicity and create a negative image in the minds of prospective visitors. So tour companies tend to avoid destinations that have a reputation for crimes against tourists. Eventually, no matter how much effort is applied to publicise the area's benefits and visitor rewards, decreasing popularity will result in failure."

Entertainment service industries complained that during the Rugby World Cup in South Africa, tourists stayed in their hotels rooms instead of spending money, due to the high crime rate in the country (**Smith, 1995:22**). Just over 100 tourists were allegedly mugged during the Rugby World Cup 1995.

It has been stated that the high crime rate was one of the many reasons which led to Cape Town's failure of hosting the 2004 Olympic Games, and that something had to be done to reduce the crime in Cape Town as well as in the rest of South Africa in order to guarantee the safety of tourists (Anon, 1997). Another statement on the Olympic bid implied that one thing that must get attention is safety. The police cannot be expected to be solely responsible for safety. This was backed by the Minister of Tourism, who claimed that: "About 500 visitors per year are mugged or assaulted" (**Keenan, 1995: 25**).

McIntosh et al. (1995:223) also found that tourism expenditure had an insignificant effect on crime, but they suggested that tourism could be a potential determinant of crime, which affect the quality of the environment negatively. This is especially the case with great sports events, where a great number of sports tourists suddenly descend on a city. The responsibility for the prevention of crime is not that of the sports tourism industry. However sports tourists are potential targets of crime, and protecting them against crime is essential to the growth and survival of the tourist industry.

Resentments

The apparent gap in economic circumstances, behavioural patterns, appearance, and economic effects can generate resentment by local people toward the tourist and it is not uncommon in areas where there is conflict of interest because of tourists. Tourists' demand for goods may lead to increased prices and cause bad feelings. A feeling of inferiority among local groups because of unfavourable contrast with foreign visitors is another form of resentment. Financial dislocation can also occur (**Bennett, 1995:337**).

In any society hosts and guests can learn from each other. Sports tourism has the ability to facilitate a transition from rigid authoritarian social structure to one that is more sensitive to the individual's need. When societies are "closed" to outside influences, they tend to become rigid. Stereotypes or the act of categorising groups of people based upon a single dimension can be broken down by one-to-one interaction between hosts and guests (**Bennett, 1995: 337**).

The following negative social effects of tourism on a host community, identified by **McIntosh et al. (1995: 224-225)**, can be applied to sports tourism:

- The introduction of undesirable activities such as gambling, prostitution, drunkenness, and other excesses.

- The so-called "demonstration effect" of local people wanting the same luxuries and imported goods as those indulged in by tourists.

- Racial tension, particularly where there are very obvious racial differences between tourists and their hosts.

- Development of a servile attitude on the part of the tourist business employees.

- "Thrinketisation" of crafts and art to produce volumes of souvenirs for the tourist trade.

- Standardisation of employee roles such as the international waiter - the same type of person in every country.

- Loss of cultural pride, if the culture is viewed by the visitor as a quaint custom or as entertainment.

- Hooliganism, especially at soccer events, for example where supporters are sometimes killed because of their affiliation. In African states like Zimbabwe and

South Africa this also happens.

- Too rapid change in local ways of life due to being overwhelmed by too many tourists.
- Disproportionate numbers of workers in low-paid, menial jobs characteristic of much hotel and restaurant employment.

Intelligent planning and progressive management methods can decrease or eliminate many if not all these negative effects. Sports tourism can be developed in ways that will not impose such a heavy social cost.

In order to protect their financial investments, organisers of sports events in the private sector should be careful when investigating the cost and benefits involved in these events. They should pay attention to possible externalities in order to make explicit any social benefits or cost that might otherwise be ignored by the organisers or promoters (**Fayos-Sola, 1997:242-243**).

4.7 SOCIAL BARRIERS

There are a number of reasons why people do not travel extensively, or do not travel at all to sports events. In order to increase sports tourism and, as a result, the benefits it brings to a country, one should identify these barriers and try to overcome them. Although some of these barriers cannot be controlled by the sports tourism industry, ways should be found in which these barriers can be minimised, by making it easier for the sports tourist to attend sport events. McIntosh et al. (1995: 238) divided these barriers into six broad categories:

1. **Cost.** Consumers operate within financial constraints, and sports travel must compete with other allocations of funds. Saying that travelling to a sports event is too expensive is an indirect way of saying that travel is not important, but, even allowing this interpretation, costs are a principal reason for staying home. **Furguson et al. (1991: 208)** makes the following remark on ticket prices: "The threat of withdrawal of patronage can serve to punish firms who set prices in excess of those perceived by customers to be fair (warranted by cost)."

2. **Lack of time.** Many people cannot leave their businesses, jobs, or professions for the purpose of visiting a sports event.

3. **Health limitations.** Poor health and physical limitations keep many persons at home.

4. **Family stage.** Parents of young children often do not travel because of family obligations and inconveniences in travelling with children. Widows/widowers and single people sometimes do not travel because of the lack of a travelling companion.

5. **Lack of interest.** Unawareness of travel destinations, such as a specific sports event, that would bring pleasurable satisfaction, is a major barrier.

6. **Fear and safety.** Things unknown are often feared, and in travel, much is often not familiar to the would-be traveller. Wars, unrest, and negative publicity about an area will create doubt and fear in the mind of the prospective sports tourist.

4.8   CONCLUSION

Sports tourism has significant effects on individuals and families who travel for this purpose, and leads to behavioural changes. Sports tourists as well as the host community encounter certain problems when the sports tourist visit the location, and these problems must be resolved.

The extent to which the sports tourist solves these problems, determines the degree of success of the trip. The traveller must therefore decide how much cultural distance he or she desires. Consideration must be given to the likely influence that masses of tourists will have on their hosts and steps must be taken to minimise the negative sociological influences and enhance the positive effects of large numbers of tourists on their host society. Social factors, such as cost, time, health, family stage, safety, as well as stadium factors which can inhibit the attendance of sports events, must be identified and dealt with in order to increase sports tourism and its benefits to the host community.

Technological innovation and the growth of communication technology not only have reduced the cost of transportation and communication but also have strengthened relationships between corporations and between individuals-relationships that were previously (and almost unavoidably) organised on the basis of the nation-state (**Harvey & Houle 1994:343**). Changes like these result in an increasing number of events in the world of sports, such as the Olympic Games or other large tournaments with a global character, which result in a huge increase in sports tourism and its benefits.

Chapter 5

Economic considerations and events

Creation of wealth is almost a duty because of the widespread benefits that flow from it.
John Gunn

5.1 INTRODUCTION

Sports tourism will continue to grow and can create opportunities to a country or region. These benefits can only be obtained if the country or region host sports events. It must therefore prevent the best bids possible to secure the event.

Since the 1930's the Olympic Games changed dramatically, when countries started to compete for the honour of hosting for the Games. The reason for this competition was pride and prestige - the Olympic Games became the "hottest" property in the world, and was sold commercially in the form of sponsorship, television rights and for the benefits it can bring to the host country (**Crockett, 1998:1**). In order to reap these benefits proper planning is paramount.

Before an organisation is funded in New Zealand for sports events, they need to demonstrate that they have the following in place (**Tow, 1997**):

- The event is linked to the organisation's strategic management plan;

- Its financially viability is illustrated with detailed income and expenditure budgets, cash flow projections, etc.

- The international importance of the event is explained; and

- The international federation's requirements are indicated.

Sports tourism is becoming an increasingly competitive industry. The bidding process therefore requires much skill, because competition is tough and there are a limited number of hallmark events. It is thus very important to choose the right event, and therefore governments should ask themselves why they are hosting the event, and what benefits they are hoping to derive from it. This chapter will deal with the economic considerations for hosting events.

Knowing why one is getting involved in hosting a sports event almost automatically determines the list of sports events one should bid for. According to Crockett (1998:1) there are basically two significant benefits one should be seeking in hosting sports events:

a) Economic Impact. The calculation of what the sports event is worth to the host area in terms of money. Prior to bidding for an event one should make an assessment of this impact, which will automatically give an indication of not only whether you should bid for the event but also how much you are prepared to pay for it. For example, the 1993 Telecom Rally in Australia had an impact of AU$19 million on the Western Australian economy.

b) Promotion of your Region. Events can be extremely effective in promoting your region in a most effective way. For example, the FIA World Rally Championship in Australia was televised in 93 countries through the world, and much of this exposure features the city of Perth and the surrounding countryside.

It would be impossible to buy this kind of exposure. Those sports events that get significant television coverage will be the best at promoting one's country or region and should be targeted when bidding for an international sports event.

Crockett (1998:2) also identifies two other aspects that should be considered:

* to find sports events that is special or unique, and
* to give preference to recurring sports events, as these are more valuable than one-offs.

It is also important to understand the sports event's financial return. Most events will not always make a profit and that is why funding is needed from sponsors, the government, and other organisations. A good example is the Olympic Games. Although it does not necessarily make a profit in the short run, in the big run it is profitable for the country and area in which it is hosted. Hotels, restaurants, retailers, and many other organisations can benefit greatly and make profits from these events, and therefore new money is poured into the local economy.

Before one decides to bid, the key question, according to **Crockett (1998:2)** is: "What is the return on investments?" After one has determined the sports event that is to be bid for, and what the cost benefit for the area will be, the process of bidding for the event starts. This process is unique to the specific sports event you have chosen, and can seldom be applied to another event.

Further it must be clear who is going to decide on the location for the event. Usually this is not only a single person or group, but more often the decision comes from senior levels and even politicians. For major sporting events, one should get the approval of the national body before the ultimate approval of the international body.

When bidding for an event, the needs of the decision-makers should be identified. A detailed checklist of criteria which must be met, can make this process much easier. This things which South Africa and Cape Town could have offered for the Olympic Games by hosting it, should rather have been accentuated in Cape Town's bid for the 2004 Olympic Games (**Anon, 1997**).

It is also recommended to work closely with the specific sport involved in the event, and to include it in the development of the bidding process. Appropriate and professional people should make the presentation, both in terms of the actual presentation and the bid documents. The way the presentation is handled is a direct reflection on one's ability to host an event (**Crockett, 1998:3**).

Although Cape Town failed in its bid for the 2004 Olympic Games, the campaign have shown South Africa's tourism-potential and the opportunities that exist elsewhere on the continent (**Anon, 1997**). This in itself is also important.

Fayos-Sola (1997) remarked on economic efficiency and redistribution that the evaluation of sports events requires going below the surface and looking at those measures of success not easily identifiable or measurable, such as emotions, friendship and experience. Since the economic impact of an event may be the deciding factor for continuing the event, it is an important task for the event manager of the sponsoring community to determine this impact. Event sponsors, such as private corporations, government organisations and non-profit organisations, demand proper evaluation of the sports event's economic impact, because of their increasingly tight budgets. In the context of sports tourism, economic impact is defined as the net economic change in a host community that results from spending attributed to a sports event or facility. The purpose of an economic impact analysis is to measure the economic benefits that accrue to a community, region or country.

Sports teams and events are business investments both for the individual entrepreneur or the department that organises and promotes them, and for the community that subsidises and hosts them. Communities may invest public tax money in sports events for a variety of reasons, but economic benefits are likely to be one of the most important. They anticipate that these events will attract visitors from outside the community, who spend money while they are there and thus create an infusion of new money in the community. Communities need to assess benefits in a public context broader, than that of the entrepreneur or department that has a directly measurable bottom line that evaluates their private economic performance (**Crompton, 1995:15**).

The following sequence of actions describes the investment of public funds in sporting events and facilities for economic purposes:

Residents of a community give funds to their city council in the form of taxes, and the city council uses a part of these funds to subsidise the production of an event or the development of a facility. The facility or event attracts out-of-town visitors, who spend money in the local community both inside and outside the event they visit. This new money from outside the community creates income and jobs in the community for residents. This completes the cycle - community residents are responsible for creating the funds, and they receive a return on their investment in the form of new jobs and more household income (**Crompton, 1995:15**).

5.3 APPROACHES TO ASSESSMENT OF EVENTS

The following table indicates the approaches to event impact assessment, according to **Getz (1994:437)**.

Table 5.1: Approaches to Event Impact Assessment

APPROACHES	GOALS	COMMONLY USED MEASURES
BREAK-EVEN OR PROFIT/LOSS	• Short-term assessment of financial efficiency or solvency	• Measure direct costs and and revenues to organisers • Determine surplus or deficit (profit or loss)
RETURN ON INVESTMENT	• Show the benefits of grants or sponsorship • Calculate ROI for private investors or owners	• Determine the relationships relationships between grants/ sponsorships and levels of visitation or economic benifits • Use standard ROI accounting practices
ECONOMIC SCALE	• Determine the economic	• Measure total attendance and

	scale of one or more events from the destination perspective	attendance and expenditure of event consumers, plus organisers' expenditure
ECONOMIC IMPACT	• Determine the macro-economic benefits to the destination area	• Estimate direct and indirect income and employment benefits • Use multipliers or econometric models
COST & BENEFITS	• Evaluate the cost and benefits from the perspective of the host community and environment • Determine the net worth or value of event	• Compare tangible and intangible costs and benefits for the short and long term • Assess opportunity costs of investments • Examine the distribution the of impacts • Judge the net worth and acceptability of events

Break-even or profit/loss assessment

According to **Getz (1994:437)** it is a challenge for many events merely to survive from year to year. To determine their solvency or to measure their efficiency and effectiveness in achieving goals within their budget, organisers tend to look at the bottom line of their own financial statements at year-end. This is a short-term approach, and the only impacts addressed are those affecting the organisation's financial performance. Direct cost and revenues will be considered, and this might include a statement of how surplus revenues or operating cost were spent; but wider economic impacts are not examined.

A surplus revenue or profit is not necessarily an economic benefit for the destination, depending on the source of revenue. An event might, for example, generate a surplus, but only because of the local government's grants, in which case the surplus does not represent new income for the area.

Return on investment (ROI)

Sponsors of sports events may want to know if their investments in events are paying off. They will be interested in sales, public relations, and other marketing goals. Their main concern is the amount of money they invested to conduct the special event and how much return occurs. Public agencies giving grants to events will be more interested in how the event achieved certain goals, ranging from qualitative evaluations of changes in public attitudes to full economic impact assessment (**Getz, 1994:437**).

According to **Turco & Kelsey (1993:34)** one portion of return on investment for local governments is the tax revenue generated by the event and returned to the community. Event organisers and private investors will want to calculate their return on investment using standard accounting practices, but this, too, is only a measure of financial performance and not of economic impact on the destination. It should be kept in mind that when calculating a return on investment, money earned today can be reinvested and money spent on events could be invested elsewhere. This is why the use of net percent value calculations is recommended (**Getz, 1994:437**).

Thus, according to **Turco & Kelsey (1993:34)**, the return on investment is calculated as the amount by which revenues exceed investment. Revenues brought into the event is therefore divided by the expenditures to conduct the event, to calculate this percentage. This can be very impressive for some events and for others it may be a measure of subsidy.

Expenditure Leakage

Sports events, especially those large-scale events, often make use of the businesses of non-residents to provide the necessary goods and services, such as entertainment, food and beverage concessions and souvenirs. After the event these non-resident businesses leave the local economy taking with them a considerable amount of revenue. This is called expenditure leakage or the vendor factor (**Turco & Kelsey, 1993:34**).

The total income effect of tourism expenditure depends on the leakages from the economy (**Flemming and Toepper, 1990**). **Saayman (1997:39)** and **Cooper et al. (1997:118)** explain that a portion of the money can either be saved or taxed or a portion can be spent outside the local economy.

McIntosh et al. (1995:327) and **Johnson (1999:37)** define leakage as a combination of savings and imports. Savings represent funds retained by households and firms. Imports result in expenditure flowing overseas, and taxes represent money taken out of the circular flow of income by the government in the form of income tax, value added tax and corporation tax, for example. Thus, to get the maximum benefits economically from tourist expenditures, a country should introduce as much of the tourist funds as possible into the local economy for goods and services rather than save the proceeds or spend it on a large amount of imports (**Tribe, 1995:187**).

Lickorish and Jenkins (1997:68) describe sports tourists as short-term visitors who bring with them certain expectations relating to accommodation, food and hygiene, to name but a few. To meet these expectations, many developing countries have to import goods and services in order to encourage and develop sports tourism. Payment for these goods and services to support the tourism sector are said to be "leakages", that is, part of tourist expenditure leaks out of the economy to pay for necessary imports. Very few countries, if any, have the resources and means to supply the total tourism demand. It is necessary, therefore, to examine the import pattern of the tourism sector and to determine whether imports can be limited and substituted by domestic production (**Gee et al., 1989:155**).

Leakages in regional economies result from two main problems. Firstly, rural economies are chronically underdeveloped, requiring importation of many goods and services. Payment for these goods and services flow directly out of the local economy. Secondly, businesses are sometimes owned by individuals or companies that are located outside the region and profits from these businesses are not retained in the local economies. Because of chronic leakages in rural, tourism-based economies, the economic benefit of tourism to local residents may sometimes be more apparent than real (**Van Harssel, 1994:165 and Niedermeier and Smith, 1995:51**).

The encouragement of domestic production will not only reduce the leakages of foreign exchange, but will generate employment and income. **Lickorish and Jenkins (1997:68); Mill and Morrison (1985); Bennett (1997:326); Koch et al. (1998:909) and Coltman (1988:225)** list a number of possible forms of leakages that may occur:

- The cost of goods and services that have to be imported to satisfy sport tourist needs;

- Importation of goods and materials for the infrastructure and buildings required for sports tourism development;

- Payment of interest, rent or profit on foreign capital invested in the country's tourism plant;

- Direct expenditure on promotion; publicity and other services purchased when promoting the country abroad; or

- Transfer pricing, particularly in the case of multinational companies, where payments are recorded in the country of tourist origin rather than in the destination country, thereby reducing profits and taxes in the destination country; and exemption of duties or taxes by host governments, on foreign-owned companies or promotion of financial inducements to attract foreign investment.

To accurately estimate net economic impact, the money collected by these businesses must be subtracted from the economic impact subtotal, because it will not remain in the local community (**Turco & Kelsey, 1993:34**). In order to create wealth and other jobs, the leakage's need to be as small as possible, otherwise the country will benefit very little (**Saayman et al., 2000**).

Economic Scale
When measuring the economic impact of a sports event, researchers end up with total size of expenditure associated with an event, but this can be problematic. **Getz (1994:437)** identified the following problems:

- The first problem that arises is that of including all the expenditure of all even-goers in the calculation of the economic benefit, while little or none of the expenditure of area residents should in fact be included.

- Problem two is that of failing to account for the reasons people attend events. If they where motivated to travel to the destination because of the event, it results in new income for the area; if they were already in the area, the impact is much less, or even negated entirely.

- The third problem is that of including grants and sponsorships in the calculation of the impact, while failing to determine if the amounts are simply internal allocations as opposed to new money for the area.

- Problem four is the failure to note that much leakage is associated with tourist expenditure - that is, much of it leaves the area immediately, without creating local income or profit.

A valid way to express the economic scale of an event is to identify how many tourists it attracted and how much the tourists spent in the area. This is very legitimate and probably all that most event organizers can and should attempt. However, it does require careful explanation of how the measure of economic scale was determined and what assumptions have been made - particularly that gross visitor expenditure is not the same as net income created for the area.

Economic impact

Turco & Kelsey, (1993:34) defined economic impact as "the net change in the host community's economy, as a result of the spending that is attributed to the special event."

This impact comes, according to them, from two sources: the spending of non-residents which can be directly tied to the event, and the degree to which residents and local businesses alter their spending because of the event. When preparing an economic impact study, both of these components should be estimated, because either one of them can influence the economic impact of the event.

Four aspects are important in determining the economic impact, namely
* the number of tourists,
* their spending,
* how long they stay, and
* the multiplier effect (**Saayman, 2000**).

The measuring of the economic impact of a sports event on a destination requires rigorous research methods. The specific goals are to determine the local income and employment created for residents of the area. Sometimes long-term, indirect impacts, such as improved ability to attract investment, are also considered. Promotion and image improvement of the destination area might also be covered but are much more difficult to measure. Major reliability and validity problems are inevitably encountered, often resulting in the making of unwarranted assumptions and the use of inappropriate techniques, especially with regard to the application of multipliers (**Getz, 1994:437**).

The tourism multipliers have been developed over some years, largely based on Keynesian principles of the recirculation of a proportion of income by recipients into consumption spending, which then engenders further income and employment (**Bull, 1993:138; Vellas and Bécherel, 1995:22; Johnson, 1999:36 and Briguglio, 1995:69**). The multiplier analysis plays an important role to determine the economic impact of tourists. It expresses the relationship between the level of income or output and the initial injection into the economy (**Cullen, 1997:130**).

Inskeep (1991:387) defines the multiplier as the number of rounds of spending with regard to the initial expenditure within the local economy, or the ways in which tourist spending filters through the economy. The term multiplier is used to describe the total effect, both direct and secondary, that an external source of income has on an economy. **Mathieson and Wall (1982:64)** define the multiplier as the number by which initial tourist expenditure must be multiplied in order to obtain the total cumulative income effect for a specified time period.

Multiplier analysis is used to estimate the ongoing implications of tourist expenditures in the economy. It is recognised that initial tourism expenditure will give rise to import demand, to cater for tourists' needs, and that much of the initial expenditure will percolate through the economy to stimulate further indirect expenditure induced by the initial expenditure. These three terms reflect the fact that tourism is a multifaceted activity. It is essentially interdependent, relying for its activity on inputs from many sectors of the economy, such as agriculture, industry and general services. The initial account of tourism expenditure will generate changes in the economy in output, income, employment, and contribution to government revenue. The changes in various categories may be less than, equal to, or greater than the initial (additional) change in tourist expenditure which started the economic process (**Lickorish and Jenkins, 1997:66-68 and Cooper et al., 1997:116**).

According to **Mathieson and Wall (1982:71)**, income multipliers are useful for assessing the short-turn economic impacts of tourist expenditure. On a short-term basis, multipliers can provide information about the impacts of sports tourism. They can help to:

- identify weak linkages in the economy;

- provide information on the degree to which such objectives as maximising income and employment, and minimising foreign exchange losses, are being met; and

- identify areas in the economy which require stimulation, and others which bring large benefits and merit expansion.

5.3.1   Different types of tourism multipliers

Lickorish and Jenkins (1997:68) accentuates the fact that there are a number of methodological approaches to calculating multipliers and the choice of methodology will give rise to different coefficients.

In addition to the income multiplier, there are other types of multipliers (**Mathieson and Wall, 1982:65**). The concept of the income multiplier is often confused with these other types of tourism multipliers, with a resulting misinterpretation of their implications. **Lickorish and Jenkins (1997:67); Cooper et al. (1997:117-118); Lea (1988:41) and Muller (1992, 68)** divide tourist multipliers into five main types, namely:

- Transaction or sale multipliers. The transaction or sale multiplier is the additional turnover created by an additional unit of tourist expenditure;

- Output multiplier. The output multiplier is a sophistication of the sales multiplier where the relative changes of inventories are taken into account as a result of the additional tourist expenditures;

- Income multiplier. The income multiplier measures the additional income created in the economy as a consequence of the increased tourist expenditure;

- Government revenue multiplier. The government revenue multiplier measures the impact on government revenue as a consequence of an increase in tourist expenditure;

- Employment multiplier. The employment multiplier is the extra employment generated by an additional unit of tourist expenditure.

Each of these types of multipliers measures a different phenomenon. Each has its own utility. For example, if one is comparing the effects of a number of projects, one may be interested in the projects' implications for both income and employment. Depending upon the priorities and the flexibility of investment, the one with the highest income or employment multiplier, or the best combination of the two, could be chosen (**Mathieson and Wall, 1982:65**).

5.3.2　Tourism expenditure and the functioning of the multiplier

In tourism the extra expenditure, which is the cornerstone of the multiplier system, can take several forms. Expenditure can be divided into direct expenditure, indirect expenditure or induced expenditure.

- Direct tourism expenditure. The term direct reflects the fact that the income is received, or generated, directly and triggers the first round of spending by businesses (**Gee et al., 1989:151**). **Mathieson and Wall (1982:65)** and **Vellas and Bécherel (1995:229-233)** state that this category consists of expenditure by tourists on goods and services in hotels, restaurants, shops and other sport tourism services. It also includes expenditure on goods exported because of tourism or investments related to tourism in the region (**Strydom and Lourens, 1995:51 and Muller, 1992:68**).

- Indirect tourism expenditure. **Muller (1992:68)** defines indirect sport tourism expenditure as expenditure in successive rounds of inter-business transactions which result form the direct expenditure (described above). **Mathieson and Wall (1982:65)** indicate that the payments of salaries and wages to local employees, and tourist establishments replenishing stocks, are indirect effects of the initial, direct sport tourist expenditure (**Vellas and Bécherel, 1995:229-233 and Strydom and Lourens, 1995:51**).

- Induced tourism expenditure. **Muller (1992:68)** defines the induced sports tourism expenditure as the increased consumer spending resulting from the additional personal income generated by the direct expenditure (described above). For example, hotel staff's salaries are used to buy goods and services. As wages and salaries within an economy rise, consumption also increases and this provides an additional impetus for economic activity (**Mathieson and Wall, 1982:65; Vellas and Bécherel, 1995:229-230 and Strydom and Lourens, 1995:51**).

It is only when all three levels of impact (direct, indirect and induced) are estimated that the full positive impact of sports tourism expenditure is fully assessed (**Cooper et al., 1997:114**).

To generate income, expenses have to incur. **Muller (1992:68)** explains that in the field of sports tourism, extra expenditure takes on various forms, such as:

- spending on goods and services by sport tourists in an area;

- investment by external sources (for example hotel groups building a new unit in an area);

- government spending on infrastructure (for example airport additions or improvements); and

- exports of goods and services stimulated by sports tourism (for example flower, fish or wine sales from an area).

To put the multiplier effect in action, additional expenditure, resulting in income, is needed. Saayman (1997:38) lists the main sources of income, namely:

- payment of salaries and wages ;
- taxation on tourists, income and profits as well as custom taxes;

- rental of tourism establishments; and
- the sale of souvenirs and goods.

According to **Lundberg, (1990) and Coltman (1988:25)** the following formula can be used to calculate the tourism income multiplier:

$$TIM = MPS + MPI \quad \frac{1 - TPI}{}$$

TIM = Tourism Income Multiplier, or factor by which sports tourim expenditures should be multiplied to determine the tourism income generated by these expenditures:

- 1 = Tourist expenditure

- TPI = Tourists' Propensity to Import, or buy imported goods and services that do not create income for the area

- MPS = Marginal Propensity to Save, or residents' decision not to spend some of their tourists' disposable income

- MPI = Marginal Propensity to Import, or the residents' decision to buy imported goods or spend money abroad.

5.3.3 The size of the multiplier

Vellas and Bécherel (1995: 229-233) state that the multiplier is a tool used to analyse the economic effects of increase in tourism expenditure and its influence on other sectors of the economy. The value of the multiplier depends on the particular features of sports tourism in the area studied and the characteristics of the local economy, namely:

- The economic composition of an area. The greater the range of economic activities in the area, the greater the chance of a high number of exchanges between the activities and therefore the greater the size of the multiplier (**Hugo, 1992:41**).

- The extent to which various sectors of the economy are linked to one another. According to **Broham (1996, 56)**, lower tourism multipliers have been associated with highly concentrated, large-scale, foreign-owned tourism complexes, while higher multipliers have been connected to more dispersed, smaller-scale, locally owned operations that tend to be better linked to the local economy.

- The area's propensity to import. A high number of imports into the area will reduce the value of the multiplier (**Hugo, 1992:41**).

In general, the higher the multiplier, the more money stays and is circulated within the local economy. The economic benefits of tourism is large when the multiplier is high, indicating that much of the original sports tourism expenditure goes to salaries and wages of local residents and to pay for locally produced goods and services (**Van Harssel, 1994:165**). The multiplier effect ranges from less than one for small island economies to more than two for large, highly integrated economies (**Inskeep, 1991:386-387**).

Tribe (1995:189) indicates in Table 5.1 how the multiplier is effected by various actions taken in the economy.

Table 5.2: Multiplier effect

Value of the multiplier	Leakages from the economy	Impact of expenditure on income
High	Low	High
Low	High	Low

(Tribe, 1995:189)

5.3.4 Weaknesses of the multiplier analysis

According to **Harvey & Houle (1994:348-349)** cities focus on strategies to promote themselves in a world tourism market by organising major sports events. This demonstrates the economic circumstances cities have to cope with in order to avoid marginalisation.

Sport complexes and major events become important tools in the race to become a "world-class" city. To reach this goal, these cities have to develop world-class complexes and events. The so-called world-class complexes and events are designed according to highly homogenised concepts, and this influences local distinctiveness. This is also true for other projects: "Many kinds of ex-urban leisure developments [...] that were once distinctive have become internationally ordinary"

(Harvey & Houle, 1994: 348-349). The end result would be the diffusion of a "highly capitalised consumer culture", in other words a "global culture".

Many opportunities exist to increase sports tourism and obtain the benefits it brings to a country. However, this requires that countries should host sports events, in order to attract the sport tourists. In South Africa alone many such opportunities exist.

The annual Comrades Marathon between Durban and Pietermaritzburg attracts thousands of sports tourists from all over the world, spending money in these cities and elsewhere in South Africa. This event creates huge benefits for the region.

It has been reported that over 13 000 athletes, thousands of spectators, and 2 000 media people and officials descended on Durban and Pietermaritzburg for the 1989 Comrades Marathon. All of the 32 000 hotel beds in Durban were fully booked from the Monday to the Thursday, and local tourist officials reported that many of the visitors stayed on to enjoy an extended mid-year holiday **(Anon, 1989:76)**.

In Pietermaritzburg, which at the time had only 800 hotel beds, accommodation was problematic. Schools and college halls, as well as private homes, were used to accommodate the hordes of visitors. The director of Pietermaritzburg's publicity association confirmed that the event is worth millions of rands to the city. "When the hotels were full, we asked citizens with spare accommodation to make it available to the Comrades Marathon Association. Many did, some for free and some on a bed-and-breakfast basis for which they would charge" **(Anon, 1989:76)**.

Many more visitors stayed in surrounding towns, and small hotels as far as 60km from Pietermaritzburg reported to have hosted Comrades runners and supporters. It is difficult to estimate exactly what the Comrades is worth to Durban and Pietermaritzburg each year. A tourism official remarked: "One can be pretty accurate in hotels, but how does one estimate what is spent in shops, on food and beverage, transport and gimmicks?" **(Anon, 1989:76)**.

Tow (1997) says the sport and leisure industry in New Zealand makes a significant and economic impact, quoting the following statistics:
- it supports 23 000 fulltime jobs;
- it contributes NZ$ 1.6 billion to the economy;
- it pays NZ$300 million in taxes each year;
- it involves 300 000 volunteers contributing NZ$200 million worth of time each

year;
- its membership total 1,4 million persons; and
- local governments invest NZ$ 300 million in sport and leisure each year.

Keenan (1996:27) remarked the following on the golf opportunities and existing benefits.

With the World Cup Golf (WCG) at Erinvale Estate in the Western Cape as catalyst, a highly profitable golf tourism industry can be started in South Africa. The great increase in golf in Japan started after the 1957 World Cup. Golf has been described as a fantastic medium for tourism because it attracts tourists who will spend a lot of money. With exception only the UK and the USA, South Africa is the most developed golf country in the world. Most golf tourists staying and playing at venues like Fancourt in George, South Africa's top golf holiday destination, will spend about R25 000, air fairs excluded, during a 10-day vacation.

The chairman of the Parallel Media group said that there is no reason why South Africa could not beat Spain's 500 000 golf visitors a year, and they are all high-spending tourists. The WCG at Erinvale was expected to attract 45 000 spectators, and it attracted the sponsorships of companies not previously associated with golf. These include international companies like Silicon Graphics, Merrill Lynch, Malaysian Airlines, American Express and the Mines Resort City.

The WCG will have a television audience of hundreds of millions in over 120 countries, which is worth about $50 million, and the event will be on prime time on the US network NBC. The WCG has an advantage over rugby in that it is a single focus event. The scenic mountain and sea views will provide an excellent visual background for the golf, and filler footage of all the Peninsula's scenic spots was done, exposing Cape Town's features prominently.

The WCG holds other benefits besides golf tourism. With the arrival of the overseas contingent, buying interest increased in Erinvale Estate. Most of the available plots were sold at two and even three times the estimated price, and record prices were achieved, R800 000 was paid for a plot with an original price of R400 000, and R1,5 million was paid for a completed house.

Major building projects on the Erinvale Estate course for the World Cup Golf took place and developers worked non-stop in anticipation of overseas interest. Ideal opportunities to buy into this top golf course were provided by the weak rand. Almost 3500 guest packages were developed for the sponsors at a value of R800 per day. All the larger hotels in the Somerset West and Stellenbosh area were fully booked months prior to the event. House rentals at the golf estate were on offer for up to R1000 per person, tickets included.

According to the commentary of Parallel Media Group in London on the World Cup Golf, South Africa's government should help with funding if they want to continue hosting world class events. The weak rand makes it very difficult to increase prize money - at the WCG players competed for $1,5 million. Service in South Africa is also an aspect that needs attention. There is a perception that in an international context South Africa is not cheap at all. The travelling distance is long and the poor service quality reduces the perceived value of a South African holiday. However, WCG will certainly highlight South Africa on the golf tourism map.

Costs and benefits
Economic costs of producing sports events, and the indirect and external costs imposed on the community or environment cannot be ignored. Often only the positive economic benefits associated with sports tourists coming to the area are reported, but sports events can also generate substantial economic cost or negative impacts. These are often ignored.

The development of cost-benefit evaluation methods can overcome this serious limitation by comparing economic cost with economic benefits and by comparing intangibles. Some progress has been made in quantifying intangibles, such as social problems or psychological benefits. Implementing cost-benefit evaluation has the advantage of focusing attention on the value or worth of the sport event, rather than merely highlighting supposed profits, income, and job creation (**Getz, 1994:438**). Social, cultural and environmental effects are considered alongside economic factors, yielding a more balanced evaluation.

When more people visit a community, an additional demand is created on the local services. Although it may bring economic benefit, it also creates negative or cost impacts such as vandalism, road accidents, police and fire protection, environmental degradation, garbage collection, increased prices in retail and restaurant establishments for residents, and disruption of residents' lifestyle.

The translation some of these impacts into economic values is difficult and that may be one of the reasons why they are usually ignored (**Crompton 1995:33**). When cost is incorporated into a study, it changes from an economic impact analysis to a cost-benefit analysis. In **Crompton's (1995:33)** view it is this information that decision-makers should be using when evaluating alternative investments. According to

Crompton the benefit-cost analysis is designed to identify the most sensible investment alternative, because it considers the long-term benefits and identify the long-term costs in hosting a sports event.

5.4 IMPACT EVALUATION PROCESS

A step-by-step process of impact evaluation for event tourism by **Getz (1994:442)** is provided below. In each step a number of rules are included which must be followed if reliability and validity mistakes are to be avoided.

Step 1: Formulate precise research goals
- Define the study area within which cost and benefits are to be calculated.
- Delimit the scope of the evaluation (which costs and benefits to measure; quantitative and qualitative evaluation techniques to be used).
- Define tourists and residents.
- Set criteria for attribution of incremental expenditure (i.e., should resident spending be included?).
- Formulate precise research and evaluation questions.

Step 2: Determine data needs and appropriate methods
- Specify types of data needed to answer the research questions.
- Determine the measures needed and the appropriate methods to collect and analyse the data.

Step 3: Determine attendance at the event - Calculate total number of tourists and tourist-visits
- Whenever possible, use controlled access and/or ticket sales to estimate attendance.
- For open events, use a systematic observation method that avoids double counting by applying weightings derived from visitor surveys (asking: How many visits have you made, on how many days?)
- Take into account the difference between total number of visitors and total person-visit and between tourist and resident visit (feasible only if a visitor survey is undertaken).

Step 4: Conduct visitor surveys
- An on-site visitor survey is necessary for estimating the number and proportion of tourists at events, their motivations, spending patterns, and whether or not visits were extended or expenditures increased due to the event.

- Ensure that a systematic sample of individuals is taken.
- Include performers, officials, competitors, and so on.
- Stratify the sample by applicable factors such as venue, time, and day; use weightings to reflect the true distribution of attendance.
- Guard against sampling bias caused by length of stay and multiple-site visits by ensuring that the individuals are not mistakenly counted twice; make estimates of average length of stay and number of visits, and weight the results to reduce the effect of length-of-stay bias.
- Use past experience or educated guesses to derive a sample size that will yield high confidence limits for statistical analysis, especially ensuring a large enough sample of tourists.

Step 5: Estimate total expenditure by tourists
- Determine average spending per visitor-day, separating on-site from off-site and within the study area from outside the study area (if total trip expenditure is estimated, the on-site, within area-amounts must be distinguished).
- Include spending by performers, officials, competitors, and so on, but also account for wages, profits, and so on, that they remove from the area.
- Avoid double counting when events overlap; create a multiple-event category of visitors.
- In small non-random samples, avoid using expenditure means if large outliners occur.
- Use expenditure categories that match available classes of multiplier.
- Take into account the special estimation problems associated with package tours (knowing what proportion to allocate to the area) and business or related trips (the traveller might not have paid).
- Minimise recall bias by conducting surveys on-site or as soon after the event as possible.

Step 6: Estimate expenditure attributable to tourists
- Determine the importance of the event in motivating the trip, an extended stay, or increased spending.
- Subtract time-switchers, who would have visited the area anyway (say, during the same year).
- Do mot confuse total incremental expenditure with economic impact.

Step 7: Calculate net income and macroeconomic impacts
- Gross visitor expenditure attributed to the event (i.e., the incremental income)

does not equal net income for the area, because of leakage.

- Apply a value-added or income multiplier with caution to account for all the direct and secondary effects of incremental expenditure.
- An econometric model can be used instead of multipliers to account for macro-impacts over time.
- Government revenue, in the form of taxes at all levels is usually taken into account when value-added multipliers are applied; otherwise it must be estimated separately.

Step 8: Do a cost benefit evaluation

- Define costs and benefits to be measured and what quantitative and qualitative measures would be applied.
- Determine the levels (local, regional, national) at which costs and benefits will be evaluated, and the time-frame.
- Include externalities, intangibles, and distributional issues; consider displacement effects; evaluate cumulative, long-term effects.
- Calculate the benefit-to-cost ratio in economic terms, while evaluating the net worth of the event in qualitative terms.

5.5 THE LONG-TERM IMPACT OF SPORTS EVENTS ON TOURISM

The long-term impact of a sports event on tourism will be demonstrated with the case study of **Kang & Perdue (1994: 211-221)** on the 1998 Seoul Olympic Games. In their paper "short-term" refers to the period immediately before, during, and after the event, and "long-term" refers to the period before and after the "short-term" period.

Kang & Perdue (1994:208) presented a conceptual framework (Figure 5.2) in which the linkages are demonstrated by which a mega event, such as the Olympic Games, may produce long-term impacts on international travel to the host country. According to them the direct effects of hosting a mega event include:

- increased mass media coverage in the world community,

- improvements and expansion of tourism infrastructure and tourism services,

- possible increase in tourism promotional activities by the host tourism industry to capitalise on favourable marketing environment, and

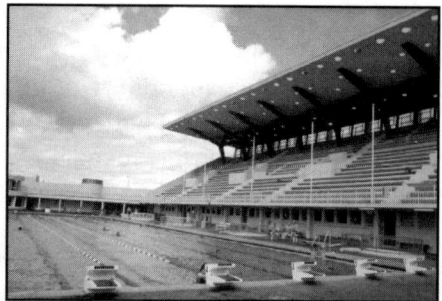

- an influx of participants and tourists during the event period.

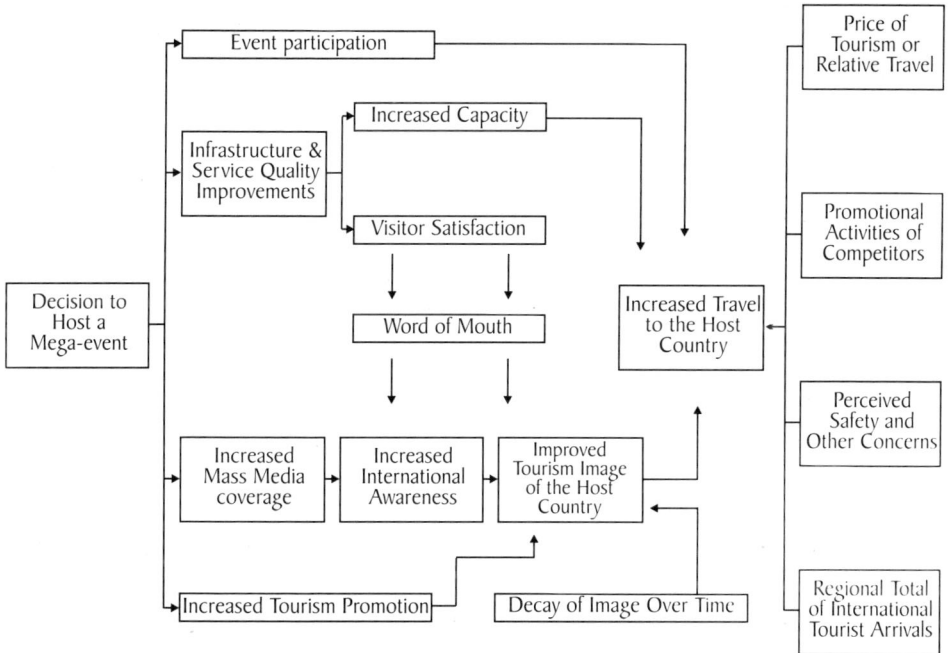

Figure 5.1: Impact of a Mega-Event on International Tourism a Conceptual Framework according to Kang & Perdue (1994:209)

Kang & Perdue (1994:208) explained the framework as follows:

Image
Carmichael (1993:94) noted that "… Gradually, a potential tourist builds up an image of a destination. The image may be stereotyped and vary greatly from reality but it reflects an individual's personal evaluations and expectations of place."

Keenan (1995:25) accentuates service as a vital factor for repeat business. Sports events have the potential to improve the awareness and image of the hosting city or country as an international tourist destination (**Kang & Perdue, 1994: 205**). Tourism products can be tangible or intangible, and the quality of these products can increase or decrease the feelings of enjoyment and comfort of the tourist (**Botha & Saayman,**

1995:53). This plays an important role in the tourist's perceived experience of the host community and therefore it influences word-of-mouth and the image of the host community. The quality of the sports tourism products and services that are offered are essential, because satisfied tourists will spread the positive image and they are very likely to return to the destination. **Botha & Saayman (1995:53)** noted that it should be the hosts objective to make the tourist's "dream" a reality, so that the planning, anticipation and memories of the visit also contribute to the enjoyment of the trip.

Service quality is an important factor in the image of a sports tourism destination. Before the Rugby World Cup in South Africa it was reported that industries worried over logistical problems during the event. They worried that the extended delays at airports and problems in transporting fans to and from the various venues could do a lot of harm to South Africa's reputation as a tourist destination (**Anon, 1995: 27**). From a marketing point of view, image is the most important aspect of any tourist attraction (**Ritchie & Goeldner, 1994:299**).

Smith (1995:22) noted that the major problem at the Rugby World Cup was looking after 16 teams flying in from all over the world, with support staff up to 46 people per team with baggage and equipment, and doing stop-over at hotels. When SA Express at one stage could not manage players and their support staff, with their baggage, they put their baggage on another plane to follow them at no extra cost (**Smith, 1995:22**). What was great service for players, however, often resulted into hassles for other tourists. Furthermore, tour busses got lost because drivers did not know the routes.

Prior to the tournament, concern was voiced that the infrastructure was not ready and the capacity and efficiency needed improvement. Low service levels and public violence was other concerns (**Ebersohn, 1995:20**). This reflected badly on South Africa's image as a sports tourist destination.

According to **Getz (1994:442)** it can be argued that because festivals and great sports events enhance the tourism image of an area, there is a "background" economic benefit attributable to these events through tourists attracted by this enhanced image. A study of Winterlude, in **Getz (1994:442)**, found that tourists believe that their visit to the event heightened their image of the Capital region.

This image-enhancing factor could have long-term, positive effects on tourism, but actual measurement of the benefits would be difficult. The value of media coverage, either in qualitative terms or by assigning financial value to free publicity should be assessed. **Van Der Walt (1997:31)** maintained that if South Africa should host a

Grand Prix, approximately 700 million to 1 billion people all over the world would watch the Grand Prix on television. This will improve South Africa's image tremendously because it will show that South Africa has the infrastructure and technology needed to host such a major event. A more subjective is that special events make residents feel proud and that heightened civic spirit will have tangible benefits for the area (**Getz, 1994:442**).

Mass Media and Awareness
Mega-events are characterised by huge numbers of tourists and worldwide publicity. The publicity of a mega-event such as the Olympic Games starts years prior to the actual event and reaches its climax during the event. Higher levels of awareness of the host city or country results from the extensive media coverage and if this is favourable, the city or country obtains a renewed, stronger and better image.

Event Participation
The duration of the sports event and the capacity of accommodation and transportation of the host region determine the number of foreign participants during the event. The sports event's immediate effect on international tourism to the host country subsequently, may or may not be significant.

Infrastructure and Service Improvements
Commercial accommodation and public transportation facilities are preconditions for future tourism growth. These facilities are renovated and expanded during the preparations for the sports event in order to provide the facilities needed for the event, as well as opportunities to improve the quality of future tourism services.

Visitor Satisfaction and Word-of-Mouth
Visitor satisfaction in later periods will be enhanced by the improvement of tourism services and facilities resulting from the sports event development. Word-of-mouth of this enhanced satisfaction is important to the long-term international tourism impact of the sports event.

Image Decay and Promotional Activities
Over time, the positive image and awareness of the host community resulting from the sports event, will decay, but the host country can prevent this by intensifying its promotional activities.

Prices and the Final Outcome
The factors mentioned above are direct or indirect consequences of hosting a mega

sports event, and except for decay of image, all of them potentially contribute to the long-term increase of the international tourism to the host country. External factors do, however, also affect tourism to countries hosting sports events such as the Olympic Games, especially those related to the actions of competitors and overall cycles in international tourism.

In order to generalise the findings of the study a number of limitations must be considered. According to **Kang & Perdue (1994:222)** these limitations include:

- A limited length of the time series. The availability of data prevented the inclusion of years before 1980 and the total long-term effect may extend to a further 10 years or more.

- The study is a case study focusing on a single region of East Asia with certain important geographical characteristics, which may not be the case for other regions.

- Before the Seoul Olympics, Korea was not a very significant country in international tourism. The impact for Korea may therefore be much larger than for other, established tourism countries.

Thus, the study have shown that mega-events do have a long-term impact on international tourism to the host country. The impact is the largest in the first years after the mega-event and decreases with time, with its effects being felt for perhaps as long as ten years. This impact can be translated into financial terms. In the case of Korea, the impact was estimated to be US $1.3 billion over a three-year period. Furthermore, visitor increase is only significant during and after the event, even though media coverage and destination awareness increase years before the event. Additionally, the event and its media coverage change the price-share relationship and there for increases the demand of the host country (**Kang & Perdue, 1994:222**).

5.6   CONCLUSION

When a country, region or destination hosts an event - whether it is big or small - the event has certain implications. These implications are of a sociological, economic and environmental nature. This chapter dealt mostly with the economic considerations.

Events have advantages such as building pride, promoting the country, creating supra- and infrastructure. Most importantly, however, it spreads money. From a business point of view, an event is about a return on an investment (ROI) that was made. In order for a region or country to benefit from an event, leakages need to be minimised. This chapter investigated ways these leakages can be addressed, for it greatly influences the value that a community or country will get from hosting events. What this chapter did not address, was the financial implications of the maintenance of structures that are developed especially for mega-events. This is something that needs to be researched, for communities normally have to carry the financial burden in terms of maintenance and other costs that arise from events. It is therefore important for planners to also take note of this important issue.

Chapter 6

Event management in tourism

The International Olympic Committee chooses a host city seven years before the Olympic games and they bring the experience of different parts of the Olympic moments to help the new organising committee. We want every Olympic Games to be even better than the last one. But each will be different. They all have their own character.

Juan Antonio Samaranch
(IOC president)

6.1 INTRODUCTION

Countries and cities compete vigorously to host mega- or hallmark events such as the Olympic Games and World Cup Sport. South Africa spent a lot of resources in their bid for the Olympic Games of 2004 but with no success. However, the country did get a lot of publicity. Recently the country was also bidding for the 2006 World Cup Soccer. These events produce large economic and tourism benefits. Even small countries can host such events and many local events originally designed to entertain local residence have grown to attract many international visitors. It was stated in **McIntosh et al. (1995:156)** that these events appeal to a very broad audience:

"...events also have the ability to spread tourism geographically and seasonally. Special events allow a region or community to celebrate its uniqueness, promote itself, develop local pride, and enhance its economic well-being."

It is further in their believe that it is beneficial for all to obtain this growth, but that it must be accomplished in an intelligent, planned, and thoughtful manner by the developers and the public.

In South Africa there is a greater awareness of the impact of events on the economy and wealth creation. Therefore it has become paramount that more emphasis should be placed on how one can be empowered to organise these events. The problem is that major events in South Africa indicated a great lack of events management, and is it the aim of this and the next chapter to address some of the issues.

Indoor and outdoor events are an important part of the leisure and tourism industry today, although not all events themselves are new. Informal gatherings for religious, cultural or sporting purposes have existed since the beginning of time. The first

Olympic Games were held in 776 BC and religious festivals and events were commonplace in the Middle Ages. In the mid-nineteenth century, Thomas Cook built his reputation as a travel entrepreneur by organising excursions to the great exhibitions in London and Paris, some of the grandest events of their day (**Youell, 1995**). The questions that need answers are: Why events? Who attend them and for what reason? What makes an event a mega-event? Do tourists attending these events alter their behaviour? Do they spend more or less money compared to other forms of tourism? What are the implication of all these questions on marketing and planning? A lot of research still needs to be done to give more clarity on these and other questions.

What have changed in recent times are the frequency, themes and locations of events. Whereas in the past, events were arranged to celebrate a specific happening, events may now be presented in order to meet specific objectives; their scope have extended beyond purely recognising the cultural importance of a particular date on the calendar (**Van der Westhuizen, 1998**).

Organisers are forever dreaming up new ideas and themes for their events, in the hope of attracting the attention of a public who is becoming increasingly sophisticated in its leisure habits. Access to private transport and new technological equipment means that events can now be staged very quickly in response to changing tastes and fashions.

The range of events that take place within leisure and tourism is equally wide. It includes:
- Swimming championship
- Athletic summer school
- Mexican evening in a restaurant
- Beer festival
- International soccer festival
- Firework display
- Town carnival
- Sponsored walk
- Holiday show
- Olympic games
- Craft fair
- Opera festival
- Music workshop
- Festival of transport
- Fitness demonstration
- Air display

- Caravan rally
- Travel trade exhibition
- Garden party
- World chess championship **(Youell, 1995)**.

If organised well, events can be a source of great enjoyment and pride, both for the organisers and those who attend. These events can generate revenue and create a positive image of the town, place or city where it is hosted. If they are organised poorly, they can have a serious impact on the credibility of the organisers, the sponsors (if any), the location/venue where the event is held and any other organisations or individuals who attach their names to it. The sort of problems that occur from time to time include:

- Failure to set clear objectives for the event.
- Inadequate funding.
- Not having the right staff to plan and manage the event.
- Having insufficient time to plan the event properly.
- Lack of team effort on the part of those organising the event.
- Overspending the budget.
- Lack of, or poor, promotional activity.
- Little regard for health and safety matters.
- Lack of consideration for those affected by the event, e.g. neighbours.
- Poor communication between staff and outside organisations **(Youell, 1995)**.

Having identified the benefits and opportunities that an event can exploit, as well as some of the problems that can hinder progress, it should be possible to draw up a checklist of what needs to be done to ensure that an event is a success. Such a checklist would include:

- Setting clear objectives
- Securing funding at an early stage
- Allowing sufficient time for planning
- Establishing a promotional strategy
- Recruiting and training staff
- Liaising with all interested parties
- Establishing a health, safety and security policy
- Having a contingency plan
- Carrying out the event according to plan
- Reviewing the event and preparing a report for future use **(Youell, 1995)**.

According to **Getz (1995)**, event tourism is the systematic planning, development, and marketing of festivals and special events as tourism attractions, image makers, catalysts for infrastructure and economic growth, and animators of built attractions.

Although the definition of a "mega-event" is still unclear, researchers began to use the term over the last decade to refer to a "mega" version of a "hallmark event", which has been defined as a "major" one-time or recurring event of limited duration, developed primarily to enhance the awareness, appeal, and profitability of a tourism destination in the short and long term **(Ritchie, 1984:2)**. In addition, mega-events also include international events that are not necessarily "developed primarily" for tourism purposes but can "serve" to promote a destination.

At the 1997 conference on the impacts of mega-events it was defined as "planned occurrences of limited duration which have an extraordinary impact on the host area in terms of one or more of the following: tourist volumes, visitor expenditure, publicity leading to a heightened awareness and a more positive image, related infrastructural and organisational developments which substantially increases the destination's capacity and attractiveness" **(Fayos-Sola, 1997:242)**.

"Hallmark events" are also classed by **Ritchie (1984)** as those which have the ability to focus national and international attention on the destination for a well defined and usually short period of time. The Olympic Games are such an event.

The justification for such events lies in their raison d'etre and they may require no further justification such as the effects upon urban tourism and/or urban regeneration **(Hughes, 1993)**. Thus, a parsimonious definition of a mega-event is "an event with (1) a large number of participants or visitors and (2) worldwide publicity" **(Socher & Tschurtschenthaler, 1987,103)**.

According to **Kang & Perdue (1994)**, the initial/direct effects of hosting a mega-event include:
- increased mass media coverage in the world community;
- improvements and expansion of tourism infrastructure and tourism services;
- possible increase in tourism promotional activities by the host tourism industry to capitalise on a favourable marketing environment; and
- an influx of participants and tourists during the event period.

The support benefits and disadvantages of tourism in urban areas are well rehearsed. There have been, however, few comprehensive evaluatory studies of their overall impact. A study done in the United Kingdom examined the effects of urban tourism from a broad perspective but it included only the effects of projects that had received United Kingdom government grants. The conclusions of that study were that "tourism projects exploit the disadvantages of inner city areas and can turn them into opportunities" **(Department of the Environment, 1990)**. Such projects not only created jobs, but also improved the environment and contributed to altering perceptions of the area. In addition the tourism projects generated visitor spending and additional employment in other businesses.

Although mega-events are frequently and often extravagantly covered by the mass media, only a limited number of studies on the impact of mega-events have been published in academic journals. **Ritchie (1984)** also acknowledges that the tourism impacts of hallmark events, although generally assumed to be positive, have not often been assessed. **Hall (1992)** cites a number of studies of the tourism effects of such events - many are multiplier studies but in respect of the "wider" and longer term tourism effects most are statements of expected outcomes rather than assessments of actual outcome.

Hiller (1989) reports that 36 000 non-Canadians visited Calgary during the two-week Winter Games period and millions of people came to Vancouver over the five-month World Expo period. Given the "mega"-attractive power of the event, the number of foreign participants during the event period varies, depending mainly on the duration of the event and the capacity - accommodation and transportation - of the host region. The immediate effect of a mega-event on international tourism to the host country, therefore, may or may not be significant **(Van der Westhuizen, 1998)**.

Carrying capacity is fundamental to environmental protection and sustainable development. It refers to the maximum use of any site without causing negative effects on the resources, reducing visitor satisfaction, or exerting adverse impact upon the society, economy or culture of the area. Carrying capacity limits can sometimes be difficult to quantify, but they are essential to environmental planning for tourism and recreation. Carrying capacity varies according to season and, over time, factors such as tourists' behavioural patterns, facility design and management, the dynamic character of the environment, and the changing attitudes of the host community.

The cultural events, museums, monuments, historic places, shopping, entertainment and conference and convention facilities of urban areas can attract large numbers of tourists. The existing infrastructure may have sufficient carrying capacity for visitors, or the capacity can be expanded as needed in ways that also benefit the local population.

However, the influx of too many tourists can lead to congestion, pollution and reduced access to amenities. **Kang & Perdue (1994)**, points out that a mega-event necessitates "mega"-facilities. Typically, commercial accommodation and public transportation facilities - prerequisites for the future tourism growth - are refurbished and expanded during the preparation of the event, providing both necessary facilities for the event and an opportunity to improve the quality of future tourism services.

Getz (1995) argues that the construction of new facilities for mega-events is not always a benefit. For mega-events like world fairs and the Olympics, and sometimes smaller special events, new facilities or community infrastructure are required. Proponents of the event might claim these additions as benefits to the community, but they are usually costs. The benefit would exist only if capital for the construction is new money to the area, such as one-time grants from central governments.

Also, once the facilities are built operational costs must be taken into account. Even if the new facilities are considered to be benefits, the permanent operating costs are borne by the host community. But some of these costs can be discounted if the facilities are able to attract new events and new tourist expenditure in the future.

Demand forecasts of event-tourism have often been unreliable. Tourist numbers at Tokyo were 54% of projected numbers and at the 1984 Los Angeles Olympics there were only 64% of anticipated arrivals (**Pyo et al., 1988; Laventhol and Horwarth, 1984**).

Notwithstanding the over-estimation of tourist numbers it may also be that the effects of any such tourism have been misrepresented and over-exaggerated. It is not clear, for instance, whether event tourists are any more beneficial than other tourists. It may be that visitors' main preoccupation is with the event and that spending on other items is limited (**Pyo et al., 1988**).

According to **Getz (1995),** not all festivals and special events create economic benefits. The evidence strongly suggests that many events have little direct economic impact on their community or region, largely because they cater mostly for residents. Only when events attract out-of-region visitors do they start to create economic benefits.

It is also debatable how much of any tourism spending during the Olympic period can be attributed to the Olympic event itself. Some visitors may already have been planning visits to the city and have merely changed their timing. Others may have been visiting the city anyway at the time and the event may have been incidental to the visit. In both cases it is doubtful if the event can be justifiably claimed as the reason for the visit and expenditure (**Policy Studies Institute, 1986**).

According to **Hughes (1993)**, increased tourism activity will depend on the extent to which the city becomes widely known and recognised as a tourism destination and the duration of that recognition. The area is given considerable exposure in the media and, hopefully, misconceptions are corrected and a positive, favourable perception is generated. There may, however, be a negative impact if poor tourism experiences lead to a poor reputation and reduced tourism flow.

People attend events for reasons. Some might want to learn, some may want to belong to or even share in the experience. **Ryan (1998)** refers to a leisure experience that is freely chosen for its intrinsic rewards. Leisure researchers have ignored events and festivals as part of their research scope and by doing this a gap was created which needs to be filled. **Horna (1994)** gives several dimensions of leisure as a construct which can be realised as events, namely absorption or concentration on the ongoing experience, lessening of focus on the self, feeling of freedom or lack of constraint, enriched perception of objects and events, increased intensity of emotions, increased sensitivity to feelings and decreased awareness of the passage of time.

Related to this is **Csikszentimihalyi's (1975)** "flow" concepts which is achieved when a person is in optimal interaction with the environment. **Smith (1990)** describes this positive feeling which is related to play as "the experience of total, intrinsically satisfying involvement in an activity in which individuals' skills are in balance with the challenges posed by the activity".

It can be argued that people need to play, and leisure therefore also need events and festivals for leisure. These may be provided in terms of what people need. People need to socialise, to meet other people, to relax, to entertain and be entertained. People need to compete to learn and experience new things and, lastly, people need to escape.

There are several types of Hallmark events, including the following:

Table 6.1: Types of Hallmark events

National Sports Event	International Sports Events	Other National Events	Other Inernational Events
Rugby Curry Cup	Olympics	Grahamstown Arts Festival	Cannes Film Festival
Rothmans Soccer Cup	Rugby World Cup	Klein Karoo Nasionale Kunstefees in Oudtshoorn Aardklop: Arts Festival in Potchefstroom	Rio-Festival
Winfield Athletics	Soccer World Cup	Oppikoppi	Miss Universe
Comrades Marathon	Million Dollar Golf Challenge	Mampoer Festival	Festival of the Dead
Two Oceans	Three Nation Series	Cherry Festival	Tomato Festival - Spain

The above are only a few examples of the countless hallmark events around the world. Whether national or international, they have the power to attract millions of tourists.

Getz and Cheyene in Ryan (1997) identified the following aspects that make events special:

- **Uniqueness**
  - ➢ An opportunity not usually available
  - ➢ Out of the ordinary type of attraction
  - ➢ Rarity
  - ➢ Something unique
  - ➢ Different activities
  - ➢ Novelty

These terms might be synonymous, although they each express something different.
- Atmosphere
  The right atmosphere in order for people to socialise, relax and enjoy the event.

- **Quality**
  > Well-organised
  > Reputation
  > Calibre of participants
  > Size
  > International scope
  > Presence of stars or very important persons.

Examples of activities that can be regarded as mega- or special events:

a. The Olympic Games

Tourism, in the sense of people travelling away from home and staying overnight, is a key element of the Olympics. The reason d'etre of the Olympics is to attract international participants and officials. Although international spectators are not implicit in the Olympics, it may well have the power to attract spectators from foreign countries (**Witt and Martin, 1987**).

The desire to stimulate tourism or to regenerate urban areas may not feature as prime objectives in seeking the Games. Nevertheless these, and other such as "honour" and "global recognition", may explicitly or otherwise feature as the objective of the host city (**Hiller, 1989**). Olympic tourists are not, though, solely international. Many athletes and officials from within the host country may be tourists, and so may domestic spectators (**Pyo et al., 1988**).

Ahn et al. (1989), report that 240 000 foreign visitors attended the Seoul Olympic Games. However, this figure does not reflect the short-term effects of the Games on inbound tourism to Korea. The Olympic Games period (17 September to October) fell within the peak season of Korean tourism. Olympic visitors may have "crowded out" or replaced a large number of potential tourists who would otherwise have visited Korea during the event period. Furthermore, an important negative aspect of mega-events is the potential short-term increase in travel prices, particularly for accommodations (**Hall, 1998; Pyo et al., 1988**).

In preparing for the Olympics, Korea dramatically expanded its tourism infrastructure. For instance, the annual growth rate in the total number of rooms registered in "tourist hostels" for 1987 was 10.8%, but in 1988 it was 20.8%, while the average growth rate for the preceding seven years was 4.6%.

Visitor satisfaction during the Olympic period was high. Based on a survey of the Olympic visitors conducted immediately before visitor departures, **Ahn et al. (1989)** concluded: "Most foreign tourists perceive Korea as a positive and favourable tourism destination. Except for some potentially negative publicity about safety issues which may have affected short-term tourism during the Olympic year".

According to **Hughes (1993)**, the Manchester Games and the process of bidding may have proven a spur to the existing tourism development in Manchester and the surrounding region. The very success of the Olympics as a tourist event would, though, create its own problems. A total of 5.5 million spectators concentrated mostly in the city of Manchester for such a short time, will clearly put considerable strain on the infrastructure. The high intensity and short-term nature of the Olympics may not fit harmoniously with long-term development strategies for tourism, and unless carefully managed it may not be very beneficial and may even be counterproductive. The city and region may gear themselves for an influx of tourists at the period of the Games (which may not be as great as anticipated) and then readjust to a much reduced level of activity. **Saayman and Van Niekerk (1996)** determined that it is best for South Africa not to host the Olympic Games, but rather the World Cup events, purely because of the size of the event.

Visitors to the 2 000 Manchester Olympics are estimated at 3.5 million "local" spectators, 1.7 million spectators from the rest of the United Kingdom and 0.3 million overseas spectators **(KPMG, 1993)**. Pre-Olympic visitor numbers are assumed to grow by 2% per year between 1996 - 1999. As a consequence of this it is estimated that at least 250 million dollars of visitor expenditure and 5 000 jobs will be generated. This also includes the additional spending of overseas Olympic visitors whose stay is extended beyond that necessary to attend the Olympics and the spending of "the Olympic family" and media.

The Olympics may result in a long-term increase in tourism after the Games, as a consequence of the enhanced awareness of the host city. Notwithstanding the tourist nature of the Olympics, it is clear that some of the more general benefits claimed for the Games are also derived from tourism. In particular, the economic benefit of hosting the Games arises in part from the "net injection" of money into the host city from outside, such as through tourism. Ticket sales to those outside the host city are ostensibly an inflow and an addition to the economic life of the city **(Burns, Hatch and Mules, 1986)**. The effect of any increased tourism inflow on income and employment may be such as to make a major impact on the local economy.

Hallmark events may also have a significant impact in a non-tourist way. Any expenditure on the construction of sporting facilities and the operation of the event itself may lead to increased income and employment, however short-term (**Hughes, 1993**).

MOBC commissioned assessments of the economic impact of the staging of the 2 000 Games in Manchester (**Hague et al., 1990; KPMG, 1993**). The study for the Games estimated that "total expenditure" as result of bidding for and hosting the Games would be 4.3 billion pounds. This total grouped together construction costs, operating costs, and visitor expenditure (other than on event tickets). 65% of the expenditure will arise from the capital programme.

The total expenditure of 4.3 billion pounds would support, it is believed, the equivalent of 11 000 fulltime jobs. About 4 000 of the jobs would be in construction and related sectors and 7 000 in other sectors, especially tourism, retail and distribution. In addition, the high profile given to an area by presenting the Games could provide an opportunity for an increase in inward investment in unrelated manufacturing and services. There may be an increased awareness among entrepreneurs of the intrinsic attractions of the area for location and the area itself may become more attractive as part of the Olympic development - either through the sporting and cultural facilities that develop and/or through any necessary infrastructure improvements.

b. **The Rugby World Cup**
According to **Ebersohn (1995)**, David Hall, managing director of Gulliver's Indo-Jet, anticipated some 18 000 visitors for the Rugby World Cup of 1995. He reported that 7 000 locals followed the big matches from city to city, but that it was the overseas contingent who brought money into the country. Each of the visitors was expected to spend R200 a day over a 15-day period, generating a total income of close to R55 million. Moreover, they were expected to be spending some R200 million on travel expenses, much of it inside South Africa.

The Rugby World Cup did not attract the masses of tourists and megabucks that public relations agencies promised, but it has probably been the greatest event since the 1994 elections. The profits made will not directly have a major impact on the gross domestic product, but that does not mean that the RWC did not generate a healthy injection in sales and created, even temporarily, jobs across a wide spectrum (**Smith, 1995**).

Koenderman (1995) also holds the view that the Rugby World Cup was not an overwhelming success. Apart from self-promotion by the sponsors and a few banners and posters along major highways, very little marketing effort was apparent. Yet, despite a perception of banks of empty seats, more tickets have been sold for the World Cup of 1995 then either of the two previous ones. According to SA Rugby Football Union (Sarfu) tournament director Rian Oberholzer, 1.1 million tickets were sold, compared with just over 1 million in 1991 when the event was held in Britain and France, and 640 000 in 1987 in Australia and New Zealand (Anon, 1989). The bald numbers sound good, though the event was some way from being a sell-out. The 250 000 unsold tickets amounted to nearly 20 % of the total capacity of 1.35 million for the 32 games. It should be mentioned though, that most unsold tickets were for the least attractive pool.

Lindsay Smiters, chairman of John Sinclair, described the marketing for the event within South Africa as been disappointing. It had been left to the advertisers and sponsors to popularise the event. Most of the awareness had been achieved through clients like Telkom and Vodacom using the World Cup as a peg for their advertising.

Koenderman (1995) also adds that the lost opportunity for organisations such as Satour to market the country was a disappointment and **Smith (1995)** commented that South Africa's abysmal service industry and poor management around production deadlines made for even more opportunities lost.

The crime rate in South Africa did not help either: just over 100 tourists were mugged. To add insult to injury, tour buses, when they weren't breaking down, got lost because of drivers who did not know their towns.

Nonetheless, The South African Rugby Football Union was happy. Rian Oberholzer estimated they would clear around R61 million in profit after they balanced their books. He said their biggest headache was to deal "with rugby administrators that run fields like old boys clubs". Ellis Park has long been an aggressive marketer. "During international isolation we had to fill the stadium by convincing the public that the best rugby they could see was a match between Northern Transvaal and Transvaal". That has paid dividends. Ellis Park now hosts 42 events a year, from the Rolling Stones to soccer tournaments, and 22 rugby matches. It is one of the best-used venues of its kind in the world (**Smith, 1995**).

c. The Comrades Marathon

The Comrades marathon is one of the world's most prestigious ultra-marathons. The race follows a hilly 54-mile course from Durban to Pietermaritzburg in South Africa and each year attracts an astounding 14 000 runners, with hundreds of thousands of people watching along the way.

The success of the Comrades Marathon is due largely to a small band of dedicated people who spend thousands of man-hours organising one of the greatest road shows on earth. This group, the Comrades Marathon Association, works throughout the year to make June the 16th the 31st the huge success that it is. From Comrades House in Pietermaritzburg, the CMA plans the event, setting up portfolios that will cover catering for 14 000 runners: the start; the finish; the finances; medical matters; and the Comrades Expo (a runners trade fair held before the race).

For the 1989 Comrades, all of Durban's 32 000 hotel beds were fully booked from Monday to Thursday. Local tourist officials reported that many visitors would stay on to enjoy an extended mid-year holiday. Schools and college halls have been called into use, while private homes played host to hordes of runners. Dick Jones, director of Pietermaritzburg's publicity association, said the event is worth millions of rands to Pietermaritzburg.

Many more visitors also stayed in surrounding towns, rather than in Durban, to face the pre-dawn traffic jam to Pietermaritzburg. Small hotels as far as 60 km from Pietermaritzburg reported that Comrades runners and supporters were booked in.

d. Fairs, festivals and tournaments

Festivals, celebrations and other "cultural performances" are rich in meaning and provide a "text" by which much can be learned of the host culture and community. As explained by **Manning (1983)**, celebration is performance: "it is, or entails, the dramatic presentation of cultural symbols". Celebration is public, with no social exclusion, is entertainment for the fun of it, and is participatory - actively involving the celebrant who takes time out of ordinary routine, and "does so openly, consciously and with the general aim of aesthetic, sensual and social gratification".

Festivals are themed, public celebration and have become one of the most common forms of modern special events. To **Falassi (1987)** the festival is unique:

"At festival time, people do something they normally do not; they abstain from something they normally do; they carry to the extreme behaviours that are usually regulated by measure; they invert patterns of daily social life. Reversal, intensification, trespassing and abstinence are the four cardinal points of festival behaviour".

MacAloon (1984) emphasised that "festival demands engaged participation, leaving little room for dispassionate behaviour; festival means being there; there is no festival at a distance". Festivals provide their own energy source, according to **Abrahams (1987)**, in the form of role playing, confrontations, noise, spectacle, movement, costumes, entertainment, games, contests and nonsense. Carnivals (and Mardi Gras) are special types of celebration, which **Turner (1983)** called a form of play embodying rituals of reversal. The term "carnival" has come to be associated with partying and licence, whereas "festival" in most instances is associated with a more sedate atmosphere. Accordingly, the name of the event can potentially influence motivations and behaviour (**Ryan, 1997**).

Turco & Kelsey (1993) identified several reasons why both public and private sectors support fairs, festivals and special events. One consideration is that the event can bring tourist money into a geographic region during the community's off-season or in periods when the number of out-of-town visitors is lower than normal. Special events may also create and stimulate economic activity on an annual basis and thereby encourage new employment opportunities. Such events may also promote and expose the community and enhance or create a desired community image. There are other benefits of special events to the community, which are difficult to quantify, including enhanced image, resident and non-resident participant and spectator satisfaction, and civic pride.

6.4   CONCLUSION

With the prospect of more international events coming to South Africa and the tourism potential that these events have, it became important to include event management in tourism curriculums. The economic and social events cut across all aspects of the tourism industry. This is one of the reasons why more countries are trying to host them.

Tourism curriculums without categories for events and sports tourism van be considered as incomplete and need to be revised. The reason is that events and sports tourism has grown to such an extent that it cannot be ignored anymore. There is also a shortage of properly trained human resources to fulfil this need.

South Africa is becoming more important in terms of a global tourist destination and attracting more events. This creates an opportunity for tourism managers to enter this market thereby growing the tourism industry. It also creates an opportunity for small, micro-, and medium enterprises to enter the tourism industry, thereby creating job opportunities and employment.

Chapter 7

Planning an event

If you don't know where you are going, you will probably end up somewhere else.
Laurence J Peter

7.1   INTRODUCTION

This chapter will deal with the aspect of how to plan an event. In order for the event to be successful it needs to be planned properly. Because of the cost involved in staging an event one cannot allow mistakes. This is one of the reasons why major or hallmark events, such as World Cup tournaments and the Olympic Games, are planned years in advance.

Major festivals are organised on a fulltime basis. The advantage of this is that the risks of failure are minimised in this way. Most of the events that did not work well, was because of a lack of planning.

7.2   HOW TO PLAN AN EVENT

The following section (see also Figure 7.1) deals with the process of planning for an event (**Kestner, 1996**). This requires a lot of work before the event, and most major events are planned two to four years in advance. One should not attempt to do it in less time.

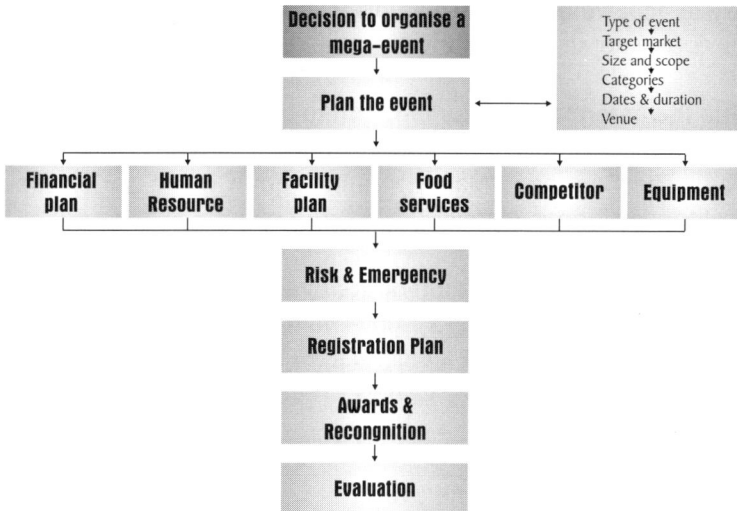

Figure 7.1: Planning of an event

The steps below must be followed to determine the objectives of an event. The size of the event might require that you form a committee to help you. A committee approach may ensure that the most appropriate objectives are identified. The committee should not be too big, however. Also, when establishing objectives, be sure to consider other factors that could impact on your objectives, such as finances

a. Determine the type of event

First of all you need to determine what type of an event it is going to be, for example a music festival, sports event or any other festival. The type of event will determine the size of the operation. The Olympic Games for example, is a mega-event that requires many people and other resources to organise. It is important to determine beforehand who is going to be involved, for example local authorities, tourism departments, and private companies.

b. Determine for whom the event is planned

Once you have identified the type of event, it is easy to determine the target market who will be involved in the event and what you want to achieve. This is a critical question to be asked and answered. One also needs to know what the primary objective or outcome of the event is. Do you want to promote a positive image, promote tourism and generate income?

c. Determine the size or scope of the event

Once again the type of event will impact on the size and scope. Most events, even the Olympic Games, started off small and developed into a mega-event. Do not try to achieve a mega-event unless it has already developed into one. This is obviously not the case with all events.

d. Determine the categories of competition to be offered

After you have determined the above, your event will dictate the different categories. The Comrades Marathon and Argus Cycling, for example, have several categories for participants.

e. Determine the dates and duration of the event

If one wants an event to grow into a mega-event, is should take place annually or bi-annually. Most mega-events are annual events, with the exception of World Championships and the Olympic Games. The type of activity or event will also determine the duration.

f. Determine the location(s) of the event

The final aspect that needs consideration is the location/venue. Even though one wants to develop tourism in all areas of a country in order for everyone to benefit from it, certain events are bound to major cities for reasons such as image, accommodation, accessibility, food supplies, or entertainment. Festivals like the cherry, biltong, mealie and other similar festivals are very successful in small towns where these products are produced. However, mega sport events need good infrastructure, which is usually only found in big cities.

7.2.2 FINANCIAL PLANNING
The following steps need to be followed:

a. Prepare a budget for the event
The smaller the event, the easier it becomes not only to budget, but also to control finances. Mega-events need a budget committee, which will include auditors, to manage finances. First of all you will have to prepare a detailed budget for all aspects of the event, which include facilities, activities, staff and marketing.

b. Develop plans to obtain all income and implement these plans
Once the budget has been prepared you will have to state how these expenses will be covered. If possible, sponsorships could be considered. All mega-events are mostly paid for by sponsors.

c. Keep accurate records
The finance committee who was involved in preparing the budget will have to be responsible for managing the funds. This includes deciding who is going to sign cheques and make all payments. Detailed financial records must be kept.

7.2.3 RISK AND EMERGENCY PLANNING
The one aspect that is neglected most in South Africa is risk management. Accidents happen and one needs to be prepared - prevention is better than cure. The following steps are important:

a. Prepare a risk management plan for this event
This plan should include inspection of all facilities, equipment, security, emergency exits, and crowd control.

b. Determine if you should use a waiver or release form
This can be a useful instrument to reduce the possibility of lawsuits.

c. **Determine if you need an emergency care and transport consent form**
If you need such a form, then it is best practise to issue it during registration.

d. **Determine your need for insurance to reduce your risk in managing this event**
One can get insurance cover for special events in order to reduce the financial implications of lawsuits and other claims.

e. **Determine your compliance with local fire and safety ordinances for this event**
This you will have to verify with your local authority. You need their co-operation with regard to traffic control, if need be.

f. **If food is to be sold, determine what steps are necessary for compliance with local or state food inspection laws**
Once again, contact your local authority. If they are part of the organising committee it will make things much easier.

g. **Prepare an emergency plan for this event**
In case of fire, natural disasters, bomb scares etc., how are people going to be evacuated? Who is going to give the signal, and who will take care of injured people? One should not take this lightly for it can greatly influence the success of your event.

h. **Develop a plan for managing spectators if large numbers are expected**
Aspects that need to be addressed are sufficient restrooms, food services, parking, access and crowd control.

7.2.4 REGISTRATION PLANS
a. **Determine the "qualifiers" for participation in this event**
It is necessary to establish certain criteria for participation. For example, the Comrades Marathon has qualifying times.

b. **Determine what information you need to get during registration**
The more information, the better your database will be. It can also be used for marketing purposes. The event will eventually determine the type of participants, which in turn will dictate the type of information required. It is also helpful to have an IT (Information Technology) specialist on the organising committee.

c. **Determine when the registration period begins and ends**
The registration period will depend on the type of activity.

d. Determine the registration process to be followed

Will you have entry forms that need to be completed and faxed beforehand, or will participants complete entry forms at the venue? Do you need any registration at all? These are the most important questions you need to answer with regard to registration.

e. Prepare the appropriate forms for the registration process

Adapt these forms to suit your purpose. Their lay-out will be determined by the type of information that you require, such as:

* Number of participants?
* Where do they come from?
* Type of activity?
* Group/team or individual?
* Age?
* Address/telephone numbers etc.?
* Gender?
* Where will they stay?

7.2.5   FACILITY PLANNING

Facility planning is a crucial aspect of the event, for it will determine the venue as well as the number of spectators and participants that can be accommodated. Facilities should be accessible and safe.

a. Determine your facility needs

The activity will determine the venue and facilities needed. An estimation of number of people expected and the event requirements will have to be made.

b. Reserve the facilities

Once again, if it is a mega-event, a facility committee should be formed to implement all aspects pertaining to the facilities and equipment.

c. Determine who will supervise the facility

This will be a function of the facility committee.

d. Arrange for access to the facility

Contact the local authority to see if the traffic department could be of assistance. Make use of volunteers to control the inflow and outflow of traffic and spectators.

e. Prepare the facility prior to the event
You need to know exactly what you need and how the different systems work, for example lights, sound, stage, security, air-conditioning and others.

f. Arrange for maintenance of the facility
This step is necessary in order for security purposes, as well as for the image of the event and future success. The restrooms in particular need to be cleaned and checked several times a day.

g. Arrange for security for all facilities
Make sure someone is assigned to do this.

h. Arrange for adequate parking
This aspect is also important to secure future success. People do not want to walk for distances to the different activities. There should be ample parking available. If not, arrange for a "park and ride" system.

7.2.6 EQUIPMENT AND SUPPLIES PLANNING

a. Inventory of what is available
An inventory has to be done in order to determine what equipment and supplies are available.

b. Determine what is needed for the event
Based on participants and spectators you will have to do an estimate of what you will need.

c. Purchase what is needed
The finance committee will have to purchase whatever else is needed for the event.

d. Inventory of new purchases
Any new equipment should be placed on the inventory and should also be mentioned if possible.

e. Distribute the equipment, uniforms and supplies
Develop a system whereby equipment, uniforms and supplies could be distributed. Mega-events require a great deal of supplies for example, T-shirts, numbers, forms and other items. This is difficult to do and should be done properly and systematically.

f. Plan for storage and security

You will have to have a short-term and long-term storage plan. Long-term plans are necessary for when the equipment is not used until the next event. Short-term plans should be place during the event and should allow access for authorised persons.

g. Inspect and maintain the equipment
Part of being proactive is to maintain and inspect equipment regularly. This will ensure that the equipment can be used over and over again.

7.2.7   AWARDS AND RECOGNITION PLANS
This might be a small aspect to manage but it is paramount for success. Word-of-mouth remains an important selling tool and if people get recognition for what they achieve, they will repeat it.

a. Determine for what achievements awards will be given and how they will be given
This will be determined by the categories of participation and any other achievements that need to be awarded. These may include awards for people who sacrificed a lot of time in order for the event to be a success.

b. Determine the types of awards to be given
Once again it will be determined by the different categories.

c. Purchase the awards
The finance committee must approve and to procure the type of awards, be it

flowers, plagues, trophies, medallions or certificates.

d. Plan for storage of the awards
A safe or strong room, depending on the type of awards, might be necessary in order to keep the awards safe.

e. Plan for the display of the awards during the event
The awards may be displayed, but it should be protected against theft.

f. Plan for the presentation of awards
Who is going to present the awards? Will there be a ceremony? Who will be invited? This is an opportunity to use sponsors, in order to ensure their future involvement.

7.2.8   FOOD SERVICE PLANS
It would be better to outsource this function. It will then generate a predetermined source of revenue. Most event committees follow this procedure, for it is a specialised function which is best done by professionals. Many local people specialise in food services and this will give them a chance to benefit from the event and to spread the wealth to a larger part of the community.

a. Arrange drinks for participants
Sponsors, for example Coca-Cola and Liqui-Fruit, are normally eager to supply/sponsor events.

b. Arrange food for participants and other personnel
Determine what type of food will be served, who is going to prepare it and where it will be stored.

c. Arrange refreshments for spectators
This can be done by outside companies.

d. Determine whether a hospitality room is needed.
Mega-events do have such facilities but these facilities should be managed properly. Establish who is going to be responsible for it. This privilege could, however, also be misused.

7.2.9   TRANSPORTATION PLANS
Local tour operators may be used to fill this gap and can supply vehicles for transportation purposes.

a. Determine what transportation is needed

You will have to determine whether you need to supply transport and if so, what type and to whom. Again the event and the scope of the event will dictate transportation needs.

b. Communicate what transportation will be offered

Once a decision has been taken, one needs to communicate with the respective groups that will be involved.

c. Arrange for the vehicles to provide the transportation

Pending on the type of transport, one will have to make the necessary reservations in order to ensure that transport is made available. If local people are going to do this, you only need to co-ordinate the routes and schedule.

7.2.10   COMMUNICATION PLANS

In order for this event to succeed, one needs a good communication strategy that will not only inform participants but also the bigger international audience, depending on what type of event.

a. Develop a communication system and strategy

Determine how you are going to communicate to:
- staff;
- media;
- sponsors;
- spectators; and
- participants.

b. Plan how to communicate with participants and coaches/managers

Keep participants abreast of any changes to programmes, events or any other important happening that might impact on them.

c. Plan a system for communication with spectators

Decide on a means to communicate with spectators. This may be a PA system, an electronic board etc. Also determine what will be communicated, for example results, new developments etc.

d. Plan a system for communicating with the media

The event may be promoted by means of:
- newspaper;

- radio;
- television;
- magazine advertisement;
- billboard; and
- brochure/flyer.

Publicity
- press releases;
- interviews;
- newspapers, radio and television press briefing ;
- competitions.

Personal selling
- speaking at meetings;
- tele-sales;
- bidding.

e. Develop promotional material
Someone has to take responsibiliy for developing the brochures and other promotional items. Mega-events normally has a public relations advertising company who does this function in conjunction with the organising committee. It is important to bear in mind that the best selling is done by people attending the event or who has already been there. Word-of-mouth informs more people effectively than advertising alone.

7.2.11 EVENT EVALUATION PLANS
a. Determine the system for evaluation
Evaluation is done in three ways, namely before the event (as part of the planning process), during the event and once the event is completed. A system will therefore have to be developed to ensure that evaluation takes place.

b. Prepare the evaluation questionnaire
Questions that you need answered are the following:
- Was the event well organised?
- Were the facilities adequate?
- Was the transport sufficient?
- Where were the problem areas?
- Where can we improve?
- Was the food good?
- Will you return next time?

c. Have the evaluation forms completed by those selected to evaluate the event
Determine who will hand out and collect the questionnaires, as well as who will prepare the results.

d. Review and summarise the evaluation comments
This should be done by the organising committee in order to ensure a better event the following year.

7.2.12 STAFFING PLANS

a. Determine the staff required to conduct the event
The organising committee will have to evaluate each aspect of the event, to be able to determine the number of people required.

b. Recruit the volunteers needed
Once you have determined the above you will know how many volunteers you need to recruit.

c. Hire the employees needed
The positions that need to be filled will have to be advertised and the selection process will have to be implemented. You will have to know exactly what you are looking for, for example qualifications, computer skills, language skills etc.

d. Make assignments to all staff
Appoint a director/chairperson or head for each committee. This person must be familiar with the terms of reference and work with a check-list in order to ensure that the job gets done.

e. Provide orientation and training
This is especially required if people are new to this event.

f. Plan the communication system with staff
Communicate the communication plan and strategy to staff so that they know who is responsible for what.

g. Plan for supervision of staff
Someone has to make sure that activities are carried out. Therefore it requires supervision and the managing of people.

h. Plan for the payment and/or recognition of the staff
The finance committee should be aware of what was budgeted for this item, and payments should be made timeously.

7.2.13 PLANNING FOR SPECTATORS AT SPORTS EVENTS
One should keep in mind that attending sports events is part of the entire experience spectators have at the stadium. Therefore, to further increase sports tourism and the benefits it brings, it should be recognised that the sports facility is an important part in the marketing planning of sports. It should be managed effectively to meet the needs of its users and to increase attendance at the event.

When spectators attend a sports event, the possibility exists that the stadium environment will play a significant part in determining how many spectators enjoy the experience. **Wakefield & Sloan (1995:153)** suggested that factors such as food services quality, fan interactions, and stadium design may influence the experience of sport tourists at events. Attendance has been found to be a function of the quality of the product or service. Spectators' desire to stay or return to a sports event is directly affected by stadium factors. When they are enjoying the stay, they are more likely to return to the stadium. Negative experiences at the stadium, on the other hand, may lead to spectators leaving early and not returning to similar situations in the future.

Wakefield & Sloan (1995:153) identified five such stadium factors that influence spectator attendance:

1. Stadium Parking
The availability, proximity, and "exitability" of stadium parking may increase or decrease the spectators' enjoyment at the stadium. Parking problems before getting to the event may influence the spectators' overall perception of the event negatively. Difficulties in leaving the stadium may cause some to leave earlier in order to avoid long waits in traffic. As a result they do not see the end of the event and leave the stadium less satisfied.

2. Cleanliness
In many stadiums restrooms and concessions may become overflowing with trash and spilled drinks by the middle and towards the end of the event. Spectators may be discouraged to use restrooms covered with trash, refuse, and dampness, and may become dissatisfied with the event. Close monitoring of facility cleanliness may encourage spectators to stay and enjoy the facilities.

3. Crowding

Stadiums that are designed poorly may have the psychological effect of making spectators feel crowded. The arrangement of aisles, seats, and service areas that should handle the crowd, may directly decrease evaluations and feelings towards the sports event's environment. The crowding effect has been found to negatively affect to the physical surroundings, and to negatively influence the pleasure of the spectator. Spectators who feel uncomfortable because other spectators are too close, may not wish to stay in the place or return.

4. Food Services

Food services are an important source of revenue during sports events. The quality of food services is determined by the taste of the food and the variety offered. Expensive food prices may encourage spectators to bring their own food or eat outside the stadium, before or after the event, which leads to dissatisfactory sales volumes. Stadiums with a good variety and quality of foods at reasonable prices are expected to enhance the experience of spectators, and they are then more likely to stay longer or return to the events.

5. Fan Control

Due to the competitive nature of sports events, it can cause offensive fan behaviour. The intensity of rivalry between teams and their fans, alcohol abuse, or the behaviour of the players may influence some spectators to become offensive or abusive toward other spectators. As a result these spectators are not likely to enjoy the game and may decide to leave early or not to return to such future events. Such negative experiences can be prevented by monitoring fan behaviour and the immediate resolvement of these unpleasant situations.

With this in mind, the sports event surroundings can be used as a tool to maintain spectator satisfaction and increase attendance. Thus, every effort should be made to increase positive experiences for spectators, and therefore to enhance the probability that more spectators will attend sports events and return to them.

7.3   DEVELOPING A BID DOCUMENT

In order to secure a major national or international event for South Africa or a specific region, one has to go through a process of preparing and submitting a bid document. A bid document is a document that contains all the information of an event in order for the organising committee to take an informed decision. The process is as follows (Figure 7.1):

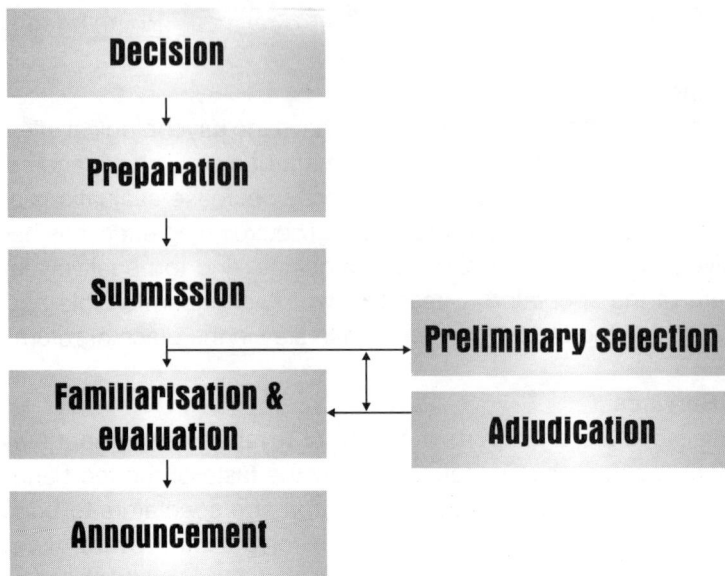

Decision
↓
Preparation
↓
Submission
↓
Familiarisation & evaluation
↓
Announcement

Preliminary selection

Adjudication

Figure 7.2: Process of developing a bid development

The process starts with a decision to host the event. After the decision is taken, a bid document has to be prepared, indicating how this event will be hosted. This is normally an expensive and cumbersome exercise of meetings, research, travel, committees, etc. When the documentation is ready it can follow two routes. If a country wants to host the event, it can go through a preliminary round. For example, Johannesburg may compare with Durban or Cape Town to host the Olympic Games. Once a city or a combination of cities has been chosen, the document is submitted to the international body who will then undertake a familiarisation tour of the country, facilities and people who support the bid. Again, their evaluation will be based on the type and size of event.

Eventually a decision is taken, which will then lead to an announcement on which country succeeded in bidding for the event. This can be a long and expensive exercise but can be economically and socially viable. It is important that it has to be done by professional people who understand what the event is all about as well as what the event can do for a region or country.

- **Elements of the bid**
  The following elements need to be reflected in the bid document.

- **Bid committee**
  Determine who will be part of the bid committee, and substructures or sub-committees, if these are necessary. Depending on the size of the event, committees will be important to make sure that all bases are covered.

- **Financing**
  Hallmark events cannot function without sponsorships. Therefore someone has to be commissioned to organise sponsorships. Financial viability studies need to be done. It is important to have contingency plans in the case of strikes, public uproar or demonstrations. This can impact negatively on the whole event and must be planned for. For hallmark events, government has to give guarantees of financial support.

- **Marketing**
  Marketing is paramount in order to have a successful event, and should be part of the bid document. This section should indicate how, when and where marketing will be done and who the partners are in this marketing drive. As part of this marketing drive it will also be essential to launch an awareness campaign to get the public's support for an event. The importance of this is that the general public can ruin the event if they do not recognise its value.

- **Human resources**
  Another important element is the human resources. How many staff will be necessary? Who will be in charge of what? What are the lines of communication? How much will it cost? How many volunteers are needed and what will their functions be? Do they need training and where will they stay? These are just some of the questions that need to be ironed out.

  The staff who are responsible for safety and security need to be identified and the role of the local police and even the defence force should be specified.

- **Facilities**
  This is normally the element that gets the most attention, although it is not necessarily the most important. Bookings have to be made well in advance. If new facilities have to be erected, models need to be prepared, with a complete plan which will indicate by when the project will be completed and who will finance it.

  Facilities should make provision for athletes, representatives at the media, doctors, spectators, catering (food and drink), proper athletic facilities, drug test facilities, warm-up areas, training areas etc.

The facilities also include the accommodation that will be required. The 1999 All Africa Games came up with the brilliant idea to develop accommodation for athletes in Alexander and to donate these facilities to the community of Alexander after the Games. This approach thus also alleviated some of the housing shortages.

- **Transport**
Transport is essential for having a successful event. Firstly, public transport should be used if it is efficient. Otherwise, tourists and participants will have to be transported by buses, which might cause huge traffic congestions. Local taxis can go a long way in alleviating the transport problem. Airports have to be equipped to handle large numbers of people and luggage.

- **Programme**
The bid document should make provision for a preliminary program of the events or event that will take place. This will be helpful in planning facilities, human resources, etc.

- **Spectator control**
It must be clear how spectators will be handled at the venue to ensure order. Furthermore, provision must be made for security. In the case of an emergency there must be proper plans to control and evacuate the crowd.

- **Community benefit**
The bid document also has to indicate how the country, region or community will benefit from hosting the activity. In most of the hallmark events, this aspect has become a paramount component of the document.

7.4   CONCLUSION

It was the aim of this chapter to give practical information on how to plan an event. Whether events are major or minor, the planning principles remain the same. This also led to the question of how to prepare a bid document which was dealt with in this chapter. This chapter indicated that organising an event is not as simple as it is believed to be. Many organisations in South Africa realised that too late, when everything went wrong. The main function of the person organising the events is to primarily manage what he/she wants people to do. This is a task that requires a lot of commitment and time. Events in South Africa are growing at a rapid rate and more international events are coming to South Africa. The important aspect is that these events have major e-commerce value and spin-offs and should be encouraged. Hence, they must be presented in a professional manner.

Chapter 8

Extreme sports

Death is not tragic. Death is universal and inevitable.
Not living is tragic.
Anonymous.

8.1 INTRODUCTION

It is the aim of this chapter to define extreme sports as well as to identify the different types of activities which can be classified as extreme sports. The latter can be practiced on land, in water and in the air. It is important to take notice of these activities because globally there are millions of people participating in them. These activities therefore have the potential to entertain thousands of tourists. Activities such as these can also generate jobs for people involved in managing and organising them. One should not underestimate the impact of these activities or events in terms of numbers of participants as well as spectators.

Extreme sports are much more than defying the boundaries of normal acceptable behaviour. They are new, perceived as being dangerous, and certainly goes against the norm. These sports cover the spectrum of outdoor sporting activities, from skydiving, rock-climbing, downhill mountain biking, to scuba-diving. Extremists are fearless, thrill-seeking athletes who thrive on challenge. Therefore, extreme sports are about:

- Individuality
- Achieving higher levels of satisfaction
- Having fun
- Excitement
- Gravity, ingenuity and technology.

The reason why these activities are important for tourism is that people travel long distances to participate in them. The activities are usually practiced at specific venues, which in most cases remain the same and cannot be moved. Extreme sports are growing at an accelerated pace and in many cases are replacing traditional sports. South Africa is a haven for many of these exciting and challenging tourism activities.

- **What are Extreme Sports?**
Extreme sports provide the participant with a combination of danger, fear and excitement. They not only offer the ultimate risk-taker an adventure, but also allow the average Joe to share the same experience. The term *extreme sports* encompasses an array of possibilities, including freestyle snowboarding, inline skating, skydiving, etc. The number of sports being referred to as extreme is constantly growing as adventurers, risk-takers and tourists continue to invent new ways to challenge themselves.

- **Why do people do it?**
Recently there has been a sharp increase in participation in all extreme sports, including skydiving, bungee-jumping, and rock-climbing. In an era where more and more leisure activities are becoming lifelike (e.g. virtual reality), people seem to be in search of something that will take them closer to the edge. They want the real thing; the rush of adrenaline, the idea of being on the edge, and the euphoria created by the entire experience. Many people, however, do it for entirely different reasons. Some may do it to overcome their fears, such as fear of heights or a fear of death. Others may pick up the sport as a new hobby whilst others might use it as team building exercises. Whatever the reason, it is clear that there is a growing number of people taking their turn at extreme sports.

- **What about the risks?**
Unfortunately, with the increase in the popularity of extreme sports there has also come an increase in the prevalence of serious injuries and deaths from participation in these activities. Marketing has encouraged many young people to participate in these activities, often without the proper training or equipment. Furthermore, extreme sport participants are now required by their insurance companies to indicate their participation in high risk activities, including extreme sports. Insurance coverage has become more expensive for these individuals, as participation in extreme sports not only increases the possibility of accidental death, but also increases the possibility of other more minor injuries and ailments such as arthritis. This chapter is divided in three parts, namely air, land and water activities.

8.2.1   AIR SPORTS

"It is fair to say that sports performed in the air are extreme. It is also fair to say that taking part in these sports can be extremely life threatening." (Joe Tomlinson)

BALLOONING

Ballooning is one of the oldest extreme pursuits in recorded history. Flight using a balloon was first successfully accomplished in late August of 1783 - a busy year - when Ann-Jean and MN Robert launched the Charles Balloon at Champ De Mars, France. One month later, Etienne Montgolfier successfully launched the first passenger-carrying balloon under a waterproof envelope made of linen. The "passengers" were a sheep, a rooster, and a duck. Only the sheep was at risk. In tourism this is an important "vehicle" for attractions like game reserves and lakes. It is often used to view game.

The first record of ballooning in South Africa was in December 1816, according to a tale that recurs in ballooning tournament literature. Apparently a certain Theodore Coussy planned to launch a balloon from the Cape Town Castle. Its passenger was to be a cat! There is no mention of whether the flight took place (**Sinclair, 1988:7**).

There was a worldwide resurgence in ballooning interest in the 1970s. In 1976 Johannesburg enthusiasts hosted the first ever balloon race on the African continent, attracting more than a dozen of the world's best hot air balloonists. Many international pilots return regularly to this country because of the ideal weather conditions and the great open spaces that give balloonists such freedom in their sport.

Balloons are not actually a method of travel, unless perhaps for Richard Branson! Balloons are an expensive, vicarious, and sometimes deadly method of long-distance travel. As a vehicle for short, breathtaking ascents, they are extremely successful. Zeppelins have fallen out of favour (and out of the sky), so for now any desire to float through the sky is limited to balloon tour operations, hang-gliding and soaring (glider flight). The newest adventure twist is bungee- jumping from balloons.

BUNGEE-JUMPING
The following types of bungee can be identified, namely (**Xtreme, 1998:79**):

(i) Conventional Bungee
The bungee cord is tied to the feet and the jumper dives head first.

(ii) Elevator Bungee
The cord is attached to a body harness and jumpers drop off backwards for a falling-lift experience.

(iii) Bridge Jump
A climbing rope is used instead of a bungee cord and is attached to a bridge parallel to the bridge on which the jumper is standing. The jumper swings down and across in an arc.

(iv) Hellswing/Bungee Swing
The climbing rope or bungee cord is attached to the same bridge that the jumper is standing on. The swing takes the jumper under the bridge.

Bungee-jumping is quite expensive. The following prices were published in **Exteme (1998:79)**:

- Victoria Falls will set you back US$90 for 100m. If you are prepared to fork out another US$40, you can get the moment recorded on video.
- Bloukrans' 216m descent costs R500, and remember the rebound tips off at 110m, the height of Victoria Falls, so in effect you are getting two for the price of one.
- The Old Gouritz River Bridge offers a variety of jumps: a straightforward bungee is R100; a bungee swing costs R90; and a bridge jump is also R90.
- Mobile jumps cost anything between R50 and R70.
- The rocket bungee will launch you up to 40m into the air for R80.

Zimbabwe and South Africa boast the highest and most scenic commercial jumps in the world, making them major drawcards for any bungee enthusiast.

BASE-JUMPING
If any of the extreme sports can be considered a truly high risk, then BASE Jumping is that sport. For those who are unfamiliar with the term "BASE", it is an acronym for

Buildings, Antenna Tower, Span, Earth. BASE jumpers are people who leap from objects which fall under the categories BASE represented by each letter of the acronym. Generally these objects are not very high off the ground, and so the jumper must deploy his parachute very quickly or risk impacting the ground at deadly speed.

CANOPYING

The sport originated from rappelling, which is a sport derived from mountain climbing in that it also uses safety climbing harnesses and ropes to displace the person from one inaccessible point to another. According to research the technique was developed by scientists in the US to study the canopies of trees in forests without disturbing the life in the limbs and trunk by having to attach ladders or climbing equipment to the tree. Apparently it was not until a few years ago that scientists were able to study the canopy ecosystems in great depth through the use of this technique, and once it was developed, the rainforest became the optimal target for its use, due to its large and complex ecosystems. It was not long before the growing tourists industry took notice of this technique and decided that it was too exciting an activity to pass. Thus the sport was born as an assisted sport which is sometimes called a canopy tour, mainly because it is targeted on tourists.

FIGHTER PLANE FLYING

Certain tour operators have fighter planes which one can fly. The tour operators will give the tourist a one hour grand course, a videotape of your experience and a one-hour debriefing afterwards. No flying experience is required. An instructor sits next to you the entire time, but even novices get to take the controls.

HANG-GLIDING

The first manned hang-glider flown was designed, built and flown by German inventor Otto Lilienthal in 1893. Hang-gliders are deceptively strong. They are built of aircraft quality aluminum and stainless steel with a sail (the wing) generally made of dacron. The structure is held together by a series of wires that create an amazingly stable geometry. A typical hang-glider is capable of handling a load of over one ton without breaking. Today's hang-glider technology allows them to be outfitted with full instrumentation, radios and even rocket deployed emergency parachutes. There are many venues in South Africa where one could participate in hang-gliding.

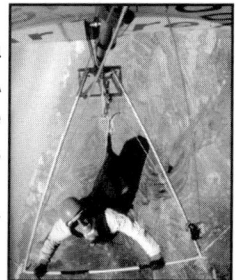

HIGH WIRE

Jay Cochrane, a 51-year-old Canadian, holds the world record for time spent balancing on a high wire - 21 days and nights spent performing six shows a day to the crowds in San Juan, Puerto Rico. This is a sport which requires split-second reflexes, and a willingness to play a life-and-death game with each record attempt.

PARAGLIDING

Paragliding is an offshoot of skydiving, Base-jumping and hang-gliding. The idea of skydiving is to get from the aeroplane to the ground as fast as possible without getting killed. Paragliding is the opposte; the more time spent in the air, the better (**Xtreme, 1998:83**).

There are three classes of glider - standard, competition and tandem. South Africa offers great opportunities for the event. South Africa also boasts being host of the World Paragliding Championships. Kuruman in the Northern Cape Province is well known for this.

World records (Xtreme, 1998:82):

- Men's open distance in a straight line: Alex Louw (SA) 283,9 km in 1992, Kuruman.
- World record for distance to a declared goal: Alex Louw (SA) 250,2 km in 1994, Kuruman.
- Women's open distance in a straight line: Kat Thurston (UK) 285 km in 1995, Kuruman.
- Tandem open distance: Richard and Guy Westgate (UK) 200 km in 1995, Kuruman.
- Highest take-off: Jean Marc Boivin (France) 8 845 m in 1988, Mount Everest, Nepal.
- Tandem altitude: Richard and Guy Westgate (UK) 4 390 m in 1995, Kuruman.
- Altitude: Robby Whittal (UK) 5 430 m in 1993, Brandvlei, SA.

The ten best places for paragliding * (**Getaway's top 10, 1998:126**);

- Lion's head, Cape Town, South Africa
- Dasklip Pass, near Porterville, South Africa
- Graaff-Reinet, South Africa
- Map of Africa, South Africa
- Brenton-on-Sea, South Africa

- Hartbeespoort Dam, South Africa
- Bulwer, South Africa
- Bitterwasser, Namibia
- Swakopmund dunes, Namibia
- Katse Dam, Lesotho

* All paragliders must have a license issued by the South African Hang-Gliding and Paragliding Association and may not fly from a site which is graded higher than their license.

PARASAILING
The ten best places for parasailing (**Getaway's top 10, 1998:118**):

- Over Buffelsjags Dam, South Africa
- Above Verneukpan, South Africa
- Sun City, South Africa
- Club Makokola, Lake Malawi, Malawi
- La Pirogue, Mauritius
- Ile Aux Cerfs, Mauritius
- Le Coco Beach, Mauritius
- La Mauricia, Mauritius
- Le Galawa Beach, The Comores
- Beau Vallon Bay, Mahé, Seychelles

SKI-JUMPING AND SKI-FLYING
To jump or fly, the skier starts down the hill to the jump site from a seated position high above the take off point. Skiers crouche down to optimise their aerodynamic form and minimise wind resistance. In this position, they accelerate to speeds exceeding 96 kph before reaching their take-off point. At the take-off point, the skiers lunge forward toward the tips of their skis, adding the final lift-generating from, their body. The take-off point is not flat, but sloped downward at 11 degrees. On landing, the skier uses a traditional telemark-style position, with one foot in front of the other. This is the correct landing position for both ski-jumping and ski-flying. Each jump is scored based on the style of the jump from take-off to the landing, and the distance traveled relative to the K-Point. The K-Point is the point at which the hill begins its transition to a flat surface. A panel of five judges award style points.

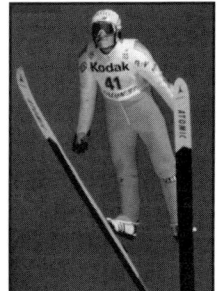

SKYDIVING

Today there are five internationally recognized competitive disciplines (**Xtreme, 1998:8-9**):

(i) **Accuracy Landings:**

Here competitors jump from 3 000 feet and attempt to land on a 5cm disc situated on an electronic recording surface. This is the oldest of the competitive disciplines and has become more competitive over the years thanks to improvements in parachute design.

(ii) **Free Fall Gymnastics:**

These are individual free fall events where competitors are judged on how quickly and precisely they perform set routines of loops and turns. The loneliest of all the disciplines, this demands a very high degree of skill and body control similar to that needed by a gymnast or high-board diver.

(iii) **Team Formation Skydiving:**

This discipline is very popular at club level and requires a team of four or eight to perform a series of predetermined formations within an allotted time. South Africa sent a team to the World Championships in November 1998.

(iv) **Individual Freestyle:**

Freestylers jump as a team of two and perform a choreographed sequence usually involving head-down flying, stand-ups and sit- flying. It has been compared to aerial gymnastics, which is not easy in wind speeds of 240 km/h.

(v) **Skysurfing:**

A new and spectacular addition to the skydiving family, skysurfing utilises a specially designed board to help the skydivers surf the airwaves. Marks are awarded for compulsory and free rounds. Loops, barrel rolls and helicopter spins are just a few of the maneuvers in this rapidly developing discipline.

A novice can be introduced to the sport in three ways (**Xtreme, 1998:12**):

(i) **A tandem skydive:**

Here the instructor with over 1000 jumps lead his/her partner, who is harnessed to the instructor, in a dive.

(ii) **Static line:**

The novice is equipped with a dual-parachute assembly and taken up to 3 500 feet (1070 m). As the jumper leaves the plane the main parachute is automatically deployed by a static cord attached to a strong point on the plane. From 3 500 feet it's a 3 minute parachute ride down to the ground.

(iii) **Accelerated free fall (AFF)**
Wearing a free fall dual-parachute assembly the jumpers leave the aircraft at 10 000 feet. Two instructors accompany the novice. The instructors fall with the parachutist for 35 seconds, after which the novice deploys the parachute by pulling the ripcord. It takes roughly four minutes for the parachutists to get down to earth.

The ten best skydiving sites (**Getaway's top 10, 1998:127**):

- Stellenbosch, South Africa
- Citrusdal, South Africa
- Grahamstown, South Africa
- Wonderboom, Pretoria, South Africa
- Leopard Rock, near Sun City, South Africa
- Pietermaritzburg, South Africa
- Swakopmund, Namibia
- Windhoek, Namibia
- Victoria Falls, Zimbabwe
- Nairobi, Kenya

SKYSURFING
Sky surfing is skydiving with a board and is extremely dangerous.

SOARING
By definition, soaring and gliding are different, although they are commonly used terms to describe the sport of soaring. *Soaring is defined as flying without engine power and without loss of altitude. Gliding on the other hand is defined as flying without engine power, and a glider is an aircraft without a power source.* Gliders are towed from airfield by towplanes using towropes of between 45-60m in length. The

towropes are light, stretchy, abrasion-resistant lines with high strength-to-weight ratios. Towropes are designed to be dropped by the glider once the desired altitude has been achieved. The glider is then left to the task of finding ways in which to increase its altitude without assistance.

Contingents of pilots from overseas are attracted to fly in South Africa because of the ideal gliding conditions and open terrain, qualities rarely found in other countries. So ideal are the conditions that visitors often make - and achieve - record gliding attempts during their visits here (**Sinclair, 1988**).

8.2.2 LAND SPORTS

ABSEILING
The ten best places for abseiling (**Getaway's top 10, 1998:124**):
- Table Mountain, Cape Town, South Africa
- Chapman's Peak, Cape Town, South Africa
- Beaverlac, near Porterville, South Africa
- Bushmanskloof Private Game Reserve, South Africa
- Kamikaze Canyon, near Gordon's Bay, South Africa
- Gouritz River Bridge, near Mossel Bay, South Africa
- Knysna Heads, South Africa
- Isibini Eco-Reserve, near Dundee, South Africa
- Amanziwayo Falls, South Africa
- Bulungu Falls, Swaziland

ACW CLIMBING
A new sport that has emerged from the creation of indoor climbing facilities is that of climbing an Artificial Climbing Wall. ACWs were first constructed as a method of training and teaching without the concern of falling rocks and other natural hazards, weather, or long hikes to good routes. For enthusiasts who do not want to venture out to the real cliffs, artificial climbing walls can be found in any major city.

ADVENTURE RACING
Adventure racing draws from many different extreme sports: climbing, whitewater, and mountain biking, for example. Surely event organisers and creators will find ways of including more and more extreme sports in their events until a decathlon style event is created, which will act to find the best all-round extreme sports athlete in the world. Racing originated with the marathon, based on the distance a messenger ran from the battlefields of Marathon to Athens (he died, of course). The concept of pushing oneself past the limits has evolved from polite joggers to Triathlons

and Ironman competitions where swimming and biking are integrated. It seems that when television and sponsors become involved these simple tests of personal best became more akin to the events held at the Coliseum of ancient Rome. The Camel Trophy, the Raid Gauloise and the Eco Challenge are the new breed of adventure racing.

AGGRESSIVE INLINE SKATING

Like skateboarding, "street" inline skaters seek to jump over and grind across just about any obstacle imaginable. These needs wound up giving birth to an entire sub-industry created to serve the needs of aggressive skaters that the corporate manufactures are only now recognising represent the future of inline skating.

BOB SKELETON

Head first on a metal toboggan (a skeleton) at speeds in excess of 80 mph down a bobsleigh run is the great sport of bob skeleton. The first downhill man-made ice canal, custom built for the sport of competitive tobogganing, was the world famous Cresta Run in St Moritz, Switzerland. Though no longer an Olympic sport, The Cresta Run still exists to this day and between January and March each year many riders attempt the Run. Until recently the Cresta style of riding was only practiced on the Cresta Run. However, in the last decade a handful of international riders have pioneered access to the bobsleigh tracks of the world. Bob skeleton is now on course to be included as an Olympic medal event once more. Each run starts with an explosive sprint as the rider pushes his toboggan for the first 20 to 30 metres before jumping aboard. Whilst descending the rider attempts to find the ideal energy saving line through fifteen steeply banked curves and is aiming to achieve the fastest possible descent of the track. This is exactly the same as two- and four-man bobsleigh and the luge, except the solo rider adopts a face down, head first, minimal drag riding position. The skeleton has no brakes or mechanical steering. Steering is effected by shifting the body's weight and aerodynamic profile and pulling on the skeleton's handles to change direction. Once the rider has broken the timing light at the bottom of the track, the rider brakes by digging his shoes into the loose snow.

BOBSLEIGH

Bobsleigh was invented by a group of Englishmen on holiday in Switzerland in 1890 when they raced down the snow-covered road between St Moritz and Celerina on primitive bobs. The first races were for 5 to 6 people and a requirement of the competition was that each crew included at least one woman. Bobsleigh is now in two- and four- person bobs, with separate events for men and women. Competitions are run down iced tracks with at least 15 banked curves. The track is approximately 1 500m long and speeds of up to 90 mph are reached. The object of modern bobsleigh is to get to the finishing line in the shortest time. Although the condition of the ice and the preparation of the bobsleigh affects its speed, a fast start and a clean drive are crucial. The passengers' role at the start is vital and in world class competition the crew are often accomplished track athletes. Once in the bob, the passengers' role is over and it is then the responsibility of the driver to steer the best line as gravity pulls down to the finishing line and, hopefully, a team's or competition's best time.

BMX (MOUNTAIN BIKING)

BMX racing went through a period when it was overlooked as the mountain bike craze hit, but it is now resurging, and many of today's mountain biking and motorcross stars are former and current BMX racers.

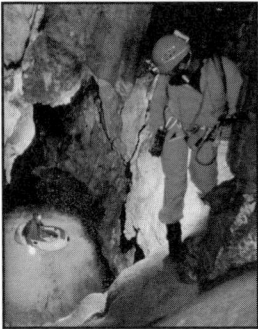

CAVING

Many activities have challenges, but they can nearly always be assessed in advance. Mountaineers can usually see the route ahead and know how high they are to climb. Scuba-divers have charts and tables to tell them of depths, reefs, tides and currents. Cavers know nothing when they enter a cave for the first time. There is a hole in the ground and somebody has to slip into it first, "Take nothing but pictures; leave nothing but footprints; kill nothing but time," sums up the attitude of people engaging in caving (**Sinclair, 1988**). Appropriately, those who do cave always travel to the inner depths of the earth in groups of two or more. Not surprisingly, cavers are subject to many dangers that one would expect could occur in a cave, such as death by starvation, falling, asphyxiation, drowning, and hypothermia from exposure.

DRAG RACING
MOTORCYCLES

The first drag strip in South Africa was built during the 60s but the sport was born 10 years earlier in the US. It was an attempt to take dicing off the streets. At that stage a top of the range superstock bike would run the quarter-mile in 13 seconds at 165 km/h. The same class today comes in around 10,7 at 212 km/h (**Xtreme, 1998:32**).

Classes of bikes include (**Xtreme, 1998:32**):

(i) **Street Eliminator Class:**
There is A, B and C Superstock, which is a standard factory bike off the showroom floor. Only minor modifications are allowed to these bikes. Hot street involves superstock bikes with extensive modifications to the engine. Pro street involves superstock bikes with extensive modifications to the engine and chassis.

(ii) **Top Eliminator Class (Wheelie bikes)**
All Top Class Eliminators feature a wheelie bar, which prevents the bike from flipping over when the horsepower kick in. The bikers steer by using their body weight. From the finish he has 650m in which to stop the bike. No nitromethane is allowed but the bikes can be turbo-charged.

(iii) **Handicap System**
The handicap system in drag racing allows bikes from different classes to race against one another.

MOTOR CARS
The first drag strip built in South Africa was in the 1960s and the Tarlton track in Gauteng is the only operation that races Top Fuelers and Funny Cars. No vehicle on the ground or in the air accelerates faster than a drag racing machine.

On the four-wheeled side there are three classes of car: Pro Stock, Top Fuel and Funny Cars (**Xtreme, 1998:34**):

(i) **Pro Stock Class**
These cars can be bought from a dealer but that is where the similarity between a Pro Stocker and a street car ends. Petrol powered, they feature extensive engine modifications, sophisticated chassis and suspension development and they weigh about a ton.

(ii) **Top Fueler**
The dragster can reach 160 km/h in one second and it takes 600m to stop even with parachutes.

(iii) **Funny Cars**
The front wheels of the machine are set further forward than a normal car, hence "funny car". The low-slung fibreglass body and the downforce created by the exhaust pipes prevent the car from becoming airborne.

EXTREME MOTOCROSS

The course is designed to reward riders who can handle the most difficult of situations. The courses have many of the bumps and ruts of traditional motoX, but the obstacles and jumps are designed to maximize the height a rider can, and must, jump to win.

The moves and obstacles are not natural, but many natural obstacles exist in areas that every rider can get to and play on.

HELISKIING

The main centre for heliskiers and helisnowboarders is Canada. The names of mountain ranges like the Bugaboos, Purcells and Monashess conjure up images of the very essence of heliskiing - endless glaciers, vast alpine bowls and old growth forest covered in metres of light, dry powder. Heliskiing was started in the late 1960s by a Swiss mountain guide based in Banff who was looking for a way to reach remote areas where incomparable powder skiing was available without having to trek many days to get there. To begin with, fixed wing aircraft were used to fly skiers into the heart of the territory. Then basing themselves at abandoned lumber camps, the skiers would set out each day to climb one of the surrounding peaks to experience the exhilaration of skiing down. Before long, fixed-wing aircraft were replaced by helicopters. These gave access to remote regions and mountain summits, giving skiers the opportunity to make many different descents in one day. Thus a sport was born. The popularity of which spread like wild-fire.

INFLATABLE BOAT RACING

South Africa has among the best teams when it comes to offshore and inland inflatable boat racing (**Xtreme, 1998:62**).

Offshore and inland rubber duck racing has its roots in South Africa but the sport has greatly improved since the introduction of "pencil boats". Before the "pencils" most inflatables featured a round nose. The pontoons or 'pencil boats ', were originally designed along the lines of the Formula One powerboats and have improved speed and manoeuvrability. The new shape proved such a hit that many overseas competitors now use the South African design. In the US they call these boats "performance inflatables".

South Africa has the largest number of registered pilots ,but the numbers in the US are fast closing in. The racing season starts in October and runs through to July.

JUNGLE TREKKING

Many people would never think of going to a tropical jungle with a tour operator, while others would not think of going without one. Because local ground operators are used, the same trips are often offered by many agencies. Top jungle destinations are Irian Jaya, Papua New Guinea, Borneo, Sumatra, Vietnam and the Amazon. The most popular are Costa Rica and Belize.

KART RACING

Off-road karting is a new form of grass roots level racing. The sensation of speed in an off-road kart is unparalled and many motocross and Formula K drivers compete in the monthly meets for just this reason (**Xtreme, 1998:58**).

Various models are available, from 100cc to 200cc 4 stroke, a baby kart, junior, sport, enduro and utility karts. The machine has an independent fully adjustable elastomer-based suspension system, available in a range of stiffness to suit any terrain, rider size or rider style. Combine the steering geometry and an unsprung weight ratio of 8%, the wide range transmission options, power to weight ratio and a low centre of gravity, and this all makes for an unbeatable ride.

KITE BUGGYING

These are carts just inches off the ground, but fast enough to excite speed extremists and tricky enough to delight freestyle kings. However, in the quest to maximise miles covered in a specified period of time, what is scientifically known as ragging it, two pilots with two kites combine into a tag-team. Urban buggying is the latest fringe of this sport, involving buggying in anything from children's playgrounds, cycle ways, golf courses, roads or car parks. It is only limited by the imagination and the confines of your local metropolis.

KLOOFING

The ten best spots for Kloofing in South Africa (**Getaway's top 10, 1998:128**):

- Suicide Gorge, Western Cape
- Riviersonderend Gorge, Western Cape
- Ratel River, Western Cape
- Steenbras River, Western Cape
- Stroms River, Western Cape
- Tonquani, Magaliesberg, Gauteng
- Blyde River, Mpumalanga
- Sekororo, Olifants River, Mpumalanga
- Ndedema Gorge, Drakensberg, Kwazulu-Natal
- Mzimkhulu Pipeline, Drakensberg, Kwazulu-Natal

LAND AND ICE YACHTING

Landsailing can be practiced on a broad range of surfaces. Dry lakebeds and abandoned airfields are a great site for sailing. However, they are more temperamental, since the asphalt direction and the wind direction do not always line up just right. Many land sailing enthusiasts enjoy sailing on beaches, which often offer a predictable breeze that is perpendicular to the required direction of travel, the preferred wind direction for beach sailing.

Ice yachts have a slightly easier time finding suitable ice to sail on. Their primary problem is finding lakes that are sizable enough to allow them to not only accelerate up to speed, but also to turn safely before coming ashore.

MOTORCYCLE TOURING

There are four types of motorcycle touring: the classic Harley/Gold Wing, BMW, sport Tourers, and off-road motorcycles.

MOUNTAIN BIKING

The images and beauty of the outdoors are really why mountain biking has grown so rapidly. Mountain bikes have opened up an entire range of remote wilderness and landscapes that recreational trail hikers had never been able to get to so easily and quickly. Not surprisingly, many of the most popular mountain biking regions are established hiking areas.

MOUNTAIN BOARDING

Mountain boards are steered just like a skateboard, by leaning the board's deck in the required direction. On dirt and loose surfaces, the boards respond much like a snowboard. Mountain boards are available in a variety of lengths, just like a snowboard. Shorter versions are for freestyle riding, while the longer ones offer better directional stability and are better suited to speed riding.

OUTDOOR MOUNTAIN-CLIMBING

Climbing mountains covers two basic categories, namely technical and non-technical. The latter requires little more than sheer energy and knowledge of one's own limitations. No special equipment are needed; just a good rugged and supportive pair of hiking shoes. Technical climbing requires the use of ropes and other specialised equipment to ascend the terrain to be climbed. The equipment is used so that, in the event of a fall, the climber is both protected from injury and securely fastened to the rock or ice.

Technical climbing can be broken into two components: ice and rock. Rock-climbing involves scaling cliffs and boulders in situations that could prove hazardous or dangerous.

Ice-climbing entails scaling cliffs and boulders that are entirely covered with ice and snow. Climbing ice requires and additional level of specialised equipment such as "crampons", the metal spikes that ice climbers attach to the bottom of their climbing shoes. In ice-climbing, even the most proficient extreme climbers require the aid of equipment that allows them to grip the ice and snow without slipping.

The ten best places for rock-climbing (**Getaway's top 10, 1998:123**):

- The Peninsula Mountain Chain, South Africa
- Cedarberg, South Africa
- Paarl Rock, South Africa
- Montagu Crags, South Africa
- Towerkop, Ladysmith, South Africa
- Magaliesberg, South Africa
- The Restaurant at the End of the Universe, Mpumalanga, South Africa
- Mount Everest Resort, Eastern Free State, South Africa
- Monteseel and Shongweni, Durban, South Africa
- Matopo Hills National Park, Zimbabwe

The ten best places for mountaineering* (**Getaway's top 10, 1998:125**):

- Du Toit's Mountains, Boland, South Africa
- Hex River Mountains, South Africa
- Blouberg Nature Reserve, Northern Province, South Af rica
- Drakensberg, South Africa
- Spitzkoppe, Southern Damaraland, Namibia
- Chimanimani Mountains, Zimbabwe-Mozambique
- Mulanje Massif, Malawi
- Mount Kenya, Kenya

- Mount Kilimanjaro, Tanzania
- Ruwenzori Mountains, Uganda

* Climbing permits are needed for all these areas.

There is little argument that the Hindu Kush in Nepal is the ultra of peaks and trekking. Only about 40 years ago the ascent of a major peak was sufficient to secure the climber fame. Now, even Mount Vinson in the Antarctica has had 130 successful summit trips. Up and coming places include the peaks of Alaska, Argentina and Pakistan. The Alps no longer present a serious challenge to these sportsmen an - women. The Holy Grail is to conquer the seven summits or climb the highest mountain on each continent. Many guides will require proof of your skills before taking you along.

OVERLANDING
Although not technically four-wheel driving, you will be sitting in a four- or six-wheel-drive Bedford as you bump and lurch across Africa. Any old African hand knows that "you use a Bedford to pull out a Land Rover and you will need a tank to pull out a Bedford." Overlanding became popular in the early seventies when companies could take you all the way from London to South Africa. Today, conditions and roads have worsened. Most overlanding is done on a communal basis.

PRO JOUSTING
Pro Jousting is a highly competitive horsesport that combines all of the elegance of classical equestrian events with the hard-hitting action of pro football. Unlike Joust Shows at Renaissance Faires, Medieval Dinner Theatres, or Las Vegas Castels, this is reality. There are no choreography, staged falls, or pre-selected winners. This is a real sport. Fully armoured competitors ride at each other at a combined speed approaching 60 mph with one goal in mind: To blast the opponent off his horse. But that is only part of what makes up Pro Jousting. Professional Jousting consists of more than only the Full Armoured Joust.

Competition includes the following disciplines: Horseback Skill Games; Light Armour Jousting; Baston Matches upon Horseback; and Heavy Armour, Xtreme and Jousting.

ROAD RACING
Road racing is high-speed competition that takes place on paved, usually oval, but sometimes irregular tracks by state-of-the-art racing motorcycles. There are various engine-size classes determining the speed and power of the vehicles involved in each race, the most spectacular of which is the "superbike" category.

ROCKBOARDING

Rockboarding involves boarding on snow-covered slopes. The equipment is challenged tremendously by these kinds of environment. However, this is the only alternative to please the desire of snowboarding in the summer time. At the high risk of getting hurt, neck-breaking stunts and sharp turns are performed by the boarders.

SAFARIS

Arguably, safaris were the first adventure or ecotour. In the past, travellers would preserve wildlife by collecting samples for museums by shooting and mounting them. Now, all you hear are the clicking of cameras and whirring of videotapes. The best safaris in the world are private tented safaris to the lesser-visited areas of Africa's parks. South Africa has an overabundance of wildlife, along with clean, efficient facilities.

SANDBOARDING

The ten best places for sandboarding (**Getaway's top 10, 1998:122**):

* Sandy Bay, Cape Town, South Africa
* Silwerstroombeach, West Coast, South Africa
* Betty's Bay, South Africa
* Alexandria, South Africa
* Maitland River Mouth, South Africa
* Port Alfred, South Africa
* Cape Vidal, Greater St Lucia Wetland Park, South Africa
* Swakopmund, Namibia
* Sossusvlei, Namib-Naukluft Park, Namibia
* Sandwich Harbour, Namibia

SCRAMBLING

Scrambling is an exciting addition for the hill walker with a head for heights. It offers a chance to explore the crenellated ridges, deep gullies and cliff faces with often only the ravens for company. Scrambling combines the techniques of climbing with the awareness of mountaineering. A walking route becomes a scramble when you start using your hands for ascent. Many of the classic scrambles date from the Victorian era and were amongst the earliest recorded rock climbs. With the rapid rise in climbing standards they slipped into obscurity. Since 1980 interest in these routes has been renewed by the growing number of scrambling guide books available. They cover all the popular areas, giving grades and route descriptions. It should be remembered that unroped scrambling leaves little margin for error. Using a rope should be a readily available option for anyone in the party needing its assurance. However, in the wrong hands, it can give a false sense of security, inviting peril. That said, only the safety skills of basic ropework are required: tying-on, anchor selection, arresting a fall and abseiling.

SKATEBOARDING

Today's skateboarding can be categorised as either "street" or "vert". Street skating is the more technical style of skating and is extremely difficult to master. Street tricks are performed on any and every available obstacle that looks like it can be ridden over or jumped. Park benches, handrails, loading ramps, garbage cans, and even monuments are fair game. Vert skating take place in a half-pipe. Pools and basins are also popular arenas for vert skating.

SKIJORING

Skijoring (pronounced SKI-joring, with a hard -j-) is a fast-growing winter sport combining mushing and cross-country skiing. It is a sport that can be enjoyed on many levels, from jaunts with the family dog, to noncompetitive fun runs, to all-out racing. Many types of dogs can enjoy skijoring. It is helpful for the skier to have intermediate skiing ability, or the willingness to take some lessons.

SNOWBOARDING

All forms of sport need an element of revitalisation or they risk becoming commonplace. Skiing has been a part of life for anyone living near snow-covered or mountainous regions of the globe. With the advent of cheap international air travel, skiing as a sport for the masses progressed until it reached saturation point - interest and participation waned. The combination of surfer-skateboarding with skiing created new interest in the sport. Steep and extreme riding requires the highest levels of technical and physical skill to get from top to bottom while seeking extra points for jumping over and off obstacles.

SNOWSHOEING

Snowshoeing as sport has grown out of the outdoor, extreme sports movement. Snowshoes were long overlooked by other extreme athletes, until it was realised that they are an effective method of transportation. In difficult and isolated terrain, snowshoes can deliver extreme skiers and snowboarders to locations that could otherwise only have been reached with the aid of helicopters or snowmobiles. In fact, snowshoes help to keep the natural spirit of these sports from being overwhelmed by machines.

SPEED-BIKING

Over the past few years, downhill mountain bike racers have been pushing the limits of speed on specially outfitted mountain bikes. The bikes are fitted with special aerodynamic fairings and tires modified with large spikes to grip the snow and ice-covered surface as they accelerate to maximum velocity before racing through a steep-trap zone (a time distance that determines the official speed established by the rider).

SPEED-SKIING

Skiing in its own right is an extreme sport, and has been for years. One skiing discipline that is as amazing as it is extreme is speed-skiing. Speeds of up to 240 kph are reached down a mountain on skis.

Speed-skiing competitions are held throughout Europe, but mostly in France, where they are major events. Speed-skiing is rapidly gaining exposure and popularity globally, as the demand for more and varied extreme sport competitions grows.

STEEP-SKIING

Extreme skiing is the last frontier of modern skiing. It fills the void for skiers who no longer find skiing in groomed terrain as exciting as it was. As skiing extreme regions becomes more and more popular, many more people are heading to the steeper challenges of technical terrain. The future of skiing are currently being defined by extreme skiers.

STREET LUGE

Like ice luge, which can trace its roots to traditional sledding pushed to the limit, street luge is an extension of another form of downhill pavement skateboarding. In fact, skateboarders have travelled downhill on their boards at speed both lying down on their backs like a street luge, on their stomachs, and standing up.

WALKING/TREKKING
This is the most laid-back method of travel. There is some danger of kidnapping and robbery, as well as the usual penalties caused by tripping, falling and general wear and tear. Most trekkers hire porters and spend the evenings in small huts or villages. The most popular trekking sites are Annapurna in Nepal, Zanskar in Ladakh, Bernese Oberland in the Alps, the Milford Track in New Zealand and Chiang Mai in Northern Thailand.

8.2.3 WATER SPORTS

Water nourishes, but also brings death. We are not naturally built to survive in it, but we are drawn to its many possibilities for extreme sports (Joe Tomlinson).

AIR CHAIR
The Air Chair is relatively easy to ride since once the foil is working, the rig creates minimal drag. Jet-propelled personal watercraft and small boats with as little as 25 hp can tow the Air Chair. These advantages enable a broader spectrum of water sports enthusiasts to enjoy the device.

BAREFOOT WATER-SKIING
Barefoot skiers adapted many of the freestyle moves of traditional waterskiers. Spins, backward maneuvers, body drags, and other tricks made barefooting an exciting new discipline. Due to the speeds

required to barefoot, the tricks are especially difficult, and dangerous, since the surface of the water becomes very hard in a high-speed impact.

BOARDSAILING
One of the great things about boardsailing is that all you need are water, wind, and a board.

The ten best places for boardsailing (**Getaway's top 10, 1998:119**):

* Misty Cliffs, Cape Town, South Africa
* Big Bay, Cape Town, South Africa

- Rietvlei, Cape Town, South Africa
- Hakgat, Cape Town, South Africa
- Langebaan Lagoon, South Africa
- Shelly Bay, Cape St Francis, South Africa
- Noordhoek, Port Elizabeth, South Africa
- Vaal Dam, South Africa
- Midmar Dam, near Howick, South Africa
- Cape Maclear, Lake Malawi, Malawi

BOOGIEBOARD OR RIVERBOARD
On a riverboard the rider is completely exposed to the elements without the protection of a boat's hull to ward off the jagged rocks and absorb some of the shock the rapids can hand out.

CANOE
Next in difficulty would be the canoe, which offers little protection from a capsize, due to the open nature of the design. Many canoeist are qualified to run rivers of sizeable power. However, canoes do not offer the "righting" performance (returning the boat to a rightside-up position) necessary in big rapids.

The ten best flat-water canoeing trips (**Getaway's top 10, 1998:135**):

- Keurbooms River, near Plettenberg Bay, South Africa
- Vaal Dam, near Parys, South Africa
- Kosi Bay, South Africa
- Kowie River, near Port Alfred, South Africa
- Orange River, South Africa
- Kavango River below Popa Falls, Namibia
- Okavango Delta, Botswana
- Zambezi River just above Victoria Falls, Zimbabwe
- Lower Zambezi, Zimbabwe/Zambia
- Lake Malawi, Malawi

FREEDIVING
To freedive to depths of 15m is an unsettling prospect for all but the strongest swimmers. To dive much deeper requires holding one's breath for minutes. In fact, the world's best freedivers hold their breath for periods that rival many marine mammals.

There are three categories of freediving for depth. First there is "fixed weight" or " fixed volume" diving. Divers in this discipline swim down as deep as they can under their own power, and resurface the same way. This means using up valuable air in the descent, limiting the speed at which they can get deep, and the depth attainable.

Second is "variable weight" freediving, in which ballast is used to aid divers descend. Up to one-third of body weight is considered legal. Variable weight divers can get down faster and with less effort than fixed weight divers, yet they must still swim back to the surface under their own power.

The third is called "absolute" diving, which allows unlimited ballast in the descent, with rates reaching between 3,65 - 4,6m per second. To return to the surface the diver grabs a lifting aid, such as an inflatable bag. Cuban diver Francisco "Pepin" Ferreras-Rodriguez holds the current record at 127m, an amazing depth. Pepin boasts an extraordinary lung capacity, and has been freediving since age seven.

JET-SKIING
Competitive jet-skiing is made up of three disciplines (**Xtreme, 1998:45**):

(i) **Circuit**
Circuit is raced on closed flat water or offshore courses over a set number of laps. The flat water races tend to be dominated by the faster skis while offshore tournaments rely more on the pilot's skill and knowledge of the conditions.

(ii) **Longhaul**
Longhaul is similar to circuit racing only over greater distances with competitors reaching speeds of 120 kph.

(iii) **Freestyle**
Freestyle is the most spectacular of the disciplines and it attracts the biggest crowds. Competitions can be held inland or offshore. Generally five foot waves are big enough for Freestyle. Anything bigger than this makes it hard to do tricks. If a big wave catches you it can also drop the ski on you, with unfortunate consequences.

KAYAKING
The most extreme method of getting down a river, is on a kayak. Kayaks offer a

completely enclosed hull design that allows the paddlers to sit in the opening of the hull and seal themselves in, using a neoprene skirt.

The ten best places for sea-kayaking (**Getaway's top 10, 1998:133**):

* Cape Point, Cape of Good Hope Nature Reserve, South Africa
* Bloubergstrand to Robben Island, South Africa
* Up the West Coast, South Africa
* Langebaan Lagoon, South Africa
* Walker Bay, South Africa
* Knysna Lagoon, South Africa
* Quirimba Archipelago, Mozambique
* Round Zanzibar, Tanzania
* Pemba Island, Tanzania
* Masoala Peninsula, Madagascar

KITEBOARDING

Kiteboarding, also called kitesurfing or flysurfing, is taking the world by storm. It combines the two most powerful forces of nature, water and wind, with the use of the surfboard and the powerkite! This is an extreme and radical sport and includes speed, spray, hang-time and adrenaline. As soon as the traction kite was introduced, a number of kite flyers started thinking of using kites to replace conventional sails in water sports such as windsurfing. To make this popular, you need a kite that can be launced directly from the water. After years of research, a number of water relauncheable kites were introduced. While the fundamental technologies are different and the degrees of relaucheability vary, these kites share the same characteristics that allows a kite flyer to launch them from the water after a fall.

OPEN WATER-SWIMMING

Open-water swimming races are held globally, and were included in many of the early Olympic Games. Course lengths are usually 5, 10, 15, or 25 km and require several hours to complete. The courses are set between two points on any large body of water. Some races require athletes to do several laps to complete a given distance, while others may consist of one very long lap.

POWERBOAT RACING

Powerboats are prone to violent crashes, largely thanks to inconsistent water surfaces. Even small waves hitting the hull in an odd or unexpected way are capable of sending boats flying out of the water, where they become uncontrollable. Sometimes landings can be smooth, but backward flips and hard impacts are more likely. Because of the excessive speeds, the results can be deadly - at 100+ mph, water behaves like cement.

ROUND THE WORLD YACHT RACING

THE TROPHéE JULES VERNE

When Jules Verne penned his classic novel Around the World in 80 Days in the late nineteenth century, he relied heavily on his imagination to propel hero Phileas Fogg and trusty servant Passepartout in their land, sea, and air circumnavigation of earth. Today, that imagination is embodied in the Trophée Jules Verne, a crewed non-stop race around the world. While Fogg and Passepartout travelled by ship for a fraction of their voyage, this race is entirely waterborne.

THE WHITBREAD RACE

The Whitbread Race sailboat racing occurs every fourth year.

THE BOC CHALLENGE AND THE VENDé GLOBE

The BOC has more stature worldwide because it led to a new generation of single-handed sailors, as well as boats. Many speed-enhancing features now key to today's single-handed sailor were developed and refined in the heat of BOC competition - water ballast systems, autopilots, twin rudders, and the use of carbon fiber as a construction material in the hull and masts.

RAFTING

Whitewater rafting is a big business, as it offer the opportunity to enjoy the rush of the ride without most of the risks associated. This is not to say whitewater rafting is easy or safe. Any time the river is entered on a watercraft, there are risks, and every year people are seriously injured or killed on rivers all over the world while on rafts. A number of rivers in South Africa have navigable whitewater. Some are truly wild, such as the Doring in the Cape, and others are mostly gentle with occasional rapids, such as the Orange. The range of climates in the country means that at any time of the year one or more of the rivers are working. Equally, since good whitewater is a function of rain, there are periods, sometimes

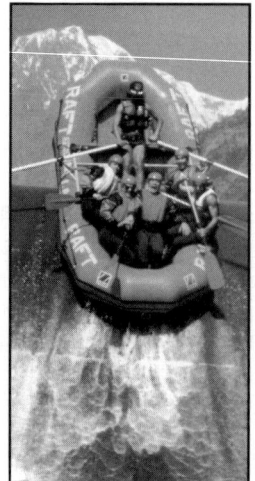

---

extended, when it is not possible to use them for canoeing or rafting. Dams regularise flow so that some rivers are navigable all year round, like the Orange. The best known river in Africa for white water rafting is the Zambezi, where tourists start below the Victoria Falls to conquer 18 rapids. This is a major tourism attraction for Zimbabwe.

The ten best whitewater rivers (**Getaway's top 10, 1998:134**):

- Molenaars River, South Africa
- Doring River, South Africa
- Palmiet River, South Africa
- Blyde River, South Africa
- Tugela River, South Africa
- Buffalo River, South Africa
- Great Usutu River, Swaziland
- Orange River, South Africa
- Kunene River, Namibia
- Zambezi River, Zimbabwe/Zambia
- Archipelago, Mozambique

SAILING
The ten best places for sailing (**Getaway's top 10, 1998:120**):

- Table Bay, South Africa
- False Bay, South Africa
- Kleinriviersvlei, Hermanus, South Africa
- Hartbeespoort Dam, South Africa
- Durban Bay, South Africa
- Lake Kariba, Zimbabwe
- Lake Malawi, Malawi
- Seychelles
- The Comores
- Bassas da India, off the Mozambique coast

SCUBA-DIVING
Deep technical diving is the extreme end of scuba. Deep divers must have a rock solid understanding of the physiology and psychology of diving as well as strong stress management skills.

The ten best diving spots (**Getaway's top 10, 1998:130-131**):

- The cichlids in Lake Malawi present a very colourful photo-opportunity.
- Go cage-diving off Dyer Island, South Africa, to see the great white shark.
- The clear warm water of Mauritius harbour many sponges, anemones and colourful corals.
- The waters round Pemba Island, Tanzania, shelter the vivid regal angelfish.
- The ragged-tooth shark frequents Protea Banks off the KwaZulu-Natal South Coast.
- Clusters of anemones encrust the full of the Nebo wreck more than 100 years old, which lies near the Aliwal Shoal, off the KwaZulu-Natal South Coast.
- Gorgonian fan corals make a garden of the sea bed round Desrockes in the Seychelles.
- Shoals of fusiliers dart above Mozambique's pristine reefs in the Bazaruto Archipelago.
- Indian longfin bannerfish graze at Bonne Adventure Reef in the Comores, a prime diving site.
- Lemon fish glide among the coral reefs of Sodwana Bay, the most southerly reefs in the world.

SNORKELING
Extreme snorkelers do not generally seek out small prey, but are in search of larger stuff, in the 90-270 kg category. Blue- and yellow-fin tuna, black marlin, and other larger game fish separate this style of spear fishing from the more ordinary sports.

SPEED-SAILING
Speed-sailing is a highly specialised sport requiring highly specialised designs. The only goal is to accelerate within a straight, closed course, and pass through a section of that course at maximum velocity in hope of recording a new speed record.

SURFING
The most famous of the tow-in spots is a particularly dangerous reef, aptly named "Jaws". The mushroom-shaped reef, located in the Hawaiian Islands, creates a wave that jumps up and breaks in a crescent shape. The wave heights in a big swell

easily exceed 15m and are certainly capable of killing anyone unfortunate enough to get caught in a bad wipeout. In South Africa Jeffreys Bay is internationally known as a surfer's mecca. Durban is the host of the Gunston 500 surfing championship which is also an important day on the surfing calendar.

The ten best surfing sports (**Getaway's top 10, 1998:132**):

- Kalk Bay Reef, Cape Town, South Africa
- Outer Kom (and Innder Kom), Noordhoek, Cape Town, South Africa
- Elands Bay, South Africa
- Victoria Bay, near Wilderness, South Africa
- Bay of Plenty, Durban, South Africa
- Bruce's Beauties, Cape St Francis, South Africa
- Supertubes, Jeffrey's Bay, South Africa
- Nahoon Reef, near East London, South Africa
- Cape Cross, Namibia
- St-Leu, Réunion

TRIFOILING

The Trifoiler design will certainly gain popularity over the next several years, when they become faster than today. As the technology improves, larger and faster versions are sure to be developed. In the meantime, these extreme sailboats will show up wherever there are wind and water.

WAKEBOARDING
Wakeboarding is a relatively new extreme sport. Its heritage can be linked to waterskiing, surfing, windsurfing, skateboarding, and snowboarding, and it is quickly redefining how we look at boat-towed sports.

8.3   CONCLUSION

It was the aim of this chapter to explain the role of extreme sports in tourism. The essence of tourism it is about an experience. People travel all over the world to have different experiences. In the world of sports tourism extreme sports are often overlooked. They are less formalised and structured activities, not normally found on the sports calendar, but people all over the world are participating in them basically everyday.

Extreme sports give an unforgettable experience and has already contributed to the success of tourism industries all over the world. Countries like Zimbabwe and Slovenia are famous for whitewater rafting, and Switzerland and Canada for skiing activities. Therefore, one should not underestimate the real value and tourism potential of extreme sports. As people's lives are getting more structured, more people will "escape' in these activities.

Chapter 9

Planning a sports tour

Change starts when someone sees the next step.
William Drayton

9.1 INTRODUCTION

Sport is an aspect of a community's culture that repeatedly plays a role in the lives of individuals and groups. Some people are active in sport, while others are just spectators. The impact of sport differs from country to country. Competition provides the medium and opportunity for competitors to work together and to interact globally. Sport unites people and nations. In this act of travelling to compete or to be a spectator, people become part of the growing industry of tourism and become sports tourists.

In today's life sport is certainly one of the most accessible and most enjoyable relaxation methods. In the light of that, it becomes clear that sport and tourism can go hand in hand. Marketing is one of the key elements that cause tourists to visit foreign countries for the enjoyment of sport in one way or another.

A sports tour might be something new to many people, but is gaining popularity among "tourists" all over the world. This chapter will address the questions illustrated in Figure 9.1.

Sports tours are organised and planned by tour operators. Tour operators can be divided into two main categories:

- Firstly, there are the so-called **"brokers"**, who compile itineraries for prospective tourists and make arrangements for their clients in terms of accommodation, transport and excursions. They do not operate vehicles or accompany tourists.

- The second category comprises the **"wheels operators"**, who own transport vehicles, be they large coaches, minibuses, or motor cars. They also make all the necessary arrangements with regard to accommodation and other matters.

Operators in both the above categories may offer fixed package tour or flexible tailor-made itineraries. Within the main categories mentioned above, there are the following sub-categories:

- Inbound tour operators - who provide services mainly for foreign visitors to South

Africa.
- Outbound tour operators - who provide services to clients in South Africa wishing to travel to destinations outside the country.

- Local tour operators - who provide services to domestic clients for tours within South Africa.

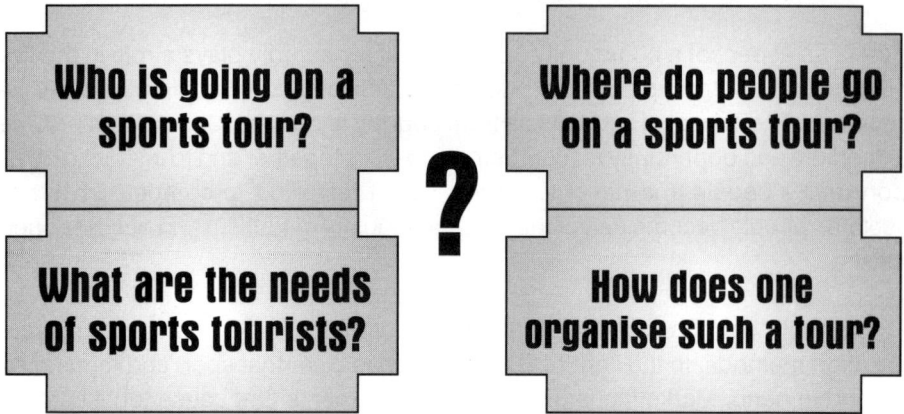

Who is going on a sports tour?	**Where do people go on a sports tour?**
What are the needs of sports tourists?	**How does one organise such a tour?**

?

Figure 9.1: Questions involving a sports tour

Sports tours are becoming more and more successful, with more and more tour operators organising specific sports tours. The latter include the competitors as well as the spectators. This is why the authors decided to spend some time on this important issue.

9.2   WHO IS GOING ON A SPORTS TOUR?

Tourists go on a tour, in this case the sports tour. Saayman (2000) describes a tourist as a person who travels from place to place, spend money and stays longer than 24 hours, but shorter than a year. Hence, when you go on a sports tour you are by definition a tourist. But what kind of tourist goes on a sports tour? One would think it would be mainly sportsmen or -women themselves, but for a South African rugby tour overseas the aeroplane is full of spectators, sport gamblers, sports administrators, sports managers, the medical team, media personnel, and of course, the players. All of these passengers travel with one goal namely participating in some way in sport, which makes them sports tourists. They are all going to experience a different culture, country, and sports experience.

9.3 WHERE DO PEOPLE GO ON A SPORTS TOUR?

Globalisation makes the world smaller and the opportunities easier to visit more different countries. Sportsmen/women have the choice of competing and participating all over the world. The latter go to sports events like Wimbledon, the Olympic Games or Formula One racing.

The choice of destination is influenced by the ability of the country's marketing skills and its fortunate position to host major events. Countries also have to provide the necessary infrastructure to host sports tourists from all over the world.

9.4 WHAT ARE THE NEEDS OF SPORTS TOURISTS?

Because there are different characteristics attached to the sports tourist, the needs differ, but they all have sport in common. The activities surrounding the sport code differ. Sportsmen would likely visit different places in their free time than the spectator with more time on his hands. The organiser of the tour must make sure that the primary goal, namely sport, is followed up with a secondary tour plan of entertainment and experiences of the country's attractions and its people. These primary and secondary goals, which are attached to timeframes, differ and the needs for them must be thoroughly investigated.

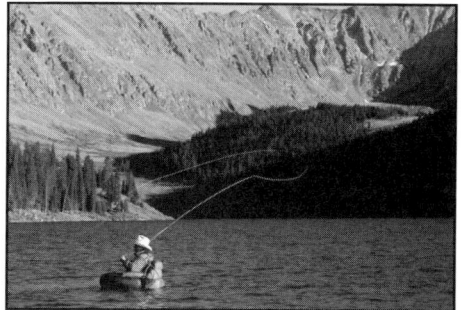

9.5 HOW DOES ONE ORGANISE SUCH A TOUR?

The organisation of a sports tour is illustrated in Figure 9.2.

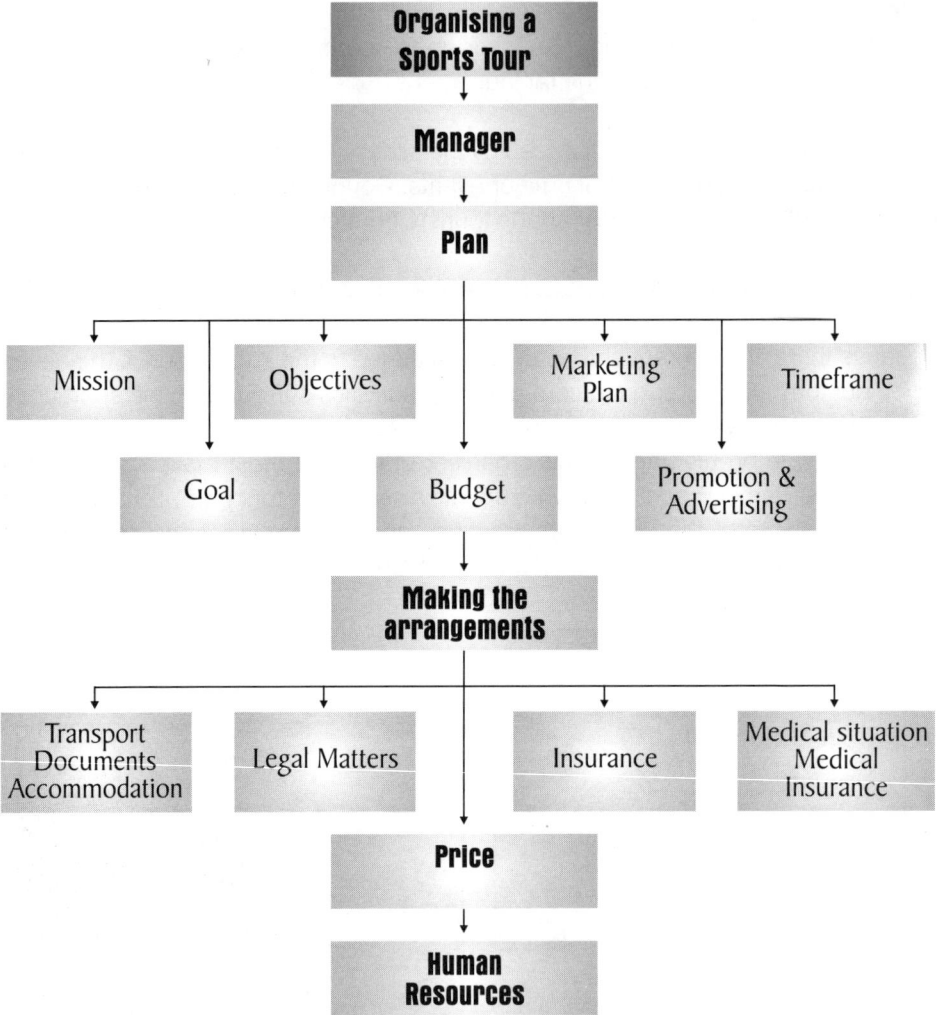

Figure 9.2: The process of organising a sports tour

The aspects of a Sports tour are discussed in the paragraphs below.

9.5.1 Manager

When deciding to be in charge of organising a sports tour, a few management skills have to be in place. These include certainty of facts, administration skills, motivation skills and a drive to success, marketing, and organisation skills. This person needs to keep track of all activities taking place.

9.5.2 Plan

First you (the tour manager) must have a plan to work with and which will act as a framework throughout the organisation of the tour, the tour itself and as evaluation for your success. The framework will consist of a few basic factors. These include your mission, goals, objectives, budget and marketing plan.

- **A Mission**

  The mission emphasises the purpose of the organisation and what it wants to achieve.

  For example:

  The business of African Sports Tours and Safaris is to provide a high quality Sports Tour for national and international tourist while touring through South Africa and foreign countries.

- **A Goal**

  A goal is a detailed statement. The goal must contain key words that describe the main thrust of the business. From the key words you will develop your objectives which will be discussed in detail.

  For example:

  Providing a high quality sports tour for the national and international tourist.

- **Objectives**

  By studying the goal you identify key words and discuss the information you as manager want to achieve by providing the service the key words describe.

  The key words in the goal may, for example, be :

  1. High quality
  2. Sports Tour
  3. Touring South Africa
  4. Foreign countries
  5. National tourist
  6. International tourist

The next step is to formulate objectives in line with every key word, for example:

1. **High quality**
   - Arrange well organised and well-planned tours.
   - Provide a professional service .
   - Recognise clients' interests, so they can enjoy themselves.
   - Provide interesting and factual information.
   - Behave with integrity and in a professional manner.
   - Handle people and situations objectively.
   - Good communication.
   - A well formed strategy.
   - Well trained staff.

2. **Sports Tour**
   - Experiencing sport and facilities.
   - Providing opportunities involving sport.
   - Answering the needs of the sports tourists.
   - Providing alternative entertainment.
   - Providing structure.
   - Providing sport systems.

3. **Touring South Africa**
   - Providing comfortable transport, in air-conditioned vehicles, with enough space.
   - High-quality accommodation during the tour.
   - Providing trained personnel, including registered Satour tourist guides.
   - Providing trained first-aid personnel, with a fully equipped first-aid kit.

4. **Touring foreign countries**
   - Providing comfortable transport, in air-conditioned vehicles, with enough space.
   - High-quality accommodation during the tour.
   - Providing trained personnel, including registered Satour tourist guides.
   - Providing trained first-aid personnel, with a fully equipped first-aid kit.
   - Taking care of all the arrangements regarding the tour.
   - Giving the necessary information to tourist.

5. **National and international tourists**
   - Accommodating local as well as foreign tourist interests and needs.
   - Other objectives.
     The objectives must be very detailed and formulated in such a manner that

they should comply with the SMART principle. The latter stands for:
Specific
Measurable
Attainable
Realistic
T imebound.

- **Budget**
  In order to determine whether you have sufficient funds to take and organise a sports tour, you must determine what you need, and a cost analysis must be done. Without proper planning the sports tour will eventually lead to financial ruin.

- **Marketing Plan**
  Decide who do you want to take on the tour? Who are your target market: the sportsmen, the spectators, the businessmen in sport, young people, old people, South Africans or foreigners? Do you organise the tour in collaboration with a big sports event where the focus is not on the tourists themselves but on the major event?

  Select your target market and be specific. You will have more success in developing a product for a specific market than in competing with people who have been in the business a long time. Determine the need of tourists or the market and then develop your product accordingly. If you do it the other way round, it may end up in a disaster.

  Once you have the plan, you must get the tourists. Market research for any kind of service or product is often missjudged, but it is very important for the basic knowledge of your service and your competitors. If the market allows a place for you, a marketing plan has to be developed. The plan will discuss the following aspects.

- **Target marketing**
  Develop the services you plan to offer. It is good to specialise rather than to try and do everything. Make your product more appealing to your target market.

  It is recommended that you establish the following before you decide on a specific category by doing market research:

- Who are your competitors in the field?
- Is there a need for your product (tour)?
- Are there similar products/tours on the market?
- What is your market potential percentage-wise?
- Which market segment do you want to target?
  - Low income, affordable, budget holidays.
  - Average, quality tours, middle income groups.
  - High quality, expensive tours (5-star treatment), wealthy clients.
- Families, congress delegates, etc.

- **Promotion and advertising**
  Advertising and promotion are sales tools that tourist organisations can utilise to sell tour packages and tour experience. These activities continually strive to build the business's identity and image. The tourist identifies with the business image if the message presented is clear, consistent and regularly brought to their attention. Advertising and promotion are worthwhile investments which significantly impact on the success of any tourism business. It is also important to get professional advice on market planning and promotions. South Africa is currently experiencing a major shortage in this field.

  ### Publicity
  If the message is not paid for, it is not considered as advertising and becomes a form of publicity or public relations.

  Advertising and publicity share two common goals:
  - To communicate clearly with people in order that they understand exactly what you mean.
  - To communicate with people in a way that will make them respond to your communication.

  ### Advertising
  Advertising is an investment. To receive the benefits of that investment, the appropriate financial commitment must be made in terms of the advertising budget. Regardless of how much is allocated for advertising, the most important factor is to make the advertising successful. This is a message that is paid for by an identified sponsor in a recognised advertising medium, such as a magazine, newspaper, etc.

  ### Advertising message
  The development of the advertising message may be the most important

aspect of advertising. The focus of the message must be directed at the needs of potential members. The possible messages must be rated on four factors:

➡ Desirability.
➡ Exclusiveness.
➡ Trustworthiness.
➡ Honesty.

The following are questions to be considered when developing the advertising message:

• Who is the receiver of the message?
• What are the best media to reach that receiver?
• What times are the best to reach the receiver?
• Where are the possible tourists you want to reach?
• What does the business have to offer the tourist?
• What types of services can the income group you have chosen afford?
• How can you get them to respond to he offer?

Additionally, each time you send a message, you must keep in mind that there are certain things which the tourist/receiver does not know. These include:

• Who you are;
• What your business does;
• What your service is;
• Where you are located;
• What you want to give to the tourist;
• Where they can contact you;
• What you are offering;
• What it is going to cost them; and
• What makes you different and worthwhile.

Keeping the message and tourist/receiver in mind will assist you in producing a desirable message and successful advertisement.

• **Time frame**
    When you just plan to organise a sports tour, for instance a dive tour to the islands, your timing will be dependent on the perfect weather for diving. In the choice of a major event, timing is important because the success of the event

also depends on variables like air tickets, accommodation, and transport that needs to be planned in advance. For events like the Olympic Games, accommodation facilities are fully booked 6 months up to a year prior to the games.

9.5.3   Making the arrangements

In the following paragraphs aspects of the arrangements for a sports tour are discussed.

- **Transport**
  Organising transport involves the arranging of the air tickets, inbound and outbound, and the transport when visiting a foreign country. With transport confirmation is extremely important. You as the manager of the tour have to make sure that the entire group of tourists' air tickets are correct and have the right time, date and place. The groups transport overseas can be managed by yourself, or you could contract the tour out to a local tour operator.

- **Documents**
  Always check the documents. Start with your tourists: their air tickets, copies of their passports, medical insurance, special medical conditions, and copies of the signed contracts with you.

  Keep a folder with all the written confirmations with accommodation facilities, tour operators, transport companies and the flight arrangements, to use as proof when necessary.

- **Accommodation**
  When booking accommodation abroad, make sure to give the full names of your tourist and all the information of your company. Make sure to get confirmation of your booking of rooms, with the correct number of people and the discount you get on making a group booking.

- **Legal matters**
  Operating a business in the tourism industry one is dependent on a number of important relationships. These include airlines, tour operators, product owners, cruise lines and car rental companies, who are the principals, and the retail travel agency or the tourist himself, who is the consumer or agent.

  There is a close relationship between the principals and the agent. The authorised acts of an agent will bind the principal as if the principal himself had carried out such acts.

In order to maintain a good relationship, there must be proper contracts to protect the principal, the agent, the tourist, and the business. The matter of contract liability of a principal and agent to each other and to clients is, perhaps the most important legal aspect of the agency concept.

*   **Insurance**
    To take people overseas or on tour in your own country is a very risky undertaking, because every day you are faced with different circumstances that can threaten your business and you as an individual. Not to have sufficient insurance is to gamble on the chances that you will never become ill, get sued, or get robbed. To invest in insurance can contribute to your agency's soundness and prosperity. Insurance will reduce the uncertainty under which you operate. Another benefit of having insurance is that it makes it easier to sell the business if you wish to do so in the future.

    > **Medical insurance**
    > Medical insurance is specified in terms of medical conditions, and is important when touring with people with poor medical coverage. Free insurance is usually included in the price of air tickets which are paid for by credit card.

    > **Medical situation**
    > When going on a tour it is important to know the medical conditions of your tourists in order to prepare yourself for any situation that may occur regarding an illness. You as the manager have the right to admit certain people to the tour but to exclude others.

9.5.4   Price

Along with product, price tends to be the key component of strategy. One of the factors that are going to make you competitive in the market, is the price of your tour, and what is included or excluded in the price. You will have to shop around for the best prices. Aspects like accommodation, air tickets, transport, entrance fees, etc. have to be negotiated. Your prices must be competitive but also give you the highest profit margin.

9.5.5 Human Resources

Planning a tour takes time and organisation. There are different tasks to complete and time are essential because of the last minute arrangements that have to be made before departure. To be successful in all of these activities, one needs a team that can work together and make things run smoothly.

Human resources is an important component in planning for the tour. Administration is essential and because of the large amount of cash involved and all the arrangements involved, a well-organised administration system must be in place. You as manager must have an administrator you can trust for this important function.

A well-trained marketer must be appointed to run a well-planned marketing campaign, to ensure that enough tourists will attend the tour.

The manager may have a personal assistant to recheck everything, to make sure that everything runs smoothly. The appointing of staff is the choice of the tour manager himself and will differ from one person to another.

9.5.6 Examples of Sports Tours

Suggested Golf Tour Itinerary :
(Places : Mumbai/ Calcutta/ Guwahati/ Shillong/ New Delhi)

Day- 01	International flight to Mumbai.
Day-02	On arrival transfer to hotel. Afternoon drive to Presidency Golf Club for a round of golf.
Day-03	City sightseeing. After lunch drive to Presidency Golf Club for another round of golf.
Day-04	Flight to Calcutta. After lunch there is time for some more golf at the Tollygunge Golf Club
Day-05	Drive to Tollygunge Golf Club for golf. Afternoon city sightseeing.
Day-06	Flight to Guwahati. Drive straight to Shillong. Evening is free for a stroll in the scenic city.
Day-07	Full day at Shillong Golf Club
Day-08	Sightseeing of Shillong. Afternoon drive to Shillong Golf Club.
Day-09	Drive to Guwahati. Afternoon sightseeing of Guwahati with a stroll in the tea gardens
Day-10	Flight to Delhi. Afternoon drive to Delhi Golf Club for a round of golf. Overnight in hotel.
Day-11	Sight seeing of New Delhi. Afternoon to Delhi Golf Club.
Day-12	Sightseeing of Old Delhi. Afternoon drive to Army Golf Club.
Day-13	Drive to Army Golf Club. Rest of the day at leisure. Drive to Delhi Golf

Club for a final round of golf. Afternoon free for Shopping or relax.
Day-14   In time transfer to airport to connect flight back home.

Horizons Sports
14 day hosted tour Durban to Sun City. A golfing and wildlife experience of a lifetime! Quality accommodation, First-class golf courses with daily competitions and regular trips to fantastic game reserves.

Day 1
Monday May 7th 2001 and
Wednesday September 5th 2001.
(NOTE: Previous September itinerary now changed.
Golf and Game Safari to start in September 2002)
Depart with South African Airways from Sydney, London or New York for Durban, South Africa.

Day 2
Arrive Durban approximately 9:30 am. Collect minibus and drive to Durban beachfront hotel. Day to relax. Optional golf at Mt Edgecombe available on request. Welcome dinner and overnight at Umhlanga Protea.

Day 3
Breakfast at the hotel.
11.00AM: Golf at Zimbali. (incl. m/carts)
A new Tom Weiskopf 5 star course. This new resort is so nice we will certainly stay for drinks at the club. Dinner tonight at local restaurant The Lord Prawn.
O/N: Umhlanga Protea.

Day 4
Early breakfast at the hotel.
10.00AM: Golf at Princes Grant. (m/carts) As a small extra you may also have caddy to guide you around the course and "ball spot" Private course in the middle of the sugar cane field area owned by local millionaires. After golf visit a Zulu village. See Zulu dancing & crafts.
Dinner and overnight at Shakaland.

Day 5
Breakfast at Shakaland. Drive north to Hluhluwe. PM game drive in Umfolozi Game Reserve with ranger. Dinner and overnight at Zulu Nyala Game Lodge.

Day 6
Another game drive before breakfast at Nyala and continuing thru the border into Swaziland. Maybe time to visit nearby local craft "stalls". O/N: Ezulweni Sun

Day 7
Breakfast at Ezulweni. Morning sightseeing. Visit African glass blowing factory and Swazi craft markets. Time to change some money in Mbabane
12.00PM: Golf at Royal Swazi.
We use local caddies on this course. (cost not incl) An "old school" course. After golf try your luck at the casino! Dinner at international restaurant Kalabash.
O/N: Ezulweni Sun.

Day 8
Breakfast at Ezulweni. Drive north east to the edge of Kruger National Park. Five star African style Intercontinental hotel/lodge overlooking the Crocodile River and the Kruger National Park.
O/N: Malelane Lodge.

Day 9
Early breakfast at the lodge. Drive into Kruger National Park from Malelane Gate to Paul Kruger Gate. This covers the most animal intense south western section of the park. Break at Skukuza. Continue to our private game reserve in the Sabi Sands area. Lunch on arrival and evenng game drive with ranger. Dinner in the boma. Full board while we are here.
O/N: Idube Game Lodge.

Day 10
Breakfast at Idube. AM/PM game drives. Midday game walk. This will be your full "African safari" experience to remember forever. The "Big Five": elephant, rhino, Cape buffalo, lion and leopard are here waiting for you. O/N: Idube.

Day 11
Early morning game drive then breakfast at Idube. Continue on to Pretoria via The Panorama Drive and Pilgrims Rest. (an original 1800's gold mining town) Stopover at motel during long drive west.
O/N: East Pretoria Motel.

Day 12
Breakfast at motel.
10.00AM: Golf at Pecanwood.
A new Jack Nicklaus "Signature" resort course. M/carts included. A new addition to

our itinerary and highly recommended. Continue to Sun City. Plenty to do here with casino and wall to wall activities. You are free to do your own thing here just turn up on time for your golf.
O/N: The Cabanas.

Day 13
Breakfast at Cabanas.
8.30AM: Golf at The Gary Player Club.
An international quality course using local caddies. Bring your camera for the baboons on the 12th. M/carts not included as you may choose to use a caddy. Competition presentation night at the Cabanas Bar.
O/N: The Cabanas.

Day 14
Breakfast at The Cabanas.
10.00AM: Golf at The Lost City. (m/carts)
A special course to complete our tour. Since restructuring and turfing late 1999 this is now a top quality course. The famous 13th bunker (full of crocodiles) is not the place to retrieve your balls! Optional alternative game drive into Pilanesberg National Park available @ apx $25.
3.00PM transfer by minibus to Johannesburg for flight home... or...

9.6   CONCLUSION

This chapter discussed the aspects that are important for planning a sports tour. The author of this chapter is also a tour operator who has been involved in numerous tours and, more specifically in the planning of these tours. The chapter addressed various issues, for example the type of sport the tours is aimed at. This will determine the target market, the place where the activity will be hosted and the planning process.

In order for a tour operator to make a success of the tour, it is important that planning should be done properly. Eventually a lack of planning will lead to financial losses.

Chapter 10

Key success factors for a sports tourist destination

*It is our responsibility to struggle firmly to convince world leaders that to hold
sport as a hostage only serves to create new sources of conflict, for thus we lose
irrevocably one of the greatest opportunities open to us to meet in a friendly
manner and to seek mutual understanding.*

M.Saayman & C van Niekerk
Evaluating the 2004 Olympic Bid document

10.1 INTRODUCTION

Saayman & Van Niekerk (1996) argue that specific requirements for the
development of a sports programme, including the future objectives of the city and
the country, urban planning, and respect for the environment, are all factors which
should be considered in planning a sports event. The question that often comes to
mind is what makes one city more attractive or better for sports events than others.
It is also important to determine how a city can go about in attracting sports tourists;
thus to identify the key success factors. The aim of this chapter is to determine
these key success factors for a sports tourist destination, particularly from the
perspective of participants who are training and competing. The reason for this is
that spectators follow competitors and events. The competitors also normally stay
for longer periods if they are using a specific destination as a training ground. Hence
their spending is greater.

According to **Halsall (1997)** a community must have objectives in hosting events.
He suggest the following ten objectives:

* To upgrade cultural activity in the community.
* To attract tourists.
* To involve the community in a civic celebration.
* To develop popular participation in arts, crafts, sports and athletics.
* To advance and promote the community for public benefit.
* To promote cultural and political exchange.
* To create or strength a spirit of goodwill between the community's social or ethnic
  groups.
* To promote the utilisation of tourist facilities in the off season.
* To call public attention to the unique characteristics or attractions of the
  community.
* To earn revenue that can be used to provide a needed but otherwise unattainable

social benefit for the community.

These objectives may be regarded as the backbone of a programme to stage events which will have a worthwhile impact on the economy of a city. Eventually these events should contribute financially to the wellbeing of the residents of a city.

10.2 DIFFERENT VIEWS ON SPORTS TOURISM

Mega-project developments, which now often include adjacent convention centres, worldclass hotels and spectacular new facilities for upscale shopping, normally involve large public subsides to large private developers. Far from being contentious, though, such "public/private partnerships" are becoming standard practice in what geographer **David Harvey (1989)** has called "the entrepreneurial city".

Mega-project developments have increased the stakes in the competitions among cities to be centres of cultural significance and have increased the importance of civic image in competitions for other kinds of growth.

The different views on sports tourism will be discussed under the following sub-headings, namely:

- Civic Boosterism
- Sport news: The creation of Continental Audiences
- Civic Ambition: The pursuit of National Status
- Federal Spending Local Interest: The Politics of Sports Facilities
- Tourism, Globalisation, and the New Entrepreneurial City
- Cities and Their Dreams: Who participates in "World Class"?

➢ Civic Boosterism

Boosterism, as a collective effort on the part of local leaders (business leaders as well as politicians) to "sell" prospective businesses and residents on the advantages of locating in their town rather than somewhere else, has a long history across the Canadian and American west. In such circumstances, local leaders vigorously promoted any sporting event or other leisure attraction that promised to bring their town to the attention of potential investors and visitors (**Voisey, 1988**).

In the early 1900s, however, local boosters soon found that sports teams, especially successful ones, were among the surest ways of attracting attention to their communities. **Betke (1983)** shows that local politicians and business leaders in Edmonton were quick to see the potential of professional sport for putting their city on the map.

Therefore it is important to make the citizens and local leaders of a city aware of this big group of foreign athletes who visit our town, and the benefits they contribute to our community.

➢ Sports News: The creation of Continental Audiences

From the media point of view, news consists of events which can be recognised and interpreted as drama. The drama most easily packaged for everyday consumption seems to be the drama of recognisable individuals: that is to say, of regulars, of celebrities, of stars (**Gitlin, 1980:146-147**).

It is useful to think here of sports coverage as constituting, cumulatively, a "shared information system" (**Meyrowitz, 1985**) that enables its audiences to follow and be knowledgeable about sports and to feel members of a wider community that is connected precisely by virtue of its shared interest in sports. In each of the professional sports, it is precisely this sports information system that allows people in far-flung towns and cities to feel an ongoing sense of membership in a community of fans. Furthermore, it is useful to recognise that in this sports information system, the primary coverage-game broadcasts, game reports, and statistics constitutes only a small part of the story. The cumulative effect of all of this sports information and imagery is the ubiquitous presence of professional sports in contemporary popular culture.

➢ Civic Ambition: The pursuit of National Status

Attracting major league sports franchises as well as other world-class entertainment events (e.g. international fairs and film festival) was important in the symbolism of these campaigns. With respect to major league sport this has typically meant putting considerable public money into a "state of the art" facility and offering a variety of other concessions and tax breaks that provide further opportunities for profitability for franchise owners (**Whitson & Macintosh, 1993:226**).

➢ The Politics of Sports Facilities

One of the most explicit goals of major games, usually, is that they leave a legacy of athletic facilities that will be important additions to the host city and will foster the development of sport, there and beyond. The first of these pertains to arenas and stadia that may be important additions to the host city as venues for spectacular sport or high-performance training centres, but whose very size and sophistication make them unsuitable for community use. The facility standards that are required for international sports competitions are required for international sports competitors are typically well beyond the needs and skills of recreational participants (**Whitson & Macintosh, 1993:230**).

Much more important than the sports legacy, for the purposes of our analysis, though, are the direct and indirect economic benefits which are supposed to accrue to a city as a result of hosting an international event (**Whitson & Macintosh, 1993:230**).

In addition, games are often the occasion for spending on urban infrastructure and, again, for more support for such projects from senior levels of government than is normally forthcoming. **Ley and Old's (1988)** history of world's fairs suggests that hallmark events have always provided cities with opportunities to get significant senior government funding for major transportation projects and other kinds of urban improvements. A best chance of attracting federal funds for such projects was deemed to be including them in a package associated with staging a world fair.

> **Tourism, Globalisation, and the New Entrepreneurial City**
A particular kind of economic strategy, of course, is bound up with tourism. **Hall (1989,263)** has proposed that the primary objective of hallmark events is to provide the host community with opportunities to secure greater prominence in the international tourism marketplace. In case of international games, events of much shorter duration than world fairs, the crucial challenge is to boost tourism in subsequent years by increasing international awareness of the destination. Unless this "destination image" is achieved, neither the public expenditures previously outlined nor private investments in new hotels, restaurants, and so forth can be recouped in the few weeks surrounding the event itself.

In addition to prospective tourists themselves, moreover, an important audience for this promotional imagery is the international tourism industry: the hotel chains and tour companies and airlines whose decisions to invest in and promote an area are what turn a good local destination into an international resort (**Whitson & Macintosh, 1993:232**). In the case of Vancouver, tourism and immigration are clearly factors in that city's dramatic growth in the late 1980's and thus its booming property values.

Cities must today compete for factories that as a result of technology and corporate integration are now much less tied to place (**Harvey, 1987:263**). They must also compete for governmental redistribution's: regional administration functions, universities, and research facilities (**Logan & Molotch, 1987**), as well as the kinds of senior government investments in tourism and cultural facilities that we have examined. They must compete for position as centres of financial and information services: head offices, advertising and public relations services, and the burgeoning management and technical consulting sectors.

The result, **Harvey (1989)** suggests, is that every city has to present itself as a dynamic and exciting place to live, play, and consume. However, the largest factor, again, in the competition to be centres of consumption, is the phenomenal growth of tourism.

Some cities already had well-known cultural or natural attractions. However, many less "attractive" cities, whose original downtown economics were built more around manufacturing and other kinds of commerce than culture and tourism, have built the modern stadia and concert halls and the upscale shopping complexes and hotels that can help them compete for conventions and other special events.

Harvey (1989, 288:295) also insists that as competition in image building became widely perceived as a key factor in the competition among cities, investments in image building (in arts, sports, etc.) became as important as investment in other kinds of infrastructure. Hence, there are a succession of spectacular stadia and concert halls, and a striving of many cities to force an image that would attract "capital and people of the right sort" (1989, 288:295)

Carmichael (1993:94) noted that "[...] Gradually, a potential tourist builds up an image of a destination. The image may be stereotyped and vary greatly from reality but it reflects an individual's personal evaluations and expectations of place."Major investments in "place identity" have only short-lived effects, and world-class comes more and more to mean simply the standards of facility and the kinds of entertainment that are expected anywhere by affluent international travellers (**Whitson & Macintosh, 1993:236**).

➢ Cities and Their Dreams: Who Participates in "World Class"?

In the case of professional teams, the annual cycles of predictions, trade talk, game discussion, and post-mortems contribute to an ongoing "buzz" of sports talk that enlivens the life of a city.

The development of the world-class city can be said to widen the gaps between the affluent residents and tourists for whom attendance at world-class entertainment is part of their lifestyle; those whose lives mostly take place a long way from downtown, except perhaps as service workers.

One needs to recognise the different interests that people at all levels of society take in these events, and indeed, the ways in which identities today are commonly constructed through leisure interests and consumer choices: clothes, movies, and music, as well as sports (**Willis, 1989**).

One is invited by promotional culture to believe that the best cities are ones that offer the famous names in entertainment and shopping, and that one is part of something important simply by living there (**Whitson & Macintosh, 1993:221-239**).

10.3 DETERMINING THE KEY SUCCESS FACTORS FOR A SPORTS TOURIST DESTINATION

The following factors play a role in becoming a sport tourist destination.

Factor conditions for a destination

The factor conditions are given through factor endowments, factor prices as well as qualities and production efficiency. An inefficient use of factors will cause mobile factors to migrate towards destinations or countries which have a higher production in tourism. The relative abundance of these resources seems to play an important role in explaining a destination's position in international tourism.

There are three categories of factor endowments:

* Natural and cultural resources,
* Capital and infrastructure resources and
* Human resources.

Natural resources consist of landscape, rivers, lakes, beaches, climate, geographical location, population, raw material, etc. Examples of cultural and historical resources are monuments, historical cities, customs, works of art, cultural heritage and attitudes, art collections.

International tourism needs developed infrastructures, suprastructures, transport system, accommodation, area and site development. Thus, the capital stock of a country or destination as well as the domestic and international investment potential heavily influence the competitiveness of the destination in question.

The human resources endowment of a country is defined through the skill level of its workforce, which in turn determines the country international competitive position. The availability of skilled labour influences tourism flows and their geographical distribution according to the specialisation of the destination and the mobility of the workers. Therefore, the lack of skilled destination or hotel and restaurant managers forces countries with a relative low education level to employ managers, who have been trained abroad.

The combination of the three factor endowments forms the basis for the competitive position of the destination. It corresponds to the theoretical model of factor endowments as applied in foreign trade theory (**Smeral, 1994**).

The factors most important to the competitive advantage of a destination or country are not inherited but created. Thus, the stock of existing factors is less important than the rate at which they are created, upgraded and specialised. For that reason an abundance of factors may have a negative instead of a positive influence on competitive advantage. Thus, if there are competitive factor creation mechanisms, selective disadvantages in factors will often contribute to the competitive success in tourism.

A checklist for the key success factors of a sport tourist destination
According to **Keenen (1995:25)** service is a vital factor for repeat business. Sports events have the potential to improve the awareness and image of the hosting city or country as an international tourist destination (**Kang & Perdue, 1994:205**). Tourism products can be tangible or intangible, and the quality of these products can increase or decrease the feelings of enjoyment and comfort of the tourist (**Botha & Saayman, 1995:53**).

This play an important role in the tourist's perceived experience of the host community. The quality of the sports tourism products and services that are offered are essential, because satisfied tourist will spread the positive image and they are very likely to return to the destination. **Botha & Saayman, (1995:53)** noted that it should be the object to make the tourist's dream reality so that the planning, anticipation and memories of the visit also contribute to the enjoyment of the trip.

To be able to determine the key success factors a checklist was set up. Sources which were used to set up this checklist was **Saayman & Van Niekerk, (1996)** and **Ritchie and Zins, (1978)**.

Primary factors: Transport, accommodation, entertainment and attractions (facilities) can be regarded as the primary components of the tourism industry. However, entertainment is a secondary factor for a sport tourist destination and climate is a primary factor. All components of the tourism industry are interdependent of each other and function in totality. These components form the heart of the tourism industry (**Saayman, 1997:20**).

Secondary factors: These have an indirect, yet determining influence. It must be emphasised that the listed aspects are not the only ones. Further aspects can be distinguished, but for the purpose of this study these will be suffice (**Saayman, 1997:21**).

The following checklist will be used to evaluate a sport tourist destination.

Table 10.1: Checklist for the key success factors of a sports tourist destination

PRIMARY	SCORE	SECONDARY	SCORE
Sport and training facilities		Political situation	
Accommodation		Management/ service	
Transportation		Media and broadcasting	
Climate		Marketing (well known)	
Location		Security/ safety	
		Altitude	
		Natural beauty	
		Cultural and social characteristics	
		Hospitality	
		Infrastructure of destination	
		Shopping facilities	
		Recreation/Entertainment facilities	
		Educational facilities	
		Image	
		Accessibility of destination	
		Price levels (value for money)	
TOTAL		TOTAL	

AVERAGE PERCENTAGE...............................

GRADE...

Explanation of the checklist scoring method:
The above are the most important aspects identified by sports tourists themselves.

A score will be given for each aspect/factor according this rating scale:
Very good = 5 points
Good = 4 points
Average = 3 points
Bad = 2 points
Very bad = 1 point

For example; The results of an empirical research will be used where all the aspects reflected in Table 10.1 have been evaluated. The factor under discussion is entertainment. The respondents have to rate the entertainment using the rating scale of Very good, Good, Average, Bad and Very bad.

The results for entertainment was   Very good -4%   Good -19%
Average -69%   Bad - 17%

The highest score, namely average 69%, which represent 3 points, will be allocated to entertainment.

PRIMARY FACTORS
Sport and training facilities
The most important aspect or key success factor is the quality of sport and training facilities. These include organisations, change rooms, medical facilities, swimming pools, grass and tartan tracks, courts and fields and running space to mention a few. These facilities should be properly maintained in a conducive environment. Therefore there should be low levels of pollution and not too many people using the facilities (overcrowding). Training facilities should not be far apart which waste a lot of time.

Accommodation
A variety of accommodation at a reasonable price is very important.

Transportation
There should be transport opportunities if one does not possess a vehicle. This include opportunities to visit tourist attractions or to go shopping. If tourists can move about more easily, it increases the score.

Climate
Climate and height above sea level are important. Athletes prefer stable weather, which implies that it should be not too cold or too hot.

Location
Most of the aspects above are influenced by the location of the city or training facilities. This implies having good weather, and being situated not too far from other major cities or attractions where major sport events are taking place. Location plays a role in the accessibility of the town or city as well as the natural environment. Open space is also important here.

SECONDARY ASPECTS
These include the following:

Political situation
The region or country should be politically stable, otherwise it creates a safety risk.

Management/service
Tourists are mindful of how facilitators are managed as well as how their arrangements were handled. Another aspect is the level of service in the country. Service is crucial for tourist.

Media and broadcasting
The level of media coverage that sports tourists will get is important, for the more coverage they get, the better the opportunity to attract major sponsorships.

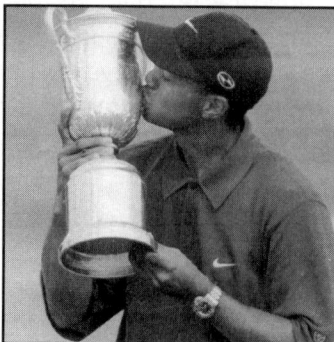

Marketing
This aspect goes hand in hand with media and broadcasting. It also includes the quality of a destination's promotion.

Security/safety
Tourists all over the world are influenced by the level of crime, or lack in safety. If it is not safe, they will not go to a destination which implies a loss of income for international athletes especially.

Altitude
Altitude has already been explained. Some sport are positively affected by a high level above sea. Other activities benefit more if facilities are closer to the coast for example long distance running. Therefore targeting the right activities is also important.

Natural beauty
Natural beauty is very important, although it is sometimes downplayed. If the area is beautiful, it creates an environment to which people want to train.

Cultural and social characteristics
These aspects are important from a tourism point of view because sports tourists do not only train and participate, but they are also tourist in the full sense of the word. Sport tourists therefore also want to be exposed to other cultures and cultural activities.

Hospitality
This aspect goes hand in hand with quality service, which implies friendliness and helpful people.

Infrastructure of destination
Basic infrastructure (therefore roads, transport systems, communication systems etc.) makes a sports tourist's life easier if it is up to standard. Fax, e-mail, internet, and telephone services should be seen as basic infrastructure.

Shopping facilities
Tourists like to shop and sports tourists are no exeption to the rule.Ttherefore these facilities are important to them. They are also important if one wants to create wealth by giving tourists the opportunity to spend money.

Recreation and entertainment

The argument stressed in the previous aspect is relevant to recreation and entertainment facilities as well. It is no good if a destination has the best training facilities but no entertainment. Athletes need to relax and to do other activities.

Educational facilities

Some sports tourist visit a destination for periods of up to a year. Then they would also want to continue their education and training. If these facilities are offered the destination gets a higher score.

Image

Image is a perception that tourist have of a place and is influenced by a number of factors, for example word-of-mouth, media, and personal experiences. A positive image contributes to a better score and perception that the destination is well worth visiting.

Accessibility of destination

This aspect has already been dealt with under topics such as transportation and location.

Price levels

Value for money is increasingly becoming more important. South Africa has a major advantage in terms of foreign exchange, compared to countries in Europe and America. Value for money also plays a role in the pricing of goods and services at the destination.

Once all these aspects were given a score, the following process needs to be followed.

* A percentage will be determined for the primary and secondary factors.
* Determine the average for further use.
  Average = Percentage of primary factors + percentage of secondary factors ÷ 2
* Lastly a grade will be given to the sport tourism destination by using the average percentage of the primary and secondary factors.

The grades are interpreted as follows:

Grade A: 80-100%   -   Very good sports tourist destination
Grade B: 70-79%   -   Good sports tourist destination
Grade C: 60- 69%   -   Average sports tourist destination

Grade D: 50- 59%   -   Bad sports tourist destination

Grade E: 40-0%   -   Very bad sports tourist destination

10.4   CONCLUSION

This chapter addressed a very important aspect, namely what it takes to become a sports tourist destination. The key success factors were identified. Some sport tourists destinations are known internationally, whilst others are battling to get recognition. This chapter was based on research done in order to determine the key success factors as identified by the competitors themselves. It gives guidelines for activities to evaluate themselves in order to see if they fit the profile.

Bibliography

AHN, J., VAR, T. & YONG-KWAN, K. 1989. An Investigation of Olympic Tourists' Perception of Korea. Study on Tourism, 13. Seoul, Korea: The Korea Academic Society of Tourism. (In Kang, Y.S & Perdue, R. 1994. Long-term impact of a mega-event on international tourism to the host country: a conceptual model and the case of the 1988 Seoul Olympics. Binghamton, New York: The Howard Press Inc.)

ALKOV, R.A. 1988. Chronic stress as a factor in aircraft mishaps. (In Comstock, J.R. ed. Mental-state estimation, 1987: proceedings of a workshop sponsored by the National Aeronautics and Space Administration, Washington, D.C., and Old Dominion University, Norfolk, Virginia, and held in Williamsburg, Virginia, June 3-4, 1987. (NASA Conference publication 2504.))

ANON. 1989. Comrades marathon: running into profit. Financial Mail: May 26.

ANON. 1995. Work Harder for Tourists. Finance Week : 5 Apr. 27.

ANON. 1997. Kanse Bekyk om in Toerisme te Belê. [Available on Internet] http://www.naspers.com/cgi/nph-bwcgis/
.

ANON. 1997. Olimpiese Blaps. Rapport : 22, Sptember. 7.

ANON. 1997. SA Spele-projekte gaan voort. [Available on Internet] http://www.naspers.com/cgi/nph-bwcgis/ (26.01.98).

ANON (a). 1999. Olympic History. [Web:] http://no-idea.com/Olympichistory.html

ANON (b). 1999. Olympic Games. [Web:] http://www.washingtonpost.com/wp.stv/sports/olympics/longterm/summer96.htm

ANDERSON, R.E. 1973. Relationship between sensation seeking and academic achievement, school attendance, academic ability, and alcohol use. Alberta : University of Alberta. (Thesis-MA).

ARNETT, J. 1991. Heavy metal music and reckless behavior among adolescents. Journal of youth and adolescence, 20:573-592.

BABBITT, T., ROWLAND, G.L. & FRANKEN, R.E. 1990. Sensation seeking and participation in aerobic exercise classes. Personality and individual differences, 11(2):181-183.

BAILEY, K.G., BURNS, D.S. & BAZAN, L.C. 1982. A method for measuring "primitive" and "advanced" elements in pleasures and aversions. Journal of personality assessment, 46:639-646.

BAKER, A.H. 1988. Sensation seeking and field independence. Journal of human behaviour, 25(2):44-49.

BAUDRILLED, J. 1970. La sociéte de consommation, ses mythes, ses structures. Paris, Denoël. (In: Piggeassou, C. 1997. Sport and tourism: the emergence of sport into the offer of tourism: between passion and reason. [Available on Internet] http://www.mcb.co.uk/journals/jst/archive/vol4no2/welcome.htm#BS4

BENNETT, J.A. 1995. Managing Tourism Services. Pretoria : Van Schaik

BENNETT, J.A. 1997. Managing tourism services. 2nd ed. Pretoria: J.L. Van Schaik Publishers.

BERKOWITZ, W.R. 1967. Use of the Sensation-Seeking Scale with Thai subjects. Psychological reports, 20:635-641.

BERLYNE, D.E. 1960. Conflict, arousal and curiosity. New York : McGraw-Hill.

BETKE, C. 1983. Sports promotion in the westhern Canadian city: The example of early Edmonton. Urban History Review, 12(2), 47-56.

BHATIA, A.K. 1983. Tourism Development, New Delhi: Sterling Publishers.

BHATIZ, A.K. 1991. International tourism: Fundamentals and practices. New Delhi: Sterling publishers.

BIERSNER, R.J. & LAROCCO, J.M. 1983. Personality characteristics of US Navy divers. Journal of occupational psychology, 56(4):329-334, Dec.

BIRON, J.E. 1990. A study of sensation-seeking and personality in an extreme-risk sport population. University Microfilms International, Ann Arbor, MICH, 1990, 2 microfiches (162 fr.).

BLACKBURN, R. 1969. Sensation seeking, impulsivity and psychopathic personality.

Journal of consulting and clinical psychology, 33:571-574.

BLENNER, J.L & HAIER, R.J. 1986. Augmenting/reducing assessed by evoked potensials and the Vando scale. Personality and individual differences, 7(6):889-891.

BONE, 1979. Is the streaker a sensation seeker? (In Zuckerman, M. ed. Sensation seeking: beyond the optimal level of arousal. Hillsdale, N.J.: Erlbaum.)

BONE, R.N., MONTGOMERY, D.D. & MCALLISTER, D.S. 1973. The relationship between sensation seeking, sex, family size, and birth order. (In Zuckerman, M. ed. 1994. Behavioral expressions and biosocial bases of sensation seeking. New York : Cambridge University Press.)

BOTHA, C. & SAAYMAN, M. 1995. IMAGE AS AN ASPECT OF STRATEGIC MARKETING. Institute for Tourism and Leisure Studies: Potchefstroom

BOUTER, L.M., KNIPSCHILD, P.G., FEIJ, J.A. & VOLOVICS, A. 1988. Sensation seeking and injury risk in downhill skiing. Personality and individual differences, 9(3):667-673.

BREIVIK, G. 1991. Personality and sensation seeking in risk sport: a summary. Unpublished data.

BRIGUGLIO, L. 1995. Perspectives on tourism policy. New York: Mansell Publishing Limited.

BROHAM, J. 1996. New directions in tourism for third world development. Annuals of Tourism Research, 23(1):56.

BROWN, L.T., RUDER, V.G., RUDER, J.H. & YOUNG, S.D. 1974. Stimulation seeking and the Change Seeker Index. Journal of consulting and clinical psychology, 42(2):311, Apr.

BUKART, A.J. & MEDLIK, S. 1981 Tourism: past, present and future. London: Heinemann.

BURKHART, B.R., SCHWARTZ, R.M. & GREEN, S.B. 1978. Relationships between dimensions of anxiety and sensation seeking. Journal of consulting and clinical psychology, 46(1):194-195, Feb.

BULL, A. 1993. The Economics of Travel and Tourism. Melbourne: Longman Chesire.

BURGAN, B & MILES, T. 1992. Economic impact of sporting events. Annals of Tourism Research. 19 : 700-710

BURNS, J.; HATCH, J. AND MULES, T. 1986. (In Hughes, H.L. 1993. The role of Hallmark Event tourism in Urban regeneration. Manchester Metropolitan University: Manchester: United Kingdom).

CALHOON, L.L. 1988. Explorations in the biochemistry of sensation seeking. Personality and individual differences, 9:941-949.

CARMICHAEL, B. 1993. Using Conjoint Modeling to Measure Tourist Image and Analyse Ski Resort Choice. (In JOHNSON, P. & THOMAS, B. eds. 1993 Choice and Demand in Tourism. New York : Mansell.)

CASSON, L. 1974. Travel in the Ancient World. London. George Allen & Erwin Limited.

CELLINI, H.R. 1982. Cognitive and personality trait differences of youthful offenders by property, violent impulsive, and violent premeditated offense groupings. Carbondale : Southern Illinois University. Dissertation (Ph.D.).

CHADWICK, A. 1994. Consepts, definitions and measures used in travel and tourism research (In Ritchie, J.R.B. & Goeldner, C.R. eds. 1994. Travel, tourism and hospitality research: a handbook for managers and researchers. 2nd ed. USA: John Wiley.

CHERON, E.J. & RITCHIE, J.R.B. 1982. Leisure activities and perceived risk. Journal of leisure research, 14(2):139-154, Second quarter.

CHU, D. 1982. Dimensions of sport studies. New York: Wiley.

COAKLEY, J.J. 1982. Sport in society - issues and controversies. St Louis: C.V. Mosby.

CLEMENT, R. & JONAH, B.A. 1984. Field dependence, sensation seeking and driving behaviour. Personality and individual differences, 5:87-93.

COHEN, L., DINGEMANS, P.M.A.J., LESNIK-OBERSTEIN, M. & VAN DER Vlugt, H. 1983. Report of findings with the sensation seeking scale in Holland. Poster presented at the meeting of the American Psychological Association, Anaheim, CA, August 26.

COLTMAN, M.M. 1988. Introduction to travel and tourism - An international approach. New York: Van Nostrand Reinhold.

CONNOLLY, P.M. 1981. An exploratory study of adults engaging in the high-risk sport of skiing. Netherland : Rutgers University. (Thesis-MA.).

COOPER, C., FLETCHER, J., GILBERT, D. & WANHILL, S. 1997. Tourism-Principles and Practice. Harlow: Addison Wesley Longman Limited.

COUSTEAU, J. 1972. New York Times. (In Zuckerman, M. ed. Sensation seeking and sports. Personality and individual differences, 4(3):285-293.)

CRANDALL, L. 1994. The social impact of tourism on developing regions and its measurement, (In Ritchie, J.R.B. and Goeldner, C.R., eds. Travel, tourism and hospitality research: A handbook for managers and researchers. 2nd ed. USA: New York: Wiley).

CROCKETT, S. 1998. Sport Tourism - Bidding for International Events. [Available on Internet] http://www.mcb.co.uk/journals/jst/archive/vol3no4/bidding.htm

CROMPTON, J.L. 1995. Economic Impact Analysis of Sport Facilities and Events: Eleven Sources of Misapplication. Journal of Sport Management. 9 : 14-35.

CRONIN, C. 1991. Sensation seeking among mountain climbers. Personality and individual differences, 12(6):653-654.

CRONIN, C. & ZUCKERMAN, M. 1992. Sensation seeking and bipolar affective disorder. Personality and individual differences, 13:385-387.

CSIKSZENTIMIHALYI, M. 1975. Beyond boredom and anxiety. San Fransisco: Jossey-Bass.

CULLEN, P. 1997. Economics for hospitality management. United Kingdom: International Thomson Business Press.

DAITZMAN, R.J., ZUCKERMAN, M., SAMMELWITZ, P. & GANJAM, V. 1978. Sensation seeking and gonadal hormones. Journal of biosocial science, 10(4):401-408, Oct.

DEPARTMENT OF THE ENVIRONMENT, 1990. (In Hughes, H.L. 1993. The role of Hallmark event tourism in Urban regeneration. Manchester Metropolitan University: Manchester: United Kingdom).

DUFOUR, R. 1977. "DES Mythes du loisir/tourisme. Week-end: Alienation ou liberation?" these de dectorat. Centre des Hautes Etudes Touristiques: Aix-en-Provence.

DUMAZEDIER, J. 1988. Révolution culturelle du teps libre 1969-1988. Paris, Méridiens Kincksiek. (In: Piggeassou, C. 1997. Sport and tourism: the emergence of sport into the offer of tourism: between passion and reason. [Available on Internet] http://www.mcb.co.uk/journals/jst/archive/vol4no2/welcome.htm#BS4

DURANT, W. & DURANT, A. 1954. Our Oriental Heritage, New York: Simon & Shuster.

EBERSOHN, W. 1995. Sport: the big dress rehearsal. Productivity SA, 21:2, March.

EDWARDS, H. 1973. Definitions and clarifications in sociology of sport. Homewood: illinois: Dorsey.

EMMONS, R.A. 1981. Relationship between narcissism and sensation seeking. Psychological reports, 48(1)247-250, Feb.

EYSENCK, H.J., NIAS, D.K. & COX, D.N. 1982. Sport and personality. advances in behaviour research and therapy, 4:1-56.

FALASSI, A. (ed.). 1987. Time out of time: essays on the festival. Albuquerque: University of New Mexico Press.

FARLEY, F.H. 1967. Social desirability and dimensionality in the Sensation-seeking Scale. Acta psychologia, 26:89-96.

FAYOS-SOLA, E. 1997. The impact of mega-event. Annals of Tourism Research. 25(1):241-244

FIRENZE, B. Sport Tourism Categories. [Available on Internet] http://www.free-press.com/journals/jst/archive/vol3no4/categor.htm (01.04.98).

FLEMMING, W.R. & TOEPPER, L. 1990. Economic impact studies: Relating the positive and negative impacts to tourism development. Journal of Travel Research. Summer 1990: 35-41.

FOWLER, C.J., VON KNORRING, L. & ORELAND, L. 1980. Platelet monoamine oxidase activity in sensation seekers. Psychiatry research, 3:273-279.

FRANKEN, R.E. & ROWLAND, G.L. 1990. Sensation seeking and fantasy. Personality and individual differences, 11:191-193.

FREIXANET, M. 1991. Personality profile of subjects engaged in high physical risk sports. Personality and individual differences, 12(10):1087-1093.

FULKER, D., EYSENCK, S.B.G. & ZUCKERMAN, M. 1980. A genetic and environmental analysis of sensation-seeking. Journal of research in personality, 14:261-282.

FURGUSON, D.G.; STEWART, K.G.; JONES, J.C.H. & LE DRESSAY, C. 1991. The Pricing of Sport Events: Do Teams Maximize Profit? The Journal of Industrial Economics. XXXIX (30) : 207-310.

FURNHAM, A.F. & SAIPE, J. 1993. Personality correlates of convicted drivers. Personality and individual differences, 14:329-336.

GAMMON, S. & ROBINSON, T. 1997. Sport and Tourism: A conceptual framework. [Available on Internet] http://www.mcb.co.uk/journals/jst/archive/vol4no2/welcome.htm#BS4.

GEE, C.Y.; MAKENS, J.C. & CHOY, D.J.L. 1989. The Travel industry. England: Van Nostrand Reinhold.

GERBING, D.W., AHADI, S.A. & PATTON, J.H. 1987. Toward a conceptualization of impulsivity: components across the behavioral and self-report domains. Multivaraite behavioral research, 22(3):357-379, Jul.

GETAWAY'S TOP 10. 1998. Published by Reader's Digest Association South Africa, Strand Street, Cape Town.

GETZ, D. 1994. Event Tourism: Evaluating the Impacts. (In RITCHIE, J.R.B. & GOELDNER, C.R., eds. Travel, Tourism and Hospitality Research : A handbook for managers and researchers. 2nd ed. USA : New York : Wiley.)

GETZ, D. 1995. Event Tourism: Evaluating the impacts. The University of Calgary: Calgary: Alberta.

GIAMBRA, L.M. 1977. Adult male daydreaming across the life-span: a replication; further analyses and tentative norms based upon retrospective reports. International journal of aging and human development, 8:197-228.

GIBSON, H.J. 1998. Active Sport Tourism: Who Participates? The Journal of Leisure Studies. 17 (2) : 155-157, Apr.

GITLIN, T. 1980. The whole world is watching: Mass media in the making and unmaking of the new left. Berkeley: University of Calfornia Press.

GORMAN, B.S. 1970. 16 PF correlates of sensation seeking. Psychological reports, 26(3):741-742, Jun.

GRUN, B., 1991. The Timetables of History. Toronto: Simon & Schuster.

GUNN, C.A. 1988. Tourism Planning. New York: Taylor & Francis.

GUTTMANN, A. 1981. Sports Spectators from Antiquity to the Renaissance, Journal of Sport History, Penn State University Press, Vol. 8, No. 2.

HAAPASALO, J. 1990. Sensation seeking and Eysenck's personal dimensions in offender sample. Personality and individual differences, 11(1):81-84.

HABASHI, Z.E. 1992. Tutankhamon and the Sporting Traditions, Paris: Peter Lang Publishing.

HALSALL, M. 1997. The impacts of major sporting events on host communities and Guidelines for event strategy preparation, Curtin university of technology. [Web:] http://www.blackmagic.com/ses/surf/apers/hallthesis.html [Date of access: 31 Jan.2000].

HART, M. & BIRELL, S. 1981. Sport in the sociocultural. Dubuque, Iowa; William Brown.

HARVEY, D.1989. The condition of post-modernity. Oxford: Blackwell.

HARVEY, J. & HOULE, F. 1994. Sport, World Economy, Global Culture, and New Social Movements. Sociology for Sport Journal. 11 (4) : 339-349.

HAYES, M.E. 1988. A motivational model of gambling behavior. Connecticut : Connecticut State University. (Thesis-MA).

HEINO, A., VAN DER MOLEN, H.H. & WILDE, G.J.S. 1992. Report VK 92-02. Haren : Traffic Research Centre, University of Groningen.

HENDRICK, S.S. & HENDRICK, C. 1987. Multidimensionality of sexual attitudes. Journal of sex research, 23:502-526.

HILLER, H. (In Kang, Y.S. & Perdue, R. 1994. The long-term impact of a Mega-Event on international tourism to the host country: A conceptual model and the case of the 1988 Seoul Olympics. Binghamton, New York: The Haworth Press, Inc.).

HORNA, J.L.A. 1994. The study of leisure: an introduction. Toronto: Oxford University Press.

HORVATH, P. & ZUCKERMAN, M. 1993. Sensation seeking, risk appraisal, and risky behaviour. Personality and individual differences, 14:41-52.

HOWELL, R. & HOWELL, M.L. 1976. Women and Sport in the Minoan Civilization, North American Society Sports History. Pennsylvania: Penn State University Press, p. 9.

HUGHES, H.L. 1993. The role of Hallmark event tourism in urban regeneration. Manchester Metropolitan University: Manchester, United Kingdom.

HUGO, M.L. & VILJOEN, A.T. 1992. Hulpbronbewaring. Pretoria: MC Drukkers.

HYMBAUGH, K. & GARRETT, J. 1974. Sensation seeking among skydivers. Perceptual and motor skills, 38(1):118, Feb.

INSKEEP, E. 1991. Tourism Planning - An integrated and sustainable development approach. USA: International Thomson Publishing Inc.

IREY, P.A. 1979. Personality dimensions of crisis interveners vs. academic psychologists, traditional clinicians and paraprofessionals. (In Zuckerman, M., ed. Sensation seeking: beyond the optimal level of arousal. Hillsdale, N.J.: Erlbaum.)

JAFARI, J. 1989. Models de turisme: Aspects socioculturels. Antropologies 2:31-38.

JANSEN-VERBEKE, M. 1988. Leisure, recreation and tourism in Inner cities. Amsterdam: Netherlands Geographical Studies.

JOHNSON, P.B. 1988. Personality correlates of heavy and light drinking female college students. Journal of alcohol and drug education, 34(2):33-37, Winter.

JOHNSON, D. 1999. Introduction to travel and tourism - Book One. Australia: Irwin/McGraw-Hill Companies.

KAESTNER, E., ROSEN, L. & APEL, P. 1977. Patterns of drug abuse: relationship with ethnicity, sensation seeking and anxiety. Journal of consulting and clicinal psychology, 45(3):462-468, Jun.

KANG, Y.S. & PERDUE, R. 1994. The long-term impact of a Mega-Event on international tourism to the host country: A conceptual model and the case of the 1988 Seoul Olympics. Binghamton, New York: The Haworth Press, Inc.

KEENAN, T. 1995. Mother Lode. Finance Week. 66 (1) : 24-25, July. 6-12.

KEENAN, T. 1996. Teeing Up for Tourism. Finance Week. 71 (9) : 27, Nov. 21.

KERR, J.H. & SVEBAK, S. 1989. Motivational aspects of preference for and participation in "risk" and "safe" sports. Personality and individual differences, 10:797-800.

KESTNER, J. AMERICAN SPORT EDUCATION PROGRAMME. 1996. Event management for sport directors. Illinois: Champaign: Human Kinetics.

KISH, G.B. & DONNENWERTH, G.V. 1972. Sex differences in the correlates of stimulus seeking. Journal of consulting and clinical psychology, 38(1):42-49, Feb.

KOCH, E.; DE BEER, G. & ELIFFE, S. 1998. International perspectives on tourism-led development - some lessons for the SDIs. Development Southern Africa, 15(5): 908-915, Summer

KOENDERMAN, T. 1995. To market, to market.... Financial Mail, 136(12):86, Jun. 23.

KPMG. 1993. "Manchester 2000. Economic benefits ad opportunities of the Olympic Games." KPMG Management Consulting.

KRIPPENDORF, J. 1987. The holiday makers: understanding the impact of leisure and travel. Oxford: Butterworth-Heinemann.

KURTZMAN, J. 1993. Inaugaural Address, sports Tourism International Council. Journal of Sport Tourism. October,1:1.

KURTZMAN, J.; ZAUHAR, J.; AHN, J. & CHOI, S. 1998. Global Understanding, Appreciation and Peace through Sports Tourism. [Available on Internet] http://www.free-press.com/journals/jst/archive/vol3no4/global.htm (01.04.98).

KUSYSZYN, I., STEINBERG, P. & ELLIOT, B. 1974. Arousal seeking, physical risk taking, and personality. (Revised version presented at the International Congress of Applied Psychology. Eighteenth. Man and sport: the psychology of physical activity. Montreal, Canada. (July 28 - August 2).)

LANDEWEERD, J.A., URLINGS, I.J.M. & DEJONG, A.H.J. 1990. Risk taking tendency among construction workers. Journal of occupational accidents, 11:183-196.

LAVENTHOL, G. AND HORWARTH. H. 1984. (In Hughes, 1993. The role of Hallmark event tourism in urban regeneration. Manchester Metropolitan University: Manchester, United Kingdom).

LAVERTY, P. 1989. Travel and Tourism, Suffolk: Elm Publications.

LAW, C.M. 1996. Urban Tourism: Attracting Tourist to Large Cities. London: Mansell.

LEA, J. 1988. Tourism and Development in the Third World. New York: Routeldge, Chapman and Hall.

LEUBA, C. 1955. Toward some integration of learning theories: the concept of optimal stimulation. Pyschological reports, 1:27-33.

LEY, D. & OLD'S. K. 1988. Landscape as spectacle world's fairs and the culture of heroic consumption. Society and space, 6:191-212.

LICKORISH, L.J. & JENKINS C.L. 1997. An introduction to tourism. Reed Educational and Professional Publishing Ltd.

LOGAN, J., & MOLOTCH, H. 1987. Urban fortunes: The political economy of place. Berkeley: University of California Press.

LOGUE, A.W. & SMITH, M.E. 1986. Predictors of food preferences in adults. Appetite, 7:109-125.

LOOFT, W.R. 1971. Conservatives, liberals, radicals and sensation seekers. Perceptual and motor skills, 32:98.

LUNDBERG, D.E. 1990. The tourist business, sixth edition. New York: Van Nostrand Reinhold.

MacALOON, J. 1984. "Olympic Games and the theory of spectacle in modern societies" (In, MacAloon, J. (ed) Rite, drama, festival,, sepctacles". Philadelphia: Institute for the study of human issues).

MARSH, N. and HENSHALL, D. 1987. Planning better tourism: the strategic importance of tourist-resident expectations and interactions. Tourism recreation research 12(2):47-54.

MATHIESON, A.S. & WALL, G. 1982. Tourism: economic, physical and social impacts. London: Longman.

MCCUTCHEON, L. 1981. Running and sensation seeking. Footnotes (publication of Road Runners Club of America), 9,8.

McINTOSH, R.W.; GOELDNER, C.R. & RITCHIE J.R.B. 1995. Tourism: Principles, Practices, Philosophies. New York: Wiley.

MELNICK, M.J. 1993. Searching for Sociability in the Stands: A Theory of Sport Spectating. Journal of Sport Management. 7: 44-60.

MEYROWITZ, J.1985. No sense of place: The impact of electronic media on social behaviour. New York: Oxford University Press.

MIRANDA, J. & ANDUEZA, J. 1997. The role of sport in tourism destinations chosen by tourists visiting Spain. [Available on Internet] http://www.mcb.co.uk/journals/jst/archive/vol4no3/jst15.htm

MILLER, S.G. 1992. Arete - Greek Sports from Ancient Sources. Oxford: University of California Press.

MILL, C.M. & MORRISON, A.M. 1985. The Tourism System: An introductory text. New Jersey, Englewood Cliffs: Prentice Hall Inc

MONTAG, I. & BIRENBAUM, M. 1986. Psychopathological factors and sensation seeking. Journal of research in personality, 20:338-348.

MOOKCHERJEE, H.N. 1986. Comparison of some personality characteristics of male problem drinkers in rural Tennessee. Journal of alcohol and drug education, 31(2):23-28, Winter.

MULLER, A.P. 1992. The importance of promoting tourism and its multiplier for local authorities. The South African Treasurer, 64 (4): 68-69, Apr.

MURPHY, P.E. 1986. Tourism: A Community Approach. New York: Methuen.

MURPHY, P.E. & CARMICHEAL, B.A. 1989. Assessing the Tourism Benefits of an Open Access Sports Tournament: The 1989 B.C. Winter Games. Journal of Travel Research. 29-; 32-36.

MUSOLINO, R.F. & HERSHENSEON, D.B. 1977. Vocational sensation seeking in high and low risk-taking occupations. Journal of vocational behavior, 10:358-365.

NAUDE, W.A. & KLEYNHANS, E.P.J. 1988. Development and Africa Economics, second edition. Potchefstroom.

NEARY, R.S. & ZUCKERMAN, M. 1976. Sensation seeking, trait and state anxiety and the electrodermal orienting reflex. Psychophysiology, 13(3):205-211, May.

NEWCOMB, M.D. & MCGEE, L. 1991. Influence of sensation seeking on general deviance and specific problem behaviors from adolescence to young adulthood. Journal of personality and social psychology, 61(4):614-628, Oct.

NIEDERMEIER, L. & SMIT, J. 1995. Tourism in Southern Africa: A Catalyst for development. Indicator SA, 12(4): 50-54.

OKAMOTO, K. & TOKARI, E. 1992. Structure of creativity measurements and their correlations with sensation seeking and need for uniqueness. Japanese journal of experimental social psychology, 31:203-210.

OLSTHOORN, J. 1998. Sport Tourism to Tap into Billion Dollar Market. [Available on Internet] http://206.191.33.50/tourism/news/17jn97.html (04.01.98).

OLIVOVA, V. 1984, Sports and Games in the Ancient World. London: Orbis.

PEARCE, P.L. 1994. Tourist-resident impacts: examples, explanations and emerging solutions. (In Theobald, W., ed. Global Tourism: the next decade. Oxford: Butterworth. .103-123).

PEARSON, P.R. & SHEFFIELD, B.F. 1978. Social attitude correlates of sensation seeking psychiatric patients. Perceptual and motor skills, 40(2):482, Apr.

PETRIE, A., COLLINS, W. & SOLOMAN, P. 1958. Pain sensitivity, sensory deprivation, and susceptibility to satiation. Science, 128:1431-1432.

PIET, S. 1987. What motivates stunt men? Motivation and emotion, 11:195-213.

PIGEASSOU, C. 1997. Sport and tourism: the emergence of sport into the offer of tourism. Between passion and reason. An overview of the French situation and perspectives. Journal for Sport Tourism. Vol 4(2):27-57.

PILKINGTON, C.J., RICHARDSON, D.R. & UTLEY, M.E. 1988. Is conflict stimulating? Sensation seekers' response to interpersonal conflict. Personality and social psychology bulletin, 14(3):596-603, Sept.

PLOG RESEARCH INCORPORATED. 1987. California travellers: perception of British Colombia and Vancouver: Results of the Research. Prepared for the Ministry of Tourism, Recreation and Culture, Government of Bristish Columbia. Victoria: Canada. May (p 33-35).

POLIAKOFF, M.B. 1987. The Will to Win: ancient perspectives, North American Society Sports History. Pennsylvania: Penn State University Press.

POLICY STUDIES INSTITUTE, 1986. (In Hughes, 1993. The role of Hallmark event tourism in urban regeneration. Manchester Metropolitan University: Manchester,

United Kingdom).

POTGIETER, J. & BISSCHOFF, F. 1990. Sensation seeking among medium and low risk sports participants. Perceptual and motor skills, 71(3:Part2):1203-1206, Dec.

PYO,S., COOK, R. AND HOWELL,R. 1988. (In Hughes, 1993. The role of Hallmark event tourism in urban regeneration. Manchester Metropolitan University: Manchester, United Kingdom).

RAIN, C. 1998. The tourist experience: a new introduction. London: Cassell.

REISINGER, Y & TURNER, L. 1998. Cross-cultural differences in tourism: a strategy for tourism marketers. Journal of travel and tourism marketing, 7(4): 79-106.

RITCHIE, J.R.B. 1984. (In Hughes, H.L. 1993. Investment and financing in the tourism industry. Manchester Metropolitan University: Manchester, United Kingdom).

RITCHIE, J.R.B. 1984. (In Kang, Y. & Perdue, R. 1994. Long-term impact of a mega-event on international tourism to the host country: A conceptual model and the case of the 1988 Seoul Olympics. The Haworth Press, Inc.).

RITCHIE, J.R.B. & GOELDNER, C.R. 1994. Travel, Tourism, and Hospitality Research. USA : New York : Wiley.

RITCHIE, J.B.R., and ZINS, M. 1978. Culture as a Determinant of the attractiveness of a Tourism Region, Annals of Tourism Research, 5.

ROBINSON, D.W. 1985. Stress seeking: selected behavioral characteristics of elite rock climbers. Journal of sport psychology, 7(4):400-404, Dec.

ROBINSON, T. 1997. Sports tourism consumer motivation. [Available on Intertnet] http://www.mcb.co.uk/journals/jst/archive/vol3no4/jst15.htm.

ROSSI, B. & CEREATTI, L. 1993. The sensation seeking in mountain athletes as assessed by Zuckerman's sensation seeking scale. International journal of sport psychology, 24:417-431.

ROWLAND, G.L., FRANKEN, R.E & HARRISON, K. 1986. Sensation seeking and participation in sporting activities. Journal of sport psychology, 8(3):212-220, Sept.

SAAYMAN, M. & VAN NIEKERK, C. 1996. A Comparative Study between the 1984 Los Angeles Olympic Games and the Cape Town 2004 Olympic Bid. Potchefstroom : PU for CHE : Institute for Tourism and Leisure Studies.

SAAYMAN, M. 1997. En route with tourism. Potchefstroom: Leisure consultants and Publications.

SAAYMAN, A. & SAAYMAN, M. 1997. Die ekonomiese impak van toerisme op die Suid Afrikaanse ekonomie. South African Journal of Economic and Management Sciences. Vol. 21. Autumn.

SAAYMAN, M. & SWART, S. 1997. Tourism management: In service training. Level one. Potchefstroom: PU for CHE: Institure for tourim and Leisure Studies.

SAAYMAN, M. 1999. What is cultural tourism and how can we benefit from it? Tourism, Environment and Conservation North West. Pilanesberg. 8 September 1999. Keynote Speaker.

SAAYMAN, M. 2000. En Route With Tourism. 2nd edition Potchefstroom. Leisure consultants and Publications.

SCHALLING, D.; EDMAN, G. & ASBERG, M. & ORELAND, L. 1988. Platelet MAO activity associated with impulsivity and aggressivity. Personality and individual differences, 9(3):597-605.

SCHEDLOWSKI, M. & TEWES, U. 1991. Physiological arousal and perception of bodily state during parachute jumping. Unpublished manuscript. Hannover Medical School.

SCHOLTZ, G.J.L., SCHOLTZ, H., SMALERGER, R. SCHOLTZ, E. & STEYNBERG, L. 1997. Gross list of leisure activities. Groslys van vryetydsaktiwiteite. 4th ed. Potchefstroom: Institute for Tourism and Leisure Studies, PU for CHE.

SCHOLTZ, G.J.L., 1999, Inleiding tot Spottoerisme: Pretoria: Departement Biokenitika, Sport en Vryetydswetenskappe, Universiteit van Pretoria.

SCHWARTZ, R.M., BURKHART, B.R. & GREEN, S.B. 1978. Turning on or turning off: sensation seeking or tension reduction as motivational determinants of alcohol use. Journal of consulting and clinical psychology, 46(5):1144-1145, Oct.

SESSA, A. 1994. Tourism production, tourism products: real situation, methodological approach, global trends. (In KELLER, P. (ed). 1996. Globilisation and tourism. Reports of the 46th Congress, Rotorua, New Zealand. Suisse: St-Gall.)

SHAW, G. & WILLIAMS, A.M. 1994. Critical Issues in Tourism: A geographical perspecive. Oxford: Blackwell Publishers.

SIMO, S. & PEREZ, J. 1991. Sensation seeking and antisocial behavior in a junior high school sample. Personality and individual differences, 12:965-966.

SINCLAIR, R. 1988. Venture Outdoors: A South African First timer's Guide. Johannesburg : Southern Book Publishers.

SLABBERT, E. & SAAYMAN, M. 2000. Kernaspekte rakende etnotoerisme in Suid-Afrika. Potchefstroom: Institute for Tourism and Leisure Studies.

SMERAL, E. 1994. Economic Models. (In: Witt, S.T. & Moutinho, L.Y. eds, Tourism Marketing and Management Handbook, second Edition, Pretice Hall.)

SMITH, V.L. 1989. Hosts and Guests. Philadelphia: University of Pennsylvania Press.

SMITH, S.L.J. 1990. Tourism Analysis: A Handbook. New York: John Wiley.

SMITH, C. 1995. Here comes the boks. Finance Week. June 22-28.

SOCHER, K. & TSCHURTSCHENTHALER, P. 1987. (In Kang, Y. & Perdue, R. 1994. Long-term impact of a mega-event on international tourism to the host country: a conseptual model and the case of the 1988 Seoul Olympics. The Haworth Press, Inc.).

SOFIELD, T.H.B. and SIVAN, A. 1994. From cultural event to international sport - the Hong Kong Boat Race". Journal of Sport Tourism. 1(3):5-22

STERNBERG, R.J. & SORIANO, L.J. 1984. Styles of conflict resolution. Journal of Personality and social psychology, 47(1):115-126, Jul.

STEVENSON, C. and NIXON, J. 1972. A conceptual framework of the social functions of sport. Sportwissenschrift. 2 Jahrgang (pp199-132).

STEYNBERG, L. 1997. Die verband tussen sensasie-soekendheid en risikovolle vryetydsaktiwiteite. Potchefstroom : Potchefstroom Universiteit vir Christelike Hoër Onderwys. (Thesis-MA).

STIRLING, J. 1977. Strength of the nervous system, extraversion-introversion, and kinestehetic and cortical augmenting and reducing. England : University of York. (Dissertation-Ph.D.)

STRAUB, W.F. 1982. Sensation seeking among high and low-risk male athletes. Journal of sport psychology, 4(3):246-253.

STRYDOM, A.J. & LOURENS, J.J. 1995. Toerisme en die Ekonomie: Die Vrystaat as Gevallestudie. Suid Afrikaanse tydskrif vir Ekonomiese en Bestuurswetenskappe, 16.

SVEBAK, S. & KERR, J. 1989. The role of impulsivity in preference for sports. Personality and individual differences, 10:51-58.

SWARBROOKE, J. 1995. The development and management of visitor attractions. Oxford: Butterworth Heineman.

THE READER'S DIGEST ASSOCIATION, 1974. History of Man, The Last Two Million Years. Montreal:

THORTON, B., RYCKMAN, R.M. & GOLD, J.A. 1981. Sensation seeking as a determinant of interpersonal attraction toward similar and dissimilar others. Journal of mind and body, 2:85-91.

TOW, S. 1997. Sports tourism - the benefits. Journal of Sports Tourism. Jan 1997. Vol 3(4).

TRAVEL AND TOURISM RESEARCH ASSOCIATION. 1986. Tourism and technology: a growing partnership. Proceedings. Seventeenth Annual Conference. Mephis: Tenesee.1986.

TRIBE, J. 1995. The economics of leisure and tourism - Environments, markets and impacts. Oxford: Butterworth-Heinemann, Ltd.

TRIGG, P. 1995. Leisure and tourism GNVQ: Intermediate textbook. Oxford: Butterworth-Heinemann.

TURCO, D. & KELSEY, C. 1993. Measuring the Economics of Special Events. Parks and Recreation : 33-37, Dec.

TURNER, V. 1983. Carnival in Rio: Dionysian drama in an industrialising society. (In, MANNING, F. (ed.) 1983. The celebration of society: perspectives on contemporary cultural performance. Bowling Green: Bowling Green University Popular Press.)

VAN DER MERWE, F.J.G. 1990, Sportgeskiedenis: 'n Handleiding vir Suid Afrikaanse studente. Stellenbosch: Words Unlimited.

VAN DER WALT, D. 1997. Grand Prix kan Miljoene na SA Bring. Finansies en Tegniek. 49 (44) : 31, Nov. 7.

VAN DER WESTHUIZEN, S.C.A. 1998. Potchefstroom: Potchefstroom University for Christian Higher Education (Unpublished mini dissertation).

VAN HARSSEL, J. 1994. Tourism: an exploration. 3rd ed. USA: Prentice Hall.

VELLAS, F. & BéCHEREL, L. 1995. International Tourism. Macmillan Press Ltd: London.

VOISEY, P. 1988. Vulcan. The making of a prairie community. Toronto: University of Toronto Press.

WAGNER, A.M. & HOULIHAN, D.D. 1994. Sensation seeking and trait anxiety in hangglider pilots and golfers. Personality and individual differences, 16(6):975-977, Jun.

WAKEFIELD, K.L. & SLOAN, H.J. 1995. The Effect of Team Loyalty and Selected Stadium Factors on Spectator Attendance. Journal of Sport Management. 9 : 153-172.

WATERS, L.K. & KIRK, N.E. 1968. Stimulus-seeking motivation and risk taking behaviour in a gambling situation. Education and psychological measurement, 28:549-550.

WATSON, J.S. 1985. Volunteer and risk-taking groups are more homogeneous on measures of sensation seeking than control groups. Perceptual and motor skills, 61(2):471-475, Oct.

WHITSON, G. & MCINTOSH, J. 1993. Becoming a World -Class City: Hallmark Events and Sport Franchises in the Growth Strategies of Westhern Canadian Cities. Sociology of Sport Journal. 10(3): (221-240), Sept.

WHITE PAPER ON TOURISM, 1996. Tourism policy document. Pretoria: Government Press.

WILLIS, P.1989. Common culture. London : Open University Press.

WILLIAMS, S., RYCKMAN, R.M., GOLD, J.A. & LENNEY, E. 1982. The effects of sensation seeking and misattribution of arousal on attraction toward similar or dissimilar strangers. Journal of research in personality, 16:217-226.

WITT, S. & MARTIN, C. 1987. (In Hughes, H.L. 1993. Investment and financing in the tourism industry. Manchester Metropolitan University: Manchester: United Kingdom).

WITT, C.A. & WRIGHT, P.L. 1993. Tourist Motivation: Life after Maslow. (In JOHNSON, P. & THOMAS, B. eds. 1993 Choice and Demand in Tourism. New York : Mansell.)

WOLOWITZ, H.M. 1964. Food preferences as an index of orality. Journal of abnormal and social psychology, 69:650-654.

WOODY, T. 1949. Life and Education in Early Societies. New York: The Macmillan Company.

WUNDT, W.M. 1893. Grundzüge der physiologischen psychologie. Leipzig, German Democratic Republic : Engleman.

XTREME. Summer 1998. Published by Eaton House, Norwich Park, Park Lane, Sandown, South Africa.

YOUELL, R. 1995. Leisure and Tourism. 2nd ed. England: Longman GNVQ.

ZALESKI, Z. 1984. Sensation seeking and risk taking behaviour. Personality and individual differences, 5:607-608.

ZAUHAR, J. 1995/6. Historical perspectives of sports tourism. Journal of Sports Tourism, 1995, 2(4) 1-46; 1996(a) 3(2): 1-31 & 1996 (b) 3(3): 1-61.

ZEIGLER, E.F. 1984. Ethics and morality in sports and physical education: an experimental approach. Chicago: Stripe.

ZUCKERMAN, M. 1974. The sensation-seeking motive. (In Maher, B.A., ed. Progress in experimental personality research. Vol. 7. New York : Academic Press.)

ZUCKERMAN, M. 1979. Sensation seeking: beyond the optimal level of arousal. Hillsdale, N.J. : Erlbaum.

ZUCKERMAN, M. 1983a. Biological bases of sensation seeking, impulsivity, and anxiety. Hillsdale, N.J.: Erlbaum.

ZUCKERMAN, M. 1983b. Sensation seeking and sports. Personality and individual differences, 4(3):285-293.

ZUCKERMAN, M. 1994. Behavioral expressions and biosocial bases of sensation seeking. New York : Cambridge University Press.

ZUCKERMAN, M., BALL, S. & BLACK, J. 1990. Influences of sensation, gender, risk appraisal, and situational motivation on smoking. Addictive behaviors, 15(3):209-220.

ZUCKERMAN, M., BONE, R.N., NEARY, R., MANGELSDORFF, D. & BRUSTMAN, B. 1972. What is the sensation seeker? Personality trait and experience correlates of the Sensation-Seeking Scales. Journal of consulting and clinical psychology, 39(2):308-321, Oct.

ZUCKERMAN, M. & HOPKINS, T.R. 1979. Unpublished data. (In Zuckerman, M., ed. Sensation seeking: beyond the optimal level of arousal. Hillsdale, N.J. : Erlbaum.)

ZUCKERMAN, M. & KUHLMAN, D.M. 1978. Sensation seeking and risk taking in response to hypothetical situations. Paper presented at the meeting of the International Association of Applied Psychology, Munich, August.

ZUCKERMAN, M. & LINK, K. 1968. Construct validity for the sensation-seeking scale. Journal of consulting and clinical psychology, 32:420-426.

ZUCKERMAN, M. & NEED, M. 1980. Demographic influences in sensation seeking and expressions of sensation seeking in religion, smoking and driving habits. Personality and individual differences, 1:197-206.

ZUCKERMAN, M., PERSKY, H., HOPKINS, T.R., MURTAUGH, T., BASU, G.K. & SCHILLING, M. 1966. Comparison of stress effects of perceptual and social isolation. Archives of general psychiatry, 14:356-365.

ZUCKERMAN, M., TUSHUP, R. & FINNER, S. 1976. Sexual attitudes and experience: attitude and personality and changes produced by a course in sexuality. Journal of consulting and clinical psychology, 44:7-19.